THE BEAUTY
OF THE TRINITY

MEDIEVAL PHILOSOPHY: TEXTS AND STUDIES

Gyula Klima, Fordham University, series editor

THE BEAUTY
OF THE TRINITY

A Reading of the Summa Halensis

JUSTIN SHAUN COYLE

FORDHAM UNIVERSITY PRESS

New York   2022

Fordham University Press has no responsibility for
the persistence or accuracy of URLs for external
or third-party Internet websites referred to in this
publication and does not guarantee that any content
on such websites is, or will remain, accurate or
appropriate.

Fordham University Press also publishes its books
in a variety of electronic formats. Some content that
appears in print may not be available in electronic
books.

Visit us online at www.fordhampress.com.

Library of Congress Cataloging-in-Publication Data
available online at https://catalog.loc.gov.

Printed in the United States of America

24   23   22   5   4   3   2   1

First edition

CONTENTS

FOREWORD

Writing as I am from Ireland, I may perhaps be excused for beginning a foreword to a book on medieval theology with a reflection on the death of God. Over here on the old island of saints and scholars, that reality—and a reality it is, on the level of social and political life—is so strong that the theologian can hardly evade it.

The expression, of course, is Nietzsche's, who uses it most notably in the story of the "madman" in *The Gay Science*. For someone who may not have read the famous passage with great care, its tone may come as a surprise. Unlike some of his followers, Nietzsche is not a vulgar atheist who glories in the triumph of enlightened modern culture as it finally leaves behind the oppressive childishness of religion. Nietzsche knows exactly what the death of God entails:

> The madman jumped into their midst and pierced them with his eyes. "Where is God?" he cried; "I will tell you! *We have killed him*—you and I! We are all his murderers. But how did we do this? How were we able to drink up the sea? Who gave us the sponge to wipe away the entire horizon? What were we doing when we unchained this earth from its sun? Where is it moving to now? Where are we moving to? Away from all suns? Are we not continually falling? And backwards, sidewards, forwards, in all directions? Is there still an up and a down? Aren't we straying as though through an infinite nothing? Isn't empty space breathing at us? Hasn't it got colder? Isn't night and more night coming again and again? Don't lanterns have to be lit in the morning?"[1]

The death of God means total chaos. It seems that the collapse of the fundamental distinction between God and non-God, between the sacred and the profane, drags with it into the night all the other distinctions that give orientation to human life. Without God the ultimate horizon of life is erased, leaving us helplessly struggling to ward off "infinite nothing."

Nietzsche, however, is not content with this nothing. He understands that one cannot be a nihilist and *live*. Since there is no path back to the faith for him—although more than one twentieth-century theologian has wondered whether Nietzsche's thought might be more open to the faith than appearances suggest[2]—there is only one way out of nihilism: we must our-selves become gods, "overmen" who create, *ex nihilo*, our own horizons of meaning. This is precisely what Nietzsche sets out to do in *Thus Spake Zara-thustra*, a palimpsest of Christian scripture composed, brilliantly, in ar-chaic German that mirrors Luther's translation of the Bible. The crucial difference between scripture and Nietzsche's attempt to erase and overwrite it is that, whereas Moses and Jesus announce the reality of the Lord, Zara-thustra, after descending from his own mountain, proclaims his death: "Could it be possible! The old saint in the forest hath not yet heard of it, that *God is dead!*"[3]

Although it is true that Nietzsche offers a philosophical critique of the Christian faith, a significant aspect of the struggle between Zarathustra and Jesus takes place on the field of beauty. In *Thus Spake Zarathustra* Nietz-sche endeavors to tell a beautiful story of what human life can and should be, a story more compelling than the Christian one, which—Nietzsche be-lieves—is ultimately life-denying and ugly.

I am convinced that one of the most decisive contemporary challenges for the Christian faith is to tell a sufficiently beautiful story of itself. Once—as has happened in Ireland—the Church is perceived not as the Body of Christ, leading the faithful on a journey to the promised land in the foot-steps of the Lord but, rather, as an "institution" led by a clique whose back-wardness *prevents* people from enjoying the happy lives to which they aspire, indeed feel entitled, then the battle is all but lost. It does not help if, moreover, that institution is seen as mired in ugly crimes.

Within the Church the rise of theological aesthetics and debates over the liturgy reflect awareness of what is at stake when the theory and practice of the faith neglect beauty: we end up in a joyless spiritual aridity. This is unlikely to be overcome by "synodal pathways" that focus on secular con-cerns with gender, sex, and power. What is needed is reflection upon, and enactment of, the beauty of the faith. (And how wonderful it would be if the reflection were able to *perform* the beauty of which it spoke!)

This is the situation against the background of which Justin Coyle's book was written. But let me put this more carefully: it is one of the situations, for there are other national churches than the Irish, and there is Christianity outside Roman Catholicism. The question of theological aesthetics, how-ever, is of universal Christian relevance, if it is important for truth to radiate beauty—and *that* I take to have been established since Plato's *Symposium*.

The truth attracts because it is beautiful; furthermore, the difficulty of scaling the mountain where Truth dwells requires a pedagogy in which limited participations of truth allow the learner to climb the ladder gradually, rung by rung.

The *Summa Halensis* to whose conception of beauty Dr. Coyle's book is devoted translates these Platonic insights into the language of the Christian faith. God himself is beauty, Brother Alexander argues, but in a way that goes significantly beyond the standard scholastic position according to which beauty is one of the Creator's essential attributes. Rather, the *Summa Halensis* suggests, the root and pinnacle of beauty is the inner trinitarian life of the three divine Persons: *pulcritudo in divinis [est] ex ordine sacro divinarum personarum, qua una persona non ab alia, a qua alia per generationem, a quibus tertia per processionem.* This statement is the center from which the beauty doctrine of the *Summa Halensis* emanates. According to it, beauty at its highest, most perfect is not an attribute, but the living relationship of three Persons bound together by relations of generation and love. Again, beauty is not a "thing" (just as God is not a thing), but a structure of personal relationships.

Dr. Coyle submits that this trinitarian grammar underlies the *Summa Halensis's* conception of beauty at the different levels of the great chain of being, from the order of inanimate creation to that of the human soul. Sin, by contrast, consists in what he calls a "palimpsest" of the order of creation which overwrites the latter's reflection of its trinitarian Source.

Methodologically, Dr. Coyle's work combines rigorous historical scholarship with an element of constructive theology. Let me draw upon the register of contemporary philosophy to explain: if Heidegger is correct that the key to a thinker's ideas lies in "that which, in what is said, remains unsaid" (*das im Sagen Ungesagte*)—in unarticulated, sometimes even unthought presuppositions underpinning an entire intellectual edifice—then it may not only be legitimate but crucial to read a work from its margins, from between its lines or, as in the case of the *Summa Halensis*, from the one explicit definition of trinitarian beauty which renders the whole fully intelligible.

There is another feature of Dr. Coyle's work to which it is worth drawing attention: the beauty of his writing. Scholars have come to be used to the notion that academic writing has to be on the dull side, as though a flat style guaranteed the objectivity of scholarly discourse. But what if the point of theological writing were not merely to state the "facts" about the teachings of some (frequently obscure) author, but to employ a discussion of these teachings to draw the reader in—in to the beauty of the Christian faith? This goal would call for a different style. Its dynamism would signal thinking rather than settled thought. Its choice of words would steer clear of the well-worn phrases and clichés that stifle curiosity; sometimes the vocabulary might even surprise. It would be pleasantly fresh, an invitation to participate in an intellectual and spiritual journey. Such is Dr. Coyle's style in this book.

The Beauty of the Trinity challenges us to articulate the Christian faith in terms of beauty while thinking beauty in terms of personal relationship. The *Summa Halensis* and Dr. Coyle's interpretation point the way, but there remains much scope for further development.

Philipp W. Rosemann
On the Feast of the Transfiguration of the Lord, 2021

ABBREVIATIONS

WORKS BY (PSEUDO-) ALEXANDER OF HALES

Glossa	Alexander of Hales, *Glossa in quatuor libros sententiarum Petri Lombardi*
SH	Alexander of Hales (inter alios), *Summa halensis/Summa fratris Alexandri*
QDA	Alexander of Hales, *Quaestiones disputatae antequam esset frater*
QDP	Alexander of Hales, *Quaestiones disputatae postquam fuit frater*

WORKS BY OTHER AUTHORS

brev.	Bonaventure, *Breviloquium*
CCSL	*Corpus Christianorum Series Latina*
CSEL	*Corpus Scriptorum Ecclesiasticorum Latinorum*
DN	Dionysius Areopagita, *De divinis nominibus*
DS	Hugh of St. Victor, *De sacramentiis*
DSA	Anonymous, *De spiritu et anima*
DSB	Ulrich of Strasburg, *De summo bono*
DT	Richard of St. Victor, *De trinitate*
Enn.	Plotinus, *Enneads*
itin.	Bonaventure, *Itinerarium mentis in Deum*
PG	Migne, *Patrologia Graeca*
PL	Migne, *Patrologia Latina*
SA	William of Auxerre, *Summa aurea*
SC	*Sources Chrétiennes*
SDA	John of La Rochelle, *Summa de anima*
SDB	Philip the Chancellor, *Summa de bono*
SDN	Albertus Magnus, *Super Dionysium De divinis nominibus*
ST	Thomas Aquinas, *Summa theologiae*
STh	Albertus Magnus, *Summa theologica*
trin.	Augustine, *De trinitate*

True beautie dwells on high: ours is a flame / but borrow'd thence to light us thither.

—George Herbert, "The Forerunner"

L'introduction des concepts artistiques dans la vie trinitaire a quelque chose d'intellectuellement saisissant et surprenant : l'analogie artistique ne sert plus seulement à penser le rapport du monde comme œuvre à Dieu créateur, mais à penser les relations internes à Dieu lui-même.

—Jean Louis Chrétien, *Corps à corps: à l'écoute de l'œuvre d'art*, 108

For the almighty truth of the trinite is oure fader, for he made us and kepeth us in him. And the depe wisdome of the trinite is our moder, in whom we are all beclosed. And the hye goodnesse of the trinite is our lord, and in him we are beclosed and he in us. We are beclosed in the fader, and we are beclosed in the son, and we are beclosed in the holy gost. And the father is beclosed in us, the son is beclosed in us, and the holy gost is beclosed in us: all mighty, alle wisdom, and alle goodnesse; one God, one lorde.

—Julian of Norwich, *A Revelation of Love*, 54.15–21

This beauty of the trinity, this orderliness of God's *perichoresis*, is the very movement of delight, of the divine persons within one another, and so the analogy that lies between worldly and divine beauty is a kind of *analogia delectationis*.

—David Bentley Hart, *The Beauty of the Infinite*, 252

Все істинно прекрасне могутнім закли-ком підносить душу до Тебе.

—Akathist to Creation, Kontakion 7

INTRODUCTION

The year is 1255. Alexander of Hales—Englishman by birth, scholastic by training, and Franciscan by calling—lay dead nearly a decade.[1] More, his promised *Summa* remains unfinished. Work on it began in 1241, long after Alexander stirred controversy by lecturing on the Lombard's *Sentences*.[2] Unlike his gloss on Master Peter, Alexander's *Summa* was not a solitary labor. It gathered the efforts of his cochair at Paris, John of La Rochelle, and another friar at least, maybe more.[3] For reasons now unclear, their labors stopped abruptly upon Alexander's death in 1245. Fearing that neglect might yield to abandonment, Pope Alexander IV penned a letter to the Franciscan Minister General. "Wisely consider that this maimed work of God," the pope writes hotly, "which divine wisdom itself through the ministry of its servant has begun with the resplendent beauty of its already finished portion, is profanely discarded if cast aside."[4] This glittering peroration closes *De fontibus paradisi*, Alexander IV's exhortation to the little friars to complete the work begun by their master.

It is interesting that Alexander IV should commend the "resplendent beauty" of the *Summa Halensis*. Which of its beauties does he praise? The cool, abstemious style of its prose, perhaps—or else the conceptual elegance of its fine-tuned distinctions. Whatever Alexander IV's intentions, I take his charge seriously. I too commend the *Summa*'s beauty as "profanely discarded if cast aside," if only under another aspect. This book has as its topic the *Summa*'s peculiar theology of beauty, or how it conceives the relation between the beauty God is and its trace upon creatures.

What is the *Summa*'s peculiar theology of beauty? When the text assays God's beauty, it teaches that "beauty in the divine is from the sacred order of the divine persons (*ex ordine sacro divinarum personarum*)."[5] "In such manner," the text continues, "that one person is not from another, one from whom another is by generation and a third is by procession." Peculiar to the *Summa*, then, is how beauty is not so much a divine name or attribute. It names instead a relation, a structure—an *ordo sacer*. But if beauty's structure is relational, it is relational only in the highly particular way of being of the trinitarian persons. And this trinitarian beauty shines out, the *Summa* teaches, when the trinity gifts its beauty to creatures. Trinitarian traces (*vestigia*)

1

thus pattern the *Summa* along theology's classic *topoi*. Being and creation and human nature and sin and salvation—all variously bear the signature style of the trinity's sacred order. And to the extent they do, they too are beautiful. So if the *Summa Halensis* was the first summa to study beauty "*d'une manière précise*,"[6] it is also the first to commit so many pages to its development. That we can and should read trinitarian beauty across the theology of the *Summa Halensis* is this book's central proposal.

This proposal is controversial. But it is only because the *Summa's* expansive theology of beauty has often eluded its readers. Most readers fix attention on other of its teachings.[7] Only the rare reader notices the text's beauty doctrine. Even those who do adumbrate its teaching. Some thumbnail-sketch it in their haste to embellish icons of beauty in other masters—mostly Thomas.[8] Others read with philosophical interest only, often with habits schooled by modern and atheological interest in beauty across medieval texts.[9] If the former readers mistake the *Summa's* idiosyncrasy for incipience, the latter surgically excise certain of its passages and rearrange them alongside other members severed from their corpora to construct a "medieval aesthetics." Whether Thomistic or aesthetic, both sets of readers remain preoccupied with questions the *Summa* did not teach them to pose. They also miss how the *Summa* always thinks beauty with trinity, *ad intra* and *ad extra*. Happily, though, not all readers indulge these errors. Some even record the connection the *Summa* braves between beauty and trinity.[10] But few readers allow this connection to propel their reading much beyond the *Summa's* cycle of questions on beauty among the transcendentals.[11] And none enlarge upon the theological implications of what the *Summa* there teaches.[12]

This book responds to the literature's lack by following the *Summa's* teaching on beauty where it points. It does so not because all lacks demand redress—still less a monograph. Rather my own reasons for writing are three. First I write to expand the literature on the *Summa Halensis*. A small but steady literature has grown up around the text since Zachary Hayes mourned its dearth in 1966.[13] To it this book offers not only the first monograph-length study of its beauty doctrine. It yields also an investigation beyond introduction—one that depicts and assays and admires the *Summa's* internal coherence on a topic despite its pseudepigraphy.[14] Second I write to texture literature on theologies of beauty across the Middle Ages. Attending to the *Summa's* unique beauty doctrine—as did Albert the Great, Thomas Aquinas, Bonaventure, Ulrich of Strasburg, Duns Scotus, and Denys the Carthusian[15]—

reveals a diversity sometimes suppressed. More, it demonstrates Andreas Speer's claim that "there is no good reason to separate this 'aesthetic' language" from medieval "teaching on the divine nature."[16]

Third and most important, I write to practice historical theology. Among other things this means that this book attempts speech about the trinity God with language on loan from a historical text (and not the other way round). This does not mean to excuse slipshod interpretation or textual docetism. But it does mean that the book's deliverances aim somehow to serve or refine or burnish normative speech about God. Its wager is that failing to recover and redisplay the *Summa*'s trinitarian account of beauty means leaving its use for theology unexamined. This book recovers and redisplays. But it does so for reasons beyond mere historical interest. It submits a theological reading of the *Summa*'s theology of beauty for scrutiny or use or rejection by theologians.

When the *Summa* identifies beauty with sacred order—the trinity's and creation's and the soul's—it forms a curriculum. This renders my method simple and clear. I submit to the *Summa*'s own pedagogy by tracing its teaching on beauty across its volumes. Or I follow its pedagogy to sites Wittgenstein calls "enormously complicated situation[s] in which aesthetic expression has a place."[17] And that means each chapter that follows studies *where* and *how* beauty does its work. Thus my method remains at once topographical and theological. It is topographical to the extent that I attend to *where* beauty crops up. And it is theological because I detail *how* beauty there instructs readers about the trinity and creation. That this method conducts my reading to sites unmapped by previous studies is a result of allowing the text rather than the reader to decide what beauty means within its pages. Lexically cataloging beauty words—*pulchritudo, decor, species, honestum,* and so on—across the text, as many readers have done, invariably wins insights. But it also risks deciding quite in advance what those beauty words must be and thus determining *a priori* where the *Summa* teaches beauty (and not). Taking seriously the *Summa*'s identification of beauty with the order of the trinity means charting another way—the *Summa*'s own. It is this way my book chances. And it does so by submitting to the *Summa*'s distinctive instruction that beauty is present wherever the sacred order of the trinitarian persons is.[18]

So my method—and the plan?

Part I begins where other of the *Summa*'s readers have: the question of beauty's transcendental status. Chapter 1 rereads the *Summa*'s account of the transcendentals—one, true, and good. There I show how already in its cycle of questions on the transcendental determinations of being the *Summa* evinces a peculiarly "trinitarian motive." Chapter 2 develops this reading to tender a stronger claim: that the *Summa's* doctrine on the transcendentals performs nothing less than an exercise in trinitarian theology. Here I propose reading the *Summa* backward—the treatise on the transcendentals after and within the *Summa's* theory of trinitarian appropriation. Chapter 3 then advocates a fresh answer to the transcendental-status question, not only reorienting the reader away from it but also showing how beauty organizes the *Summa's* theological vision. The *Summa* argues that divine beauty is the "sacred order" (*ordo sacer*) of the trinitarian persons. Just as certain of the transcendentals are appropriated to certain persons, so too beauty names their mutual indwelling.

But to say that the *Summa* defines beauty as the "sacred order" of the divine persons is to admit that beauty hews to the trinitarian taxis. So part II and chapter 4 consider the *Summa's* teaching on trinity. It studies specifically the "sacred order" or taxis of the trinitarian processions. This—on the definition of beauty canvassed above—constitutes the uncreated ground and measure of all beauty.[19]

Part III moves *ad extra* and opens the final movement of the book. Beauty as trinitarian order now in place, chapter 5 treats the *Summa's* doctrine of trinitarian causality. This accounts for creation's trinitarian traces (*vestigia*), analogous orders that reflect the very structure of their Lord. If the creature most intimate with the trinity is the human person, chapter 6 surveys the *Summa's* trinitarian anthropology. It shows that and how early Franciscan texts—beginning with Alexander's undisputed disputed questions— develop a psychology whose controlling conceit is the trinitarian *imago*. If that *imago* suffers sin's damage, its restoration comes under grace's sign. Chapter 7 concludes the book with a study of the *Summa's* theology of grace from an aesthetic angle of vision. Alexander construes sanctifying grace (*gratia gratum faciens*) as a "grace making trinitarian." This allows the Christian life to terminate in shared "delight" (*fructus*) between the trinity's beauty and the soul's, restored now by grace.

Two notes on matters of convention: the first on the question of authorship, the other on matters of textual reference.

As to authorship: although Roger Bacon (d. 1292) warned that the *Summa* bearing Alexander's name was not his only (or at all), its readers quickly forgot or ignored its joint authorship.[20] Bonaventure's editors remembered it in 1891. But against their dubia the Quaracchi editors of the *Summa*'s first three volumes asseverated authorship by "Alexander himself" (*ipse Alexander*).[21] Soon after, editorial oversight fell to Victorin Doucet, who confessed that collective authorship was now "beyond all doubt" and proposed the solution most scholars now accept.[22] Whatever Alexander's presence, the *frater inquirens* who penned or arranged *SH* I and III was likely John of La Rochelle. The identity behind the *Summa*'s massive second part (*frater considerans*) remains hidden.[23] And the (as-yet) unedited *SH* IV was probably finished long after Alexander's death in 1245—almost certainly by William of Middleton.[24]

How, then, to refer to the authors of the *Summa*? Scholars have adopted different strategies. Some invoke Doucet's characters: *frater inquirens* (likely John of La Rochelle) and *frater considerans*. Others still invoke "summists" or even "the Halensist."[25] My own preference is to read the *Summa Halensis* as scholastic pedagogy—as a theological performance or set of them. Performances turn on characters for the unfolding of the drama, not on the personal identity of the actors behind them. The text's authors preferred to write and perform scenes under their master's name—"Brother Alexander." This, then, is the name I too adopt for referencing the *Summa*'s authors. If many of the *Summa*'s readers remember that Bacon alerted us to the text's collective authorship, few recall that his qualification that "still, it is reckoned and called *Brother Alexander's Summa* (*Summa fratris Alexandri*) out of reverence."[26]

I take this approach to have several advantages. The first is a remembering of the premodern grammar of authorship.[27] Premoderns rarely thought about texts romantically—as expressions of singular genius.[28] Still less did they worry much at intellectual property. Whoever its authors, the *Summa* reflects a habit of writing that is more collaborative, more communal, more fraternal. Perhaps the business of composing a summa even mirrored the "common mendicant pattern of working."[29] Regardless of the *Summa*'s origins, its authors did not bother forensically to distinguish whose pen wrote what and when.

A second and related advantage to my approach is a refocusing of attention on the *Summa*'s theology. If this seems intuitive, it is not always common. Many readers of historical theology presume that history's canons for getting-the-text-right must be theology's too. I demur. The literature professor reads *Richard III* to explore its tension between free will and determinism; the

St. Thomas More biographer to trace Shakespeare's borrowings; the archaeologist to wonder at the unsettling similarity between Shakespeare's depiction and the scoliotic skeleton before her. None of these errs in any obvious sense—their ends simply differ. The same is true of the *Summa Halensis*. Fingerprinting, manuscript juxtaposing, redaction hypothesizing—these procedures belong to the historian. By contrast, a text's coming-to-be will matter to the theologian only in the rare case that this question bears directly on a theological one. So a *theological* reading of the *Summa* asks principally not "Whose is it, really?" but rather "What claims does it make about God and God's creatures? Are these claims true?"[30] That theology ought to be principally and primarily about God I learn too from the *Summa*, whose stated purpose is to "inculcate a pious disposition by means of divine instruction" that God might appear "to holy souls as sweet and delectable."[31] And so this book sidelines the authorship question precisely to allow the beauty of the *Summa*'s divine instruction to shine through.

As to matters of textual reference: there is not yet a received norm for citing the *Summa Halensis*. Here I prefer and (mostly) follow Kopf and Schumacher's proposal for shorthand reference over the longer-form[32]— so *SH* I, n. 103 (1:162) rather than *SH* I, tr. 3, q. 3, tit. un., c. 1, a. 2 (or, in the 1622 Cologne edition, *SH* I, q. 17, m. 2). The numbers following the *SH* stand for the *Summa*'s books (I, I–II, II–II, and III—I do not reference the unedited book IV). This is followed by a reference to the Quaracchi editor's section number. Within the parentheses the first number identifies the tome of the Quaracchi edition considered, the second the page number. This model of reference, I confess, has the disadvantage of wresting sections from their larger dialectical cycles. But then those cycles are hardly formally consistent across the *Summa* anyhow.

PART I

BEAUTY AMONG THE

TRANSCENDENTALS

When readers encounter scholastic aesthetics, they ask first about its transcendental status. They want to know whether beauty belongs alongside the one, the true, and the good. Why? Long debates over beauty's transcendental status in Thomas Aquinas's texts have trained readers to pose the question. Perhaps the question forms a kind of barometer—it sorts *this* strain of Thomist from *that*. Whatever the case, these debates over Thomas's texts have drawn other texts into their gyre. Among these is the *Summa Halensis*. And its answer to the question of beauty's transcendental status commands as much scholarly consensus as Thomas's texts do: almost none.

I begin, then, with Brother Alexander's teaching on the transcendentals. I do so mostly to show how his account of the transcendentals proves idiosyncratic. To ask after beauty's transcendental status in the *Summa Halensis*, we must first attend to its peculiar grammar of the transcendental determinations of being. Chapter 1 shows that Brother Alexander's interest in the transcendentals is already deeply theological—even trinitarian. He is at least as interested in discerning being's trinitarian structure as he is in mapping metaphysical categories. Chapter 2 confirms this. Not only do the transcendentals bear a trinitarian structure, but they also form trinitarian appropriations. Speaking the transcendentals, then, means already speaking the Trinity. Chapter 3 brings this trinitarian peculiarity to bear on the transcendental question. That Brother Alexander at length denies beauty's transcendental status does not render it epiphenomenal. Beauty as "sacred order" rather accounts for the very trinitarian structure of the transcendentals.

CHAPTER 1

TRANSCENDENTALS AND TRINITY

Nothing is more peculiar to Christians than their confession of the three-personed God. The doctrine of the trinity structures all Christian reflection on, sacrifice to, and worship of the God we confess. In this way it functions more like a "meta-doctrine."[1] That God is triune constitutes the rock upon which all other truth claims are either built or dashed. So the trinity enjoys epistemic primacy in Christian God-talk—or should.[2] Learning to speak Christian—patterning speech after and ordering it to the trinity God is—means rigorously subjecting reality to trinitarian discipline.

Brother Alexander does exactly this. His *Summa* conceives reality trinitarianly by indexing its teaching on the transcendental determinations of being to its doctrine of the trinity. For Alexander, I propose, being itself yields to trinitarian discipline. His very ontology betrays a "trinitarian motive."[3] Under this motive, the *Summa*'s expansive and influential doctrine of the transcendentals eschews a purely metaphysical account of what there is. Instead, Alexander's doctrine of being introduces the same trinitarian preoccupation that haunts all of the *Summa*'s pages.[4]

Before disclosing this trinitarian motive, I preview Brother Alexander's transcendental doctrine. I do not construct a genealogy of the transcendentals as they entered into the scholastic idiom. Neither do I draft a blueprint of the transcendental doctrine in the *Summa*.[5] Rather I merely introduce readers to the *Summa*'s peculiar construal of the transcendental determinations of being. However deep its sometime parallels, the account of the transcendentals the *Summa* writes is not Thomas's or Scotus's or Henry of Ghent's.[6] Indeed, these differences have much to do with the trinitarian motive my second section treats.

TRANSCENDENTALS IN THE *SUMMA HALENSIS*

The teaching on the so-called transcendentals follows hard upon the *Summa*'s cycles on theological epistemology and God's essential attributes. The first argues that God-talk is necessarily from God, to God, about God.[7] The-ology speaks its subject matter in two ways: *circa quam* and *de qua*. *Circa quam*, theology concerns "everything," that is, "being according to all its difference" or "different divisions of being."[8] *De qua*, theology has as its topic "being that is one in act, which is the first substance on which every-thing depends." Just here lies a tangle, however. It seems that the *Summa* fails the canons of Aristotelian science on at least two points. First, the *Posterior Analytics* stipulates that a science take one (and only one) sub-ject.[9] Has not Alexander registered two—creaturely and creative being? A second Aristotelian stipulation demands that a science possess essential knowledge of its subject.[10] To this, however, Christian theology should not pretend. Essential knowledge of "divinity itself and the trinity of per-sons" (*ipsa divinitas et trinitas personarum*) cannot be had—not here below anyway.[11]

Is theology less than scientific for fighting shy of Aristotelian canons? Not for Alexander. For him, theology names another, higher manner of knowing. Theology's knowledge begins with God's self-revelation.[12] Theol-ogy, that is, names a science "about the divine substance known through Christ in the works of restoration."[13] On the Halensian view, theology names "more a wisdom than a science (*sapientia magis quam scientia*)."[14] This introductory question[15] features an impulse that drives the *Summa*'s transcendental thinking: to think the relation between divine and created being through the grammar of God's self-revelation.[16]

The very title of the *Summa*'s third tractate bears this impulse. Next to consider, Brother Alexander teaches, is divine unity, truth, and goodness, "since these three notions (*tres intentiones*) are connected and related one to another."[17] It seems curious that the text should flag the transcendentals as somehow divine. Are they properly determinations of being, divine at-tributes, or divine names? Whatever the case, surely the *Summa*'s transcen-dental thought is already "integrated into a theological synthesis" to the extent that it establishes a "metaphysical ground for the explanation of the divine attributes."[18]

But the transcendentals invite a problem. It seems Brother Alexander wants to predicate unity, truth, and goodness not only of God, but also of creatures. And this seems impossible. There perdures, Alexander later writes, no similarity between God and creatures.[19] Later still, Alexander insists that "there is no fittingness (*convenientia*) of the creature to God."[20]

Can predication bridge the infinite interval that yawns between God and creation? Yes, Alexander answers, but only with the golden thread of analogy:

> Things may agree univocally in genus, form, or number. An example of analogical likeness would be substance and accident: they agree in that they are both [a sort of] being, which is predicated of them in terms of priority. Substance as [a sort of] being serves as a substrate to its accidents, and so "being" is predicated of substance primarily, which is "being" essentially, and of accidents secondarily, which are "beings" [by virtue of being] in something else. Thus we should say that there is no univocal agreement between God and creatures, but there is an analogical one. For example, if "good" is predicated of God and of creatures, it is predicated of God naturally (*per naturam*) and of God by participation (*per participationem*). This suggests that the predication "good" of God and of creatures is analogical (*secundum analogiam*).[21]

Here the *Summa* describes—but hardly explains—analogy analogously. How?

Being, the long Aristotelian tradition held, extends across the primordial division of substance from accident. If substance names that which has its being in and through itself (*per se*), accident names that which has its being in and through another (*ens in alio*). Properly and principally, then, being refers first to substance as *sine qua non* of accidents. Or, in Alexander's terms: being names substances *per prius*. Not that this robs accidents of being—they too have being, however derivative or *per posterius*. So both substance and accident are said to be, though not univocally. Univocal predication turns on generic identity. But being, Aristotle repeats like an antiphon, is no genus.[22] Thus being is predicated of substance and accident "according to analogy" (*secundum analogiam*), a bit of technology that allows predication between "before and after" (*prius et posterior*).[23] Let us call this the "transcendental analogy."[24]

The *Summa* uses this transcendental analogy to thicken what we might call a "theological analogy." Just as substance has its being "in itself" (*per se*) and accidents "in another" (*in alio*), so it is with God and creatures. God *is* God's very being—creatures only participate it. To the extent that 'good' describes both God and creatures, it will name God "by nature" (*per naturam*) and creatures "by participation" (*per participationem*). Hence "good" is properly and principally said of God *per prius* and of creatures *per posterius.* Philip the Chancellor wrote nearly the same,[25] though the *Summa* never registers this debt.[26] Absent Philip's account, though, is the theo-logic behind the substance-accident analogy. The *Summa's* account highlights ontological dependency: both accident and creature have their being "in another" (*in alio*). This allows the *Summa* to weave a "dependency of being"[27] into the grammar of participation. Accidental being derives from that substantial being just as created being derives from and participates God.[28] In both cases, "being" is said analogously.

This analogy redresses the preliminary difficulty, or how it is that the *Summa* applies the transcendental notions of unity, truth, and goodness across the ontological distinction. Or so it seems. The doctrine of analogy clarifies *that* the transcendental notions describe both God and creatures. But it remains unclear *what* about God and creatures these notions describe. What, we might ask, do these transcendentals pick out?

Here I commit a mild anachronism. The *Summa Halensis* never uses the term *transcendentalia*, itself an early modern term of art.[29] Neither does it use *communissima*, as Philip the Chancellor preferred. What we call "transcendentals" the *Summa* most often calls either "first intentions" (*primae intentiones*) or "first impressions" (*primae impressiones*). These descriptions function differently.

"First intentions" (*primae intentiones*) work mostly to show the notion's logical irreducibility.[30] They enjoy a sort of conceptual primacy with being and are thus simple.[31] As such, the first intentions "cannot be defined or made known by something prior to them."[32] This means that they are definable (*definibiles*) only through a "superadded *ratio*" (*ratio superaddita*) that they confer upon being. But it follows from their simplicity that this *ratio superaddita* cannot be defined. Why? On the Aristotelian view, definition means determining an essence by its genus and differentia.[33] But of course being is no genus. And to the extent that these "first impressions" are coextensive with being, they too lack a genus. A definition of the "first impressions" by something prior (*per priora*) cannot be had.[34] These are referenced only negatively *per posteriora,* by what is logically posterior— either *per abnegationem,* by negation, or *per positionem effectus consequentis,* by a position of consequent effect.[35] Logically speaking, a first intention "stands first" (*stare in primo*).[36]

So much on the "first intentions" (*primae intentiones*). But the *Summa* also calls one, true, and good the "first impressions" (*primae impressiones apud intellectum*).[37] Do these differ from *intentiones*? If "first intentions" emphasize the transcendental notions' logical irreducibility, the "first impressions" secure their epistemic priority.

What are these "first impressions"? The *Summa* offers a clue later in book I–II, where Alexander cites a certain "philosopher" who argued that "being is the first impression of the understanding."[38] This time the masked philosopher is Avicenna, not Aristotle.[39] Avicenna had argued that concepts like thing (*res*), being (*ens*), and the necessary (*necesse*) write primordial impressions upon the soul. That is, the soul receives these notions by "first impression"— not, notice, by acquiring them through "things better known than themselves."[40] Aristotle had said that the first principles of a science cannot be demonstrated. Rather they must be known immediately.[41] Yet what for Aristotle was mostly logical was for Avicenna *onto*logical: that is, Aristotle's first principles become first concepts or "first impressions." These first concepts— variously called *primae intentiones, primae conceptiones,* or *prima intelligibilia*— are "impressed" from without. In Avicenna's system, being so impressed means being given by the Agent Intellect.[42] To wax Kantian, these first concepts name the conditions for the possibility of knowing at all.[43]

As in Avicenna, so too in the *Summa Halensis*—or very nearly. The *Summa*'s quotation of Avicenna animates a discussion of the first principle. An objection suggests that what comes first commonly (*in communitate*) must also fall first causally (*in causalitate*). On this account the first impression must be of the first being, known through itself according to the intellect.[44] The *Summa* then endorses this argument. "It is by itself that the first principle," Brother Alexander writes, "is in the intellect and understood."

Notice how Alexander alloys the Augustinian form—innate knowledge of the first being[45]—with an Avicennian one—being as first known.[46] This compound recurs in the *Summa*'s teaching on divine naming. We name God either by his effects or by the impression of notions impressed upon the intellect. By the first we name the divinity "creator," "all-powerful," even "God." By the second we call God "one," "true," and "good." "These notions," the *Summa* explains, "are impressed upon us (*nobis impressae sunt*)." But of these notions "being" is first, since "being is the first intelligible (*primum intelligibile*)." And it is through this notion of "being," impressed by God, that we know God as being.[47] Thus the "first impressions" carry a double connotation. They are both what is most common and what is proper to God.

How exactly these different connotations relate one to another does not much exercise Alexander.[48] He says only that the *rationes* of the transcendental notions are "identical in God" but "distinguished in creatures." "Thus these *rationes* bear a certain likeness to their cause, as though they were impressions (*impressiones*) of it. And for this reason they are called traces (*vestigia*)."[49] The relation between them, then, seems to turn on the logic of analogy canvassed above.[50] At any rate, it is right to conclude with Aertsen that it is the *Summa*'s line on the first being as first known that becomes the style signature of Franciscan theology.[51]

A TRINITARIAN MOTIVE

So much, then, for what the transcendentals are: at least *primae intentiones* and *primae impressiones*. Yet attention to the first notions and their extensional unity is neither original to nor remarkable in the early thirteenth century—nor still unique to Christians. Avicenna had taught the same centuries before. Original to and remarkable in the early thirteenth-century scholastics was rather their emphasis on the *internal* structure or *order* of the first notions.[52] Christian scholastics wonder, in other words, if and how exactly the first notions differed one from another. The focus across the scholastic idiom, then, fell heavily and squarely on the notion's *intentional* relation. William of Auvergne, Philip the Chancellor, and the *Summa duacensis* already ask after the relation of these "firsts."[53] More remarkable still is how the *Summa Halensis* in particular adopts and adapts scholastic interest in transcendental order. If Philip innovated the limitation of being's conditions to three (one, true, good), the *Summa Halensis* baptizes it by discerning within it trinitarian traces.[54] It is this, the literature argues, that evinces the text's "trinitarian motive." If that is right, then attending to how the text orders the transcendentals means discerning a trinitarian discipline.[55] Does this bear out?

With the expansion of the doctrine of the transcendentals came their systematic ordering. But this incites quick and deep difficulties. How, if at all, are the transcendental notions to be organized? What accounts for their internal arrangement? Which is their order? The problem of order is introduced in the *Summa* by the convertibility thesis.[56] If being can be properly predicated of some thing *t*, the convertibility thesis holds, then so too can being's determinations—in this case the transcendental notions. But if by virtue of the simple fact that *t* exists, *t* is also one, true, and good, then it remains unclear whether and how the doctrine of the transcendentals escapes tautology.

Showing how the transcendentals contribute to, restrict, or otherwise determine being forms the snarl the third tract of the *Summa* seeks to disentangle. The snarl tangles the following threads of thought: If "one is convertible with being," as Dionysius argues;[57] and if unity and truth are both that by which beings are distinguished one from another, as Augustine suggests;[58] and if unity and goodness are both that which everyone desires, as Boethius writes,[59] then it seems that the intentions of every and each transcendental are identical with (and so add nothing to) being.[60] If the convertibility thesis amounts to this only, then the entire investigation of the transcendentals courts tautology. Are the transcendentals more than metaphysical pleonasms?

The solution drawn by the *Summa* to this aporia has two stages. At the first stage, Brother Alexander distinguishes being as the first intelligible (*primum intelligibile*) from the transcendentals as its first determinations (*primae determinationes*). He seems quite aware, however, of the difficulties with applying "determination" to being. Fleet of foot, he adds that *determinationes* are said to constrain (*coartabit*) being in two ways. A second distinction between the order of being (*actum existendi*) and the order of knowing (*ratio intelligendi*) allows the *Summa* to clarify what is meant by "constraint." According to the latter, the determination of unity indeed constrains being under what Alexander calls the "*ratio* of indivision" (*ratio indivisionis*). Note here, however, that the *Summa* understands the *ratio* of indivision to be wholly negative. It forms a more excellent determination. This itself is a form of negation. When I say something bears unity, for example, I mean only that it possesses no division. I have thus conceptually "constrained" or "contracted" being under the determination of being, if only negatively. And yet such constraint does not apply to a supposit—not in the order of being, anyway. As Dionysius argues, "no being exists without participating unity."[61]

The *Summa* here cribs a solution from Philip the Chancellor, whose *Summa de bono* first employed the *ratio indivisionis* to distinguish extensional from intensional unity.[62] "The attraction of this model," Aertsen notes, "is that 'one' adds something to being without limiting the extension of 'one'. 'One' retains its comprehensive, transcendental character because it does not add a positive reality but only the negation of division."[63] On the indivision model, the transcendentals as the first determinations of being differ intentionally (*secundum intentionem*) but not really (*secundum rem*).[64] In each case, indivision adds a conceptual negation to being. "One" denies that being contains any division whatever.[65] "True" denies that being contains a division between being itself and that which is.[66] And "good" denies that pure being contains a division between act and potency.[67] The last of these descriptions makes clear that the *esse* Alexander has in mind is uncreated.[68] Only in simple substances, after all and per Boethius, are *esse* and *id quod est* one. And God alone is truly *simplex*.[69] In all of these ways, Alexander traces patterns written by Philip the Chancellor. His treatment had applied the *ratio* of indivision established by unity to every determination. Only Alexander departs from Philip's picture at one point. Unlike Philip, Brother Alexander explores various systematic arrangements for how the transcendentals hang together.

It is within these systematic arrangements on the order of the transcendentals that the *Summa*'s "trinitarian motive" surfaces. Where? Alexander rehearses the question of their order each time he introduces a new transcendental determination. He writes of their arrangement, for instance, first in the question of unity, next in the question on truth, and last in the question on goodness.[70] In each place, the order given mirrors the first and longest description. The order listed in the question on truth even refers readers back to its elaboration in the question on unity.[71] For that reason, I dial in attention to the first account of the transcendentals' order.

This compressed passage outlines a triple model for ordering the transcendentals:

> We should say that being is the first intelligible. But the first determinations of being are one, true, and good: for these determine being insofar as the being of things is considered in their own genus (*in proprio genere*), and according to the relation of the being of things to its divine cause (*secundum relationem esse earum ad divinam causam*), and according to the relation of things to the soul (*secundum relationem rerum ad animam*), which is the image of the divine essence.[72]

Let us call these three modes the ontological (*in proprio genere*), the theological (*secundum relationem esse earum ad divinam causam*), and the anthropological (*secundum relationem rerum ad animam*).[73]

Only the second "theological" order, it seems, limns the determinations of being in bright trinitarian shades:

> Similarly, to the extent that the being of things is taken in relation to the divine cause, it has three determinations. For the divine cause causes in three ways: as an efficient cause, as a formal or exemplary cause, and as a final cause. And though all this causality is common to the whole trinity, its efficient aspect is appropriated to the Father, exemplary to the Son, and final to the Holy Spirit. In accord with this [triple causality], the being of creatures, which emanates from its cause, is impressed in three ways, in conformity with the [three sorts of] cause. The impression that results from conformity to efficient causality in creaturely being is unity: as the efficient cause, which is one and undivided, impresses upon a multitude of creatures, each acquires, to the extent possible, undivided being.[74]

As with unity, so with truth and goodness. Brother Alexander continues:

> Next, the impression that results from conformity to formal or exemplary causality [in creaturely being] is truth: as the exemplary cause is the primary art of truth, so every creature, insofar as it is possible, receives an imitation of this art, which amounts to possessing truth. More, the impression that results from conformity to final causality [in creaturely being] is goodness: as the final cause is the highest goodness, every creature has proclivity and conformity to the highest goodness, which is the goodness of creatures. So the unity of the being of creatures demonstrates the unity of the efficient cause; the truth [of the being of creatures demonstrates] the truth of the exemplary cause, and the goodness [of the being of creatures] demonstrates the goodness of the final cause.[75]

The *Summa* "triples" the determination of being according to Aristotle's immaterial causes. Causality as such belongs properly to the "whole trinity in common" (*commune toti trinitati*). But the logic of appropriation—on which more anon in chapter 2—allows that efficient causality belongs to the Father, formal or exemplary causality to the Son, and final causality to the Spirit. Exactly because the cause remains in the effect,[76] the trinity out of which creation flows (*fluit*) thus signs every creature with a triple impression (*triplicem impressionem*). Through this and to the extent that it is able, a creature conforms to its triune cause. The course of a creature's conformity to its efficient cause (the Father) is inscribed into the corresponding *impressio*. So far as a creature bears the impression of one, that is, the creature manifests its relation to and dependence upon the Father's efficient causality.

Next Alexander transposes this pattern. The impression of the true upon the creature, an *imitatio artis*, displays its conformity to the exemplary causality of the Son, here called the first art (*ars prima*).[77] And the good's mark discloses the creature's relation to the "highest good" (*summa bonitas*) or the final cause, both of which, Alexander assumes, belong to the Spirit's business. That these causes cohere within a singular creature, finally, demonstrates exactly how a single notion—on this model, causality—might bear a threefold determination "according to intention" (*secundum intentionem*).[78] This is the *ratio* of indivision at work.

No doubt the strong trinitarian dimensions of this passage confirm the presence of a "trinitarian motive." "The *Summa* is not interested in a consideration of being in itself," Aertsen suspects. Rather it "sees the ontological determinations of being as 'the vestiges' of the trinity in the created world."[79] However razor-sharp his suspicion, Jan A. Aertsen leaves it unproven.[80] Proving what he only suspects would entail discerning a trinitarian motive within Brother Alexander's two other modes of ordering the transcendentals.

So I take up where Aertsen leaves off. Had he kept reading, Aertsen would have noticed the trinitarian motive slinking beneath the other modes of ordering the transcendentals too. Consider Alexander's second, "anthropological" ordering of the transcendentals:

> Again, in comparison to the soul the determination is tripled. For the being of things is compared to the soul in three ways, namely as things ordered in the memory (*memoria*), perceived in the understanding (*intelligentia*), and loved in the will (*voluntate*). And so unity is in some beings from the efficient cause, through which unity is ordered and preserved in the memory. For memory organizes the things that it retains according to a pattern of unity and difference among them. Again, truth is in some beings from the exemplary cause, through which truth might be perceived by the understanding. Again, goodness is in some beings from the final cause, through which goodness is loved or commended by the will.[81]

The being of things (*esse rerum*) is here tripled again to form a psychological triad, one Alexander learns from Augustine's *De trinitate*.[82] Things relate to the soul (*per comparationem ad animam*) according to its three faculties. The soul's objects are, the text explains, ordered to the memory (*memoria*), perceived by the understanding (*intelligentia*), and desired by the will (*voluntas*). Perhaps predictably, efficient causality gifts every being its unity, which is in turn ordered to and stored by the memory. Truth inheres within a being by virtue of its exemplary causality, a reality grasped by the intellect. And the will seeks and desires a thing's goodness, which it has through its relation to its final cause. This passage anticipates a protracted lesson on the trinitarian *imago dei* in *SH* I–II, whose keynotes are already sounded here.[83]

Read together with the theological and anthropological orders, even the ontological order that considers being in its proper genus (*in proprio genere*) figures trinitarianly:

> Now to the extent that the being of things is considered in their own genus, there are three determinations of being. Indeed, being is considered either absolutely or relatively. In its turn, relative being is considered either as far as difference is concerned or as far as agreement is concerned. To the extent that a being is considered absolutely, undivided in itself, and separated from other [beings], it is determined by oneness. Yet to the extent that a being is considered in relation to another [being] in terms of its difference, it is determined by truth, for "true" stands for the ability of a thing to be detectible. Yet to the extent that [a being] is considered in relation to another [being] in terms of fittingness or order, it is determined by goodness, for "good" stands for the ability of a thing to fit into an order.[84]

Here Alexander considers being either absolutely (*absolutum*) or relatively (*comparatum*). He sorts the latter further into being according to difference (*secundum differentiam*) and fittingness (*secundum convenientiam*). Absolute being corresponds to one. The other two determinations belong to relative being. The true names that by which beings are discerned and so matches being *secundum differentiam*. And the good is that by which a thing is ordered, corresponding to being *secundum convenientiam*.

The trinitarian shape of these distinctions is present, if subtle. The *Summa* here deploys an ontological distinction present in Alexander's own

Glossa in quatuor libros Sententiarum Petri Lombardi. There Alexander distinguishes uncreated and created being as being not from another (*ens non ab alio*) and being from another (*ens ab alio*). Then he sorts being from another into being *in* another (*ens in alio*) and being *not in* another (*ens non in alio*).[85] This distinction affords Alexander an analogy to the trinity's inner life. There the same distinction works to identify the divine persons by means of origin—a choice that would come to typify Franciscan trinitarian theology.[86] To be a divine person, Alexander says, means to be God not from another (*alius non ab alio*) or else from another (*alius ab alio*).[87] Of course the former category applies to the Father alone as the only person to whom the divine notion of innascibility belongs.[88] The latter variously describes both the Son and the Spirit, who through generation and procession respectively remain distinct from the Father.[89]

Hence all three modes of ordering the transcendentals—the theological, anthropological, and ontological—elicit trinitarian interest. The theological mode correlates one, true, and good to efficient, formal, and final causality. It then appropriates each to a trinitarian person. The anthropological mode indexes the transcendentals to the Augustinian *memoria-intelligentia–voluntas*. Augustine's *De trinitate* identifies this psychological triplet, of course, as the highest analog of the *trinitas quae deus est*. The ontological mode sorts being into absolute and relative, then relative being according to difference or fittingness. These Brother Alexander links to one, true, and good. As noted and as I will show later, dividing being into absolute and relative, then relative into two sorts, recalls trinitarian distinction by origin. The point for now is that in Brother Alexander, the trinity thus appears behind every sequence of ordering the transcendentals. Indeed, the *Summa*'s peculiar doctrine of the transcendentals discloses a "trinitarian motive."[90]

CONCLUSION

Thirteenth-century metaphysics underwent a "transcendentalisation."[91] In this the *Summa Halensis* played no small role. Its expansive and innovative teaching on the transcendental determinations of being has proved deeply influential. Among its many innovations is the close attention it pays to the internal ordering of the transcendental determinations of being. Brother Alexander seems unsatisfied to receive uncritically transcendental terms inherited from various traditions—Latin, Arabic, and so on. Instead, he adopts a list of terms from Philip the Chancellor. But Alexander also adapts them by recasting them in a trinitarian light. Somehow, the transcendental determinations of being—uncreated *and* created—relate one to another as the trinity does. This means that the *Summa*'s systematic arrangements of the transcendentals do not represent a disinterested metaphysics untouched by theological commitments. No, Brother Alexander's trinitarian preoccupation suffuses his very ontology.

All of which confirms and deepens recent literature's suspicions of a "trinitarian motive" behind the *Summa*'s teaching on the transcendentals. Still unaddressed, however, is exactly what theological difference this makes—if indeed any. So the question becomes: Is correlation of the transcendentals with the trinity evident elsewhere across the text? If not, Brother Alexander's trinitarian ontology will turn out to be largely ornamental. Might this connection prove more substantive?

CHAPTER 2

TRANSCENDENTALS AS TRINITARIAN APPROPRIATION

Brother Alexander's *Summa* conceives being trinitarianly. It does this, my last chapter showed, by correlating the transcendentals—one, good, true—to the persons of the trinity. Other of the *Summa*'s readers have noticed this correlation too.[1] Less noticed is not where or whether the *Summa* thinks the transcendentals trinitarianly, but rather *how* it does so. After all, trinitarian logic demands more than the mere association of triplets. If they are truly trinitarian, the transcendentals must betray more than just a "trinitarian motive."[2] They must, rather, operate inside the very *logic* of the trinity—its three-in-oneness.

How then does Brother Alexander hew one, true, and good to trinitarian logic? He hides a clue at *SH* I, n. 73. "But certain causality," he writes, "though it be common to the whole trinity, is appropriated (*appropriatur*) as efficient cause to the Father, exemplary to the Son, final to the Holy Spirit."[3] Here the *Summa* "appropriates" causality to the persons of the trinity. In turn, the text links these causes to the transcendentals themselves, yielding the following picture: one–efficient cause–Father, true–exemplary cause–Son, good–final cause–Holy Spirit.

Tripling of this sort is hardly limited to this passage. Indeed, Brother Alexander consistently relates the transcendentals to the persons of the trinity according to the scholastic logic of appropriation shows how this trinitarian relation amounts to more than mere "motive." But how exactly? According to the *Summa*'s own account of appropriation, the practice of appropriating actually exposits the doctrine of the trinity. For Brother Alexander, then, to appropriate the transcendentals is already to practice trinitarian theology. And this is precisely what the transcendental teaching of the *Summa* does.

A GRAMMAR OF TRINITARIAN APPROPRIATION

"Appropriation" for the scholastics names a highly technical habit of speaking the trinity—a grammar.[4] And constitutive of every grammar is a syntax and a lexicon. The lexicon provides the nonnegotiable terms of art by means of which trinitarian appropriation happens. The syntax offers the rules of their combination. Here I display the syntax and the lexicon of appropriation in the *Summa* before showing that Brother Alexander expands both to include the transcendentals. I seek first a clear picture of how appropriation works and to what end. Getting this right, I suggest, allows us to see how the *Summa* employs appropriation across its transcendental doctrine in the next section.

The *Summa* assumes a syntax of appropriation that it never fully describes. Perhaps the most compressed and precise conspectus of appropriation's syntax is found in Bonaventure's *Breviloquium*:[5]

> As to the plurality of appropriations, holy scripture teaches us to hold the following: that even though all the essential attributes apply equally and without distinction to all the persons, yet oneness is appropriated (*appropriari*) to the Father, truth to the Son, and goodness to the Holy Spirit. . . . Now, these are said to be appropriated, not because they are proper (*propria*) to these persons, since they are always common (*communia*) to them all, but because they lead to a better understanding and knowledge of what is proper (*propriorum*), that is the three persons themselves.[6]

Bonaventure distinguishes between what is proper (*propria*) to the three persons and what is common (*communia*) to them. The distinction trades on a more fundamental one between personal properties and essential attributes.[7] The *Summa* evinces the same distinction. If attributes that describe God as God concern what is said commonly (*dictum communiter*), those that name God as (say) Holy Spirit are *propria*.[8] The *Summa*'s very preface to its teaching on appropriation flags this distinction.[9] Let this distinction account for the first syntactical law of appropriation: Whatever is properly said to be common x to the divine substance s applies properly to the trinity of persons (p_1, p_2, p_3) precisely *as* their substance s. More simply: divine simplicity guarantees that the persons are the divine substance, which is its attributes. Each is coextensive with the other; none is divisible. And, as Bonaventure and Alexander explain, the only thing distinctive among the persons is their respective properties of relation.[10] So the Son is not the Father nor the Father the Son, and neither is the Holy Spirit—nor is the Spirit they. But each is the divine substance.

So far, so orthodox. But a difficulty arises when theologians impute an essential attribute to one or another of the persons. What of Paul's description of the Son as "the wisdom of God" (*dei sapientia*)? Bonaventure and Brother Alexander allow for this to the extent that it does not confuse an essential attribute with a personal property. This, then, is the second syntactical law of appropriation: An essential attribute x may be "appropriated" to a person ($p2$, say) of the trinity s as fittingness demands, as long as x is understood to apply properly to the substance s and so to all persons ($p1$, $p2$, $p3$).[11]

So much for the syntax of appropriation. What of its lexicon? Following the Lombard, the *Summa*'s cycle of questions on appropriation catalogs four triplets: eternity-form-use, unity-equality-harmony, power-wisdom-goodness, and from whom-through whom-in whom.

A brief word on each. The triplet eternity-form-use (*aeternitas-species-usus*) is Hilary's,[12] or rather Hilary's as it struck Augustine.[13] Most scholastics learned it through Peter Lombard's *Sentences*.[14] Immediately Brother Alexander sets to work, showing that Hilary's appropriation bears an internal order that reflects that of the trinity. The logic of appropriation (*ratio appropriationis*) demands that eternity (*aeternitas*) be appropriated to the Father, since eternity is "not from another essentially" (*non ab alio essentialiter*) and the Father is "not from another personally" (*non ab alio personaliter*). Thus the Father is named eternity: neither depends on another for its existence (*non esse ab alio*). The same holds for the Son and the Spirit. The Son is generated by the Father "like knowledge from the mind," so both form (*species*) and the Son traffic in the *ratio cognoscendi*. And the Spirit is use (*usus*) precisely because the procession of the Holy Spirit is like that of the will from knowledge and mind."[15] What is the point? Brother Alexander seems to connect Hilary's triad to Augustine's trinitarian thought to show the coherence of appropriation, particularly with *these* words. Hilary's words are not arbitrary—they stand in for and exposit *propria* by means of *communia*. Brother Alexander aims to show, then, that Hilary's triad betrays an internal structure that reflects that of the trinity.[16]

Brother Alexander discerns the same trinitarian structure in the Lombard's second appropriative triad, unity-equality-concord (*unitas-aequalitas-concordia*).[17] The triad derives from Augustine's *De doctrina christiana*.[18] Unity belongs to the Father for two reasons. First, because he *non est ab alio*, is not from another; second, because *unitas per se multiplicata non generat nisi unum*, unity multiplied in itself produces only one. Equality belongs to the Son, since it presupposes *pluralitas*. As Augustine says, "the Image is co-equal to the Father, not the Father to the Image." And concord to the Holy Spirit? Alexander quotes Richard of St. Victor: "The origin of unity is in the Father, the inchoate status of plurality is in the Son, and the completion of the trinity (*completio trinitatis*) is in the Holy Spirit."[19] A question immediately follows: what might it mean to call the Holy Spirit the *completio trinitatis*? Without the Holy Spirit, Brother Alexander worries with Richard, there would be none in the trinity to connect plurals.[20] So the logic of the triad unity-equality-concord mirrors the logic of the trinity. The Father remains singular in his unbegottenness, the Son in his equality with the Father and cospiration of the Spirit, and the Spirit in his binding together of Father and Son.[21] Here again, Brother Alexander's point seems the same. The words of appropriation are hardly arbitrary.[22]

For the moment, I skip the *Summa*'s third triad and jump to the fourth, from whom-through whom-in whom. Obviously it evokes Paul's phrase in Romans 11:36. But the Lombard found its more proximate champions in "les maîtres chartrains."[23] Brother Alexander receives it thus: "ex" belongs to the Father as "first principle who lacks a principle"; "per" to the Son as "principle from the principle, through whom everything was made, as an artist works through art"; and "in" to the Spirit as "the enclosure of everything good." He concludes: "The sense is this: *ex ipso* all things are created *per* the highest wisdom or through the Son *in* the highest good or the Holy Spirit."[24] This appropriative triplet deepens Alexander's emphasis on just how deliberate appropriated terms are.

The third triplet, power-wisdom-will, interests Brother Alexander most. A detailed genealogy of this particular triplet would reveal his debts alongside his dividends. But perhaps it is enough to say here that the triad features prominently (if controversially) in Peter Abelard's threefold work on the trinity;[25] that it enters deeply into the theology of the Victorines,[26] especially in the thought of Hugh[27] and Richard of St. Victor; that it passes from these twelfth century denizens into the *Sentences* of Peter Lombard; and that it finds its first expansive and "*bien organisé*" expression in the *Summa*.[28] The structure of his treatment already renders Alexander's pet interest in this triplet rather plain. The previous two triplets occupy a single question over the span of two or three pages. By contrast, Alexander's treatment of the power-wisdom-will triplet runs to nearly thirteen bicolumned pages in the Quaracchi edition. More, Brother Alexander affords each term within the triplet a *membrum* of its own, sometimes with attendant chapter and article distinctions. However deep his interests in this particular triad, Alexander treats it very much as he treats the other two, which is to say he discerns within it a trinitarian *ordo*. "Power is prior to knowledge and will, just as the ability to know and to will are prior to knowing and willing. And in this way the appropriation is assigned, namely of power to the Father, wisdom to the Son, and will to the Spirit."[29]

For now, I bracket extended exegesis of the power-wisdom-will triplet. More important here is what Alexander considers the *ratio appropriationis horum trium*, the logic of this appropriative triplet. Beyond explaining why Alexander finds this particular triplet so interesting, this passage alludes to the purpose of trinitarian appropriation in general. "The reason," Alexander writes, "for appropriating power to the Father, wisdom to the Son, and will or goodness to the Holy Spirit is twofold: first, by reason of negating error (*remotionis erroris*); and second, by reason of showing the truth (*ostendendae veritatis*)."[30]

The first reason—the *via remotionis erroris*—borrows from Hugh of St. Victor.[31] Against Abelard, Hugh protests that these appropriated terms work destructively—they disrupt Abelard's insistence that power-wisdom-will map neatly onto personal properties. Instead, these terms function first to make strange again what Brother Alexander will call the *nomina propria personarum*: "Father," "Son," and "Holy Spirit."[32] In typical patterns of speech, "father" sometimes conjures images of frailty or impotence. And "son" might connote immaturity or inequality with his father. Even "spirit" might suggest swollen pride or enthusiasm. The triplet thus checks the slippage of ordinary language. Against impotence stands *potentia*, against immaturity *sapientia*, and against swollen pride *bonum*.[33] For Hugh, this triplet primarily discloses the limits of our language about so transcendent an object.[34]

Brother Alexander then tempers Hugh's *via remotionis erroris* with Richard's *via ostendendi veritatem*, the way of "showing the truth." Richard's way meets Hugh's apophatic diffidence with speculative mettle.[35] Richard appropriates not to deny ordinary experience's intimacy with God, but rather to deepen it. Experience shows that wisdom presupposes power (and goodness both), just as the Son presupposes the Father (and the Spirit both).[36] Thus the triplet hints at an intelligible order that discloses the structure of God's essential attributes. Both wisdom and goodness (or will) presuppose power, but power presupposes neither. Wisdom, in turn, hangs upon power, and goodness upon both power and wisdom. Absent this order there is only disorder. "Lucifer, who shined like the morning," for example, "had much power and cognition, but not a good will." The *Summa* thinks it important that these essential attributes (power-wisdom-will) bear an internal structure.

Why focus on the order of the essential attributes? Richard does so because he thinks their order reveals something about the trinity's personal properties (*proprietates summae trinitatis*). Power evokes unbegottenness, the *proprium* of the Father. Wisdom's dependence upon power but not goodness evokes the Son's begottenness. And goodness's dependence upon both wisdom and power calls to mind the Spirit's procession from both the unbegotten and the begotten.[37] For both Richard and Alexander, then, the point remains the same. The order of God's essential attributes itself follows a trinitarian taxis. God, we might say, is God's attributes trinitarianly.

Gilles Emery notices that the *SH*, like Bonaventure, "strictly limits appropriations to attributes which connote an order or an origin: the other attributes cannot be appropriated."[38] He continues: "In and of themselves, the appropriated names remain shared by the whole trinity, but considered *as from within their relationships*, they induce us to grasp the personal properties."[39] This line on appropriation—the Richardian-Franciscan one— aims to correlate essential attributes (*communia*) with personal properties (*propria*). Put otherwise: it refuses to conceive God's essential attributes without trinitarian discipline.[40] So for the *SH*, the second reason for appropriating ("showing the truth") involves discovering the trinitarian structure of God's essential attributes. Not that this sunders the distinction between essential attributes and personal properties—this was Abelard's crime. The point for the *Summa* has rather to do with the *way* God is God— as trinity. And if truth itself is trinitarian, showing that truth will mean tracing trinitarian patterns. When this means speaking, our speech will be trinitarian appropriation.[41]

The grammar of appropriation in the *SH*, like every grammar, has a syntax and a lexicon. Its syntax here involves the application of essential attributes to one or another of the persons because those attributes somehow relate to a personal property. The lexicon of appropriation in the *Summa*, the terms of art ruled by that syntax, borrows from the Lombard. Alexander's lexicon consists in four triplets: eternity-form-use, unity-equality-concord, power-wisdom-will, and from whom-through whom-in whom. But why learn to speak this recherché scholastic grammar? Alexander offers two reasons: to point up the limits of our God-talk and to point out the truth of our faith. On the *Summa*'s view, appropriation does not indulge a frivolous name game. No, appropriation names a practice of figuring the trinity through careful attention "to the *words* of Scripture, the *words* of tradition, which characterizes scholastic method."[42]

ONE, TRUE, AND GOOD AS TRINITARIAN APPROPRIATIONS

The *SH* extends the lexicon of trinitarian appropriation it received from its twelfth-century predecessors. To the Lombard's lexicon, that is, Brother Alexander now adds the transcendentals themselves. Or one, true, and good also name what is common to the divine essence with special reference to a certain person's *proprium*. What does this mean, and why does it matter? Remember the *Summa*'s two stated reasons for appropriating: to point up the limits of our God-talk and to point out the truth of our faith. So if the text speaks the transcendental terms as trinitarian appropriations, then it evinces something more than just a "trinitarian motive." The *Summa*'s transcendental doctrine already teaches trinitarian theology.

There is a preliminary objection to reading the transcendental determinations of being as trinitarian appropriations. In *SH* I, n. 73, an imagined dissenter might object, it is the *causes* and not the transcendentals that the *Summa* appropriates to the persons.[43] The middle term does not drop out until Bonaventure appropriates the transcendentals to the persons in his *Breviloquium*. The innovation belongs, it seems, to Bonaventure—not to Brother Alexander.

This is true enough, at least in several places across the *Summa*.[44] But then my imagined dissenter overlooks a crucial passage. As Brother Alexander catalogs definitions of "true," he lingers over one from Anselm:

> But another [definition of truth] describes uncreated truth according to what is taken personally and appropriated to the Son (*accipitur personaliter et appropriator Filio*), just as unity [is] to the Father (*unitas Patri*) and goodness to the Holy Spirit (*bonitas Spiritui Sancto*), which is: "Truth is the highest likeness to the principle," etc. . . . Because this definition

is of first truth, taken personally and by appropriation (*accipitur person-aliter et per appropriationem*), there is thus nothing to the objections concerning the essence or the Father or the truth of creatures. Hence that description is shown through the personal property (*per proprietatem personae*) of the Son and through his distinction from the other persons (*per distinctionem ab aliis personis*) and through his distinction from creatures.[45]

The language could scarcely ring clearer. Truth is "received personally and *appropriated* to the Son, just as unity is to the Father and goodness to the Holy Spirit." More, Alexander shows that he means "appropriation" in its technical sense. Does this definition sunder truth from the Father, the divine essence, and creatures?[46] It need not—and that it need not has everything to do with the logic of appropriation. As an essential attribute, truth belongs properly to the divine essence. But on this particular definition, truth belongs in a special sense to the Son as "the highest likeness to the principle" (*summa similitudo principia*). That is, truth corresponds to a particular personal property that distinguishes the Son from the other persons—that "likeness" guaranteed by his begottenness from the Father. Still, Alexander hardly sequesters truth to the Son without remainder. Again, the syntax of appropriation demands a sharp distinction between personal properties and essential attributes. Applying that syntax means that truth belongs to the divine essence and, it follows, to the Father. And creatures also participate this truth by imitation. Hence the preliminary objection entertained above does not hold. It cannot, since this passage conspicuously extends both the syntax and the lexicon of appropriation to the transcendental terms.

More can and should be said about this—much more, in fact, since this passage hardly exhausts appropriation's relation to the transcendentals in the *Summa*. Even so, my task here is not to compile an index of such sites. It is rather to show that and how the *SH* conceives the transcendentals—one, true, good—as trinitarian appropriations. I undertake it to deepen the literature's consensus over a "trinitarian motive" that animates Alexander's teaching on the transcendentals. How? If the transcendentals function as trinitarian appropriations, as speech meant to "show the truth" of the faith, then the text evinces something considerably more than a "trinitarian motive." It forms nothing less than an exercise in trinitarian theology.

Although many scenes in the *Summa* support this conclusion, I assay only three. Each relates a transcendental determination of being to a divine person. When each scene does so, it performs work typically classed as trinitarian theology proper. I treat each transcendental term in turn: one first, true next, and good last.

In the question on the unity of the divine nature, Brother Alexander wonders whether divine unity in itself is compatible with plurality. In thick Richardian brogue,[47] Brother Alexander responds. Yes, "the unity of divine being is unity in plurality; and this shows its perfection."[48] A rhetorical Platonist objects: why not unity in one (*unitas in uno*)? This holds according to the logic of natures, Alexander responds—not of persons.[49] Nothing "demonstrates the power and perfection" of true unity more than "the unity which is in plurals personally different or according to relation." In this sense, the distinction between *esse ab alio* and *non esse ab alio* does not imperil divine unity. Rather it *constitutes* that unity. And what underwrites this unity in plurality? A prototypical Franciscan answer:[50] "by speaking of commonality according to origin, there is one common, namely the person of the Father, by which the others have origin."[51]

Notice that the question considers the unity of the *divine* nature. Only the third membrum considers created unities. Throughout, Brother Alexander wants mostly to assay the peculiar mode of God's unity—whether it is compatible with a plurality of persons, for instance, or of principles, or of ideas. Whatever the case, the peculiar mode of divine unity owes to the Father, "principle without principle."[52] That the Father lacks origin means he is "the fontal fullness of the Godhead . . . the richest source of all the immanent processions and the external productions."[53] And even though unity names an essential attribute, the *Summa* appropriates it to the Father because it evokes his personal property: innascibility.[54] Assaying divine unity, then, already invites technical trinity-talk. For the *SH*, "one" is not an abstract metaphysical principle. It is a paternal appropriation.

And the true? When Brother Alexander repeats Pontius Pilate's question—*quid est veritas?*—he compiles several answers. One of Anselm's feels rather spinous. Truth, Anselm seems to suggest, is necessarily constrained to the order of bodies.[55] Is God not true, then? Remember, Alexander counsels, that *rectitudo* means "an arrangement of the middle to extremes." Does this dethorn the problem? "True order consists in three (*consistit in tribus*). Thus "truth is found in all things like a medium irreducible to extremes"—as in creation, so in the creator "in a loftier sense." In God there are the extremes of efficient and final causality. Suspended between them "like a medium irreducible to extremes" hangs the formal cause—"the truth according to which everything is made."[56]

But is this truth personal or essential? Both:

> Considered in itself, this is [in] two modes: personal and essential. Personally, there is found the sacred order of the trinity: the Father as one extreme who is not from another, the Holy Spirit as the other extreme from whom there is no other, and the Son as an irreducible medium, who is from another and from whom there is another, and he is truth personally. . . . Essentially, there is found [in God] according to the *ratio* of understanding being, understanding, and loving, since God is himself and understands himself and loves himself. And as unity he understands himself as truth and loves himself as goodness. Being is one extreme, loving the other, and understanding is like a medium irreducible to either.[57]

That this passage imagines *veritas* as trinitarian appropriation scarcely requires argument. Let us trace the logic anyhow. The passage opens with an attempt to rescue truth as a divine attribute. Truth on the definition in view entails rectitude. Can this apply to God? Yes, so far as rectitude spells an order among three terms. There truth names the suspended middle, a pose between extremes that buckles to neither. In God this middle bears a name. He is Son, spirator and generated at once. The logic here turns on the *Summa*'s correlation between truth as a suspended middle irreducible to extremes and the Son's *proprium*, namely being *Filius*.[58] This personal property suggests the Son's double notions: filiaton or passive generation (*filiatio vel generatio passiva*) and spiration in common (*spiratio communis*).[59] As generated by the Father and with him generating the Spirit, the Son is middle or center.[60] Or so the true conceived *personaliter*. The *Summa* affirms the true in its essential acceptation too, where it functions as a divine attribute. That Alexander construes the true both *essentialiter* as attribute and *personaliter* as connoting a personal property reveals the grammar of appropriation at work. In this passage and others, then, truth functions as a term appropriated to the Son.

The good as pneumatic appropriation proves more elusive. Yes, Brother Alexander personally appropriates goodness to the Holy Spirit.[61] Yes, he also appropriates final causality to the Spirit.[62] And yes, he connects these: "goodness is appropriated to the Holy Spirit, to whom is also appropriated the *ratio* of final causality."[63] But does all this amount to an appropriation in the technical sense? Compared to his lurid appropriation of one and true, Brother Alexander appears rather oblique on the good. However clearly the transcendental doctrine enunciates the good as pneumatic appropriation, it lacks a passage explicitly correlating the good to the Spirit's personal property.

Not that this connection is absent the *Summa*. For whatever reason, Alexander prefers to hide it in texts outside his teaching on the transcendentals. He shades his connection between the good and the Spirit's "passive spiration" (*spiratio passiva*) from a double source in two passages. In the first, his argument begins by stipulating a definition of the highest good (*summum bonum*).[64] The highest good is the most productive. The axiom is broadly Platonic—its application will not be. Production takes two forms: the natural (*per modum naturae*) and the voluntary (*per modum voluntatis*).[65] If the highest good is the highest really, it will actualize both modes of production. So the trinity comprises both: the Son by natural production, the Spirit by voluntary production.[66] And the Spirit must proceed from both Father and Son. Otherwise, the text argues, the trinity would feature twin Sons. So while the "good" here seems to describe the Father, it really names the Spirit as the "product" of God's double production.[67]

A second argument correlating the good to the Spirit's personal property comes from Richard of St. Victor—I glossed it already above. Again, and very briefly: goodness depends upon power and wisdom. The Spirit's antithesis here, recall, is Lucifer, whose power and wisdom run without goodness. The good's twin dependence on power and wisdom "expresses the properties of the highest trinity," especially that of "the person of the Holy Spirit, who is from the unbegotten as much as from the begotten." In this way—and here Richard ventriloquizes Brother Alexander—"in goodness the property of the Holy Spirit is especially attributed to the Spirit."[68] As well as Alexander hides these passages, the connection across them is plain. The good names an essential attribute sometimes predicated specially of the Holy Spirit. In short, it is a pneumatic appropriation.

One to the Father, true to the Son, good to the Spirit—these name the determinations of being as trinitarian appropriations. Yet Alexander says more still. In a question on the relation between one and good, he dons his trinitarian commitments almost garishly. Not only do these determinations function as trinitarian appropriations. We should also say, he writes, "that these intentions—one, true, good—indwell one another (*se circumince-dunt*)."[69] Brother Alexander's use of *circumincedere* is hardly accidental. It is a trinitarian term of art, one Alexander likely learns from Burgundio of Pisa's translation of *De fide orthodoxa*.[70] Perhaps Brother Alexander learns to apply it beyond the confines of trinity talk from Philip the Chancellor.[71] Whatever the case, Alexander proceeds to highlight an "intra-entative relationality."[72] Neither true nor one is desired apart from good. Neither are one and good understood apart from true. Neither are true and good ordered to the memory without one. Had Alexander stopped here, he would scarcely have left the shores of Neoplatonism—its principle of pre-dominance demands much the same. But Alexander braves Christian waters when he writes of the transcendentals that their *rationes induunt*. Their logics, that is, like the persons they connote, interpenetrate one another (*se circumincedunt*).[73]

CONCLUSION

My last chapter noted the idiosyncratic forms the transcendentals take in the *SH*. It stressed, too, a philosophical contrast between Brother Alexan-der's forms and more familiar ones. The present chapter supports and deep-ens the conclusion that the *Summa*'s account is idiosyncratic. How? However idiosyncratic its philosophical eccentricities, more idiosyncratic still is the text's "trinitarian motive." Yet I argued above that the trinitarian dimension of Brother Alexander's transcendental thought evinces something more than a mere motive. (After all, motives do not always accomplish what they seek.) The *SH* includes the transcendentals within the lexicon of trinitarian ap-propriation. Reading the transcendentals backward through the sections on appropriations shows how the transcendental doctrine already per-forms trinitarian theology. One, true, and good, that is, already invoke the peculiar grammar of trinitarian faith.

Why highlight this trinitarian idiosyncrasy? A first reason is broadly his-torical. Conceiving transcendentals as trinitarian appropriations remains distinctive to the *SH*. It is absent the *Summa*'s predecessors (William of Au-vergne, William of Auxerre), contemporaries (Philip the Chancellor and Albert the Great), and many of its inheritors alike—Bonaventure excepted.

Thomas Aquinas even notes the strangeness of Alexander's account when he registers, misrepresents, and rejects something like it in his disputed questions *De veritate*.[74] This distinctiveness alone—the writing and near immediate forgetting of a pattern of thought—elicits historical interest.

Another reason concerns the interpretation of the *Summa* itself. Often readers study Brother Alexander's teaching on the transcendentals without noticing or conceding its strangeness. These readers praise the text for its systematic expansion of the doctrine of transcendentals without attending explicitly to the transcendentals' appropriative function. Even when they detect a "trinitarian motive" across the transcendental doctrine, they rarely detail what difference it might make. I have here sought only to accentuate that difference. Detailing the difference it makes for the *SH* to subject being's determinations to trinitarian discipline remains too heavy a yoke. Easier and lighter (if barely) is the question of what this trinitarian difference has to do with beauty, whose seat among the other transcendentals in the *SH* remains contested. It is under this burden that my next chapter labors.

CHAPTER 3

BEAUTY AS TRANSCENDENTAL ORDER

S o I think, Hippias," Socrates muses in Plato's *Hippias Major*, "that I have been benefited by conversation with both of you; for I think I know the meaning of the proverb, 'Beautiful things are difficult.'"[1] Among beauty's difficulties, at least for readers of scholastic texts in the last century, is the question of its transcendental status. Is beauty a transcendental determination of being, like one, true, and good? The transcendental question kindles debate in recent literature. Probably it burns hottest in Thomistic camps.[2] Sometimes scholars pose the question to the *SH* too. Beauty's place there, as in Thomas's texts, lacks consensus among its readers. That a single interpretive reading of scholastic arcana should fail to command consensus is hardly cause for scandal. What is problematic, however, is how this literature conducts its investigation of beauty's transcendental status without registering the peculiarities of Alexander's transcendental thought.

I assay beauty's status among the transcendentals by registering those peculiarities. Doing that, I show, reveals something unexpected. The *SH* conceives beauty very differently than its readers allow or notice. Brother Alexander evinces little interest in sorting beauty's transcendental status (which he finally denies).[3] He prefers to speak beauty with trinitarian grammar. For Alexander beauty does not name one transcendental determination of being among others. Instead, he identifies beauty with the very taxis of the trinitarian persons—it forms their structure, their taxis, their "sacred order."[4] It is exactly this taxic shape of Alexander's aesthetics that the literature pays little mind. Little wonder why: the trinitarian grammar of beauty in the *SH* transgresses the constricted boundaries of the question of transcendental status. This chapter, then, meets the transcendental question in Alexander's *Summa* mostly to transfigure it. Only a transfiguration of the question renders Alexander's elegant and highly distinctive trinitarian aesthetic visible once again, revealing its considerable promise.

That, anyway, is what this chapter seeks: the public display of Alexander's trinitarian aesthetic for appreciation and scrutiny. But it must first be recovered from depths that have long since passed out of theological memory.

IS BEAUTY A TRANSCENDENTAL? AN AESTHETIC APORIA

I begin by opening an aporetic gap,[5] one that yawns between two answers to the question of beauty's transcendental status in the *SH*.

The *Prima pars* of the *Summa* seems to subordinate beauty to the good, at least structurally. Alexander affords one, true, and good each a cycle of questions all their own.[6] Beauty merits no such treatise, not even a membrum or chapter. It claims only a single article[7] within a larger dialectical cycle of questions on the good's relation to other terms—to being, to beauty, to the final cause.[8] Some readers parlay Alexander's structural subordination of beauty to the good into a metaphysical hierarchy. Beauty, they think, "*wird mehr oder weniger zu einem Epiphänomen des Guten.*"[9] Often these readers say vanishingly little about how beauty relates to other transcendentals. In their view it matters only that beauty does not number among them. That beauty appears indexed to the good means it forms a second-class transcendental, whatever indeed that might mean.

But Alexander's *prima secundae* weaves another story. Its long section *De pulchritudine creati* begins thus:

> Next to consider, after the conditions of creatures with regard to quantity, are the conditions of creatures with regard to quality, and these are true, good, and beauty. But truth and goodness were discussed above in the treatise on the essential things said of God. Now follows a consideration of the beautiful or beauty.[10]

True, good—and beauty? Beauty appears here to stand among the other transcendentals without qualification. Gone are its structural chains to the good. That beauty appears here alongside "true" and "good" persuades other readers to confer upon it a transcendental status.[11] These readers rarely notice that "one" has vanished. Neither do they ask after it. They notice only beauty's sudden presence among true and good. And that's proof enough, it seems, of beauty's transcendentality.

So opens the aporia before us, clear and vivid: How to construe beauty's transcendental status as Alexander imagines it? Is beauty a transcendental in its own right? Or is it otherwise accessory to the good?

Recent interest in the *SH* on beauty prizes its novelty. "Hales is the first," de Bruyne argues, "to formulate this question in a precise manner."[12] Minor qualifications aside, this is very nearly right. Scholars agree that the

Summa marks an axial moment in the transcendental question and its development across the scholastic idiom. Among the most prominent interpretive lines on the transcendental question in the *SH* and its influence are those traced by Umberto Eco and Jan Aertsen. Both thread the *Summa* into their broader work on medieval aesthetics.

It is to Eco that scholars defer, and it is his reading that Aertsen disputes. Eco tenders a bashful "yes" to the transcendental question. Yes, he writes, "the *Summa* of Alexander of Hales . . . decisively solved the problem of the transcendental character of beauty, and its distinction from other values."[13] There is no question for Eco that the *Summa* gifts to beauty all the benefits proper to a transcendental. It does all this, too, "in an act of speculative courage."[14]

But how, on this reading, recalling the aporia before us, can one explain beauty's apparent subordination to the good in *SH* I? Here Eco assumes that the *Summa*'s speculative courage yields to the prudence of convention. Alexander hesitates to catalog beauty among the transcendentals, Eco claims, "no doubt because of the usual prudent reluctance of the scholastics to give an open and unambiguous welcome to philosophical innovation."[15] Whatever the reason, Eco meets the aporia by affirming the transcendental status of beauty. And doing that, it seems obvious to say, means favoring *SH* I–II, n. 75, over *SH* I, n. 103. Still Eco's "yes" remains qualified exactly to the extent that he thinks scholastic decorum required Alexander to innovate in hushed corridors, in whispers, in secret. "The boldness of [Alexander's] innovation," Eco concludes, "required caution in its implementation."[16]

Aertsen disagrees. In his final book Aertsen razes Eco's arguments with dispatch and without remainder in two moves.[17] The first rejects as flaccid Eco's argument from scholastic prudence. The doctrine of the transcendentals, Aertsen writes hotly, was itself a recent innovation. Eco cannot explain, for instance, why Thomas Aquinas announces some *six* transcendental terms only ten years later and without much hand-wringing.[18] Second, Aertsen thinks Eco's fevered search for beauty rides roughshod over textual difficulties. Principal among these difficulties, of course, runs the subordination of beauty to the good in *SH* I, n. 103.[19]

Better to class beauty an "epiphenomenon of the good,"[20] Aertsen admits soberly. After all, beauty is present only where the good is also. Hidden within his critique of Eco lies Aertsen's own position on beauty's transcendental status. The position he draws is, as the above suggests, weighted heavily toward protestation. For Aertsen, the extent to which beauty runs subordinate to the good is just the extent to which beauty cannot prove a transcendental under its own steam.[21]

So run the two interpretive lines on beauty's transcendentality in the *SH*, neither of which overcomes the aporia. Both finally boost one text only to knock the other. With Pouillon, Eco privileges *SH* I–II, n. 75, to defend beauty's transcendentality. Is not beauty there named a *conditio creaturae* alongside true and good? With Halcour, Aertsen privileges *SH* I, n. 103, precisely to deny the same. Beauty stands there as an "epiphenomenon of the good," not as a determination of being on its own.

There is more. Readers familiar with sea battles over beauty's status in Thomistic waters will recognize that the *SH* floats far from safe harbor. The positions Eco and Aertsen draw on beauty's status in Alexander already anticipate their positions on the same in Thomas. The contest over Alexander's *Summa*, it turns out, is hardly neutral. It is a skirmish—an exercise in reconnaissance for the gathering battle over Thomas Aquinas.

Look again at Eco. Which are his criteria for transcendentality? He stipulates convertibility with being and intensional distinction. The *SH*, Eco concludes, quietly allows beauty to meet this canon without trumpeting it. On this point, Aertsen is no doubt correct to register doubt over Eco's indulgent psychologizing. But notice the work this does for Eco: he flags Alexander's hesitation to blazon beauty's transcendentality exactly because he finds the same in Thomas Aquinas. "Not many years separate [Thomas's *Summa theologiae*] from the work of John of La Rochelle. Some element of caution must have remained."[22] Thomas "tackled the themes of his *Summa* with reserve; moderation had to be reestablished."[23] Put differently, Thomas also endorsed beauty's transcendentality furtively—he mimicked the *SH*. So much seems clear: Eco's answer to the transcendentality question in the *Summa* remains overwritten by his answer to the same in Thomas Aquinas.

Aertsen too seems preoccupied with the Thomistic question. In near perfect counterpoint to Eco, Aertsen's denial of beauty's transcendentality in Alexander betrays his preoccupation. Consider Aertsen's transcendental criteria: he discounts beauty as a transcendental in the *Summa* on the grounds that it fails to name an expression of *being*. Yet that transcendentals ought to add something conceptually to being is one of Aertsen's central criteria for transcendentality in *Thomas*.[24] This new canon renders "indisputable that [Aertsen] has made the greatest contribution of any scholar to the debate over beauty's transcendental status."[25] Why? Because Aertsen "has manifested the only principle by which one can determine whether beauty is a transcendental in Thomas's thought." This seems right-headed, at least for the Thomistic question. That debate raging around it needed clear criteria. And these criteria, Aertsen argued, reveal that Thomas denies beauty's transcendental status.[26] Whatever the success of Aertsen's transcendental canon within Thomistic circles,[27] he transposes it now onto the *SH*. And as we might expect, his conclusion there portends his conclusion concerning Thomas's texts. To the extent that the *SH* does not write of "the beautiful as expressing a universal mode of *being*," beauty cannot prove a transcendental.

Together, these notes yield two conclusions: first, that the literature has drawn but scarcely overcome an aporia over beauty's transcendental status in the *Summa*; and second, that the literature has read the *Summa* mostly as a cipher for Thomas's texts. Deeper reading reveals the debate between Eco and Aertsen to be heavily coded. Their respective criteria for transcendentality derive from and anticipate their interpretation of Thomas. As a result, their collective reading of the *SH* assumes conclusions borrowed from their arguments over Thomas. More, both Eco and Aertsen do this without registering differences between transcendental thought in the *Summa* and in Thomas (we explored some in the last chapter). Neither reader has adopted Alain de Libera's axiom that sometimes to read other scholastics well, "we must forget Thomas Aquinas."[28] Neither has either reader allowed the text to surprise him, to disrupt his expectations. This can be forgiven Eco—whose interest in the *SH* remains peripheral— but not Aertsen. It is Aertsen, after all, who stresses the distinctive notes sounded in Alexander's transcendental thought.[29] It is Aertsen too who discerns the peculiarity of Alexander's "trinitarian motive."[30] Why, then, does Aertsen uncritically transpose his canon for transcendentality in Thomas onto the *SH*?[31]

AN ANONYMOUS PROPOSAL

Aertsen is not content merely to overturn Eco. He wants to locate the site of the aesthetic confusion, to map its genesis. He wants to learn who first accords beauty a transcendental status. He discovers a candidate—or a culprit—in an anonymous Franciscan gloss on the *SH* called the *Tractatus de transcendentalibus entis conditionibus*.[32] The title commits an anachronism: it was furnished by an editor, not the author. In any case, that text, circulated under Bonaventure's name but of unclear provenance,[33] seems the first text to register beauty among the determinations of being. Or so Aertsen claims, following rather closely Dieter Halcour's introduction to his edition of the text.

The passage in question comes early in the *Tractatus*:

> We should say that these conditions are established above being, for they add a certain *ratio*. Hence one, true, good, and beauty presuppose the understanding of being, in which they share and redound upon one another: for beauty foreknows good, and good true, and true one, but one being itself, for which reason being is said to be absolute. One adds indivision beyond being; for one is the indivision of being. But true is called the indivision of form from matter or "quod est" et "quo est." But good is called the indivision of potency from act. Hence, according to appropriation (*secundum appropriationem*), one considers the efficient cause, true the formal, and good the final. But beauty circulates through (*circuit*) all causes and is common to them.[34]

Aertsen discerns the logic of appropriation at work. This lends evidence to Halcour's claim that the *Tractatus* probably comments or glosses the transcendental doctrine of Alexander's *Summa*. Perhaps the anonymous friar penned it "as a draft for teaching purposes" or perhaps "as an outline for his own commentary on the *Sentences*."[35] Whatever its intimacy with Alexander, Aertsen registers a difference. He thinks the anonymous friar's decision to accord beauty "a place of its own in virtue of its synthesizing function" represents a "surprising" innovation.[36] Aertsen argues that the text's definition of beauty as "circulating through all causes" concocts "an isolated statement," not "explained or grounded." Aertsen's point is clear. If the *Tractatus* is the first to crown beauty with transcendental status, it does so only by innovating the *SH*—by transgressing it.

Perhaps this is an innovation. But is it a transgression neither "explained" nor "grounded"? Consider now a passage in the *Tractatus* that Aertsen misses (or ignores). An objection issues from Augustine's by-then trite definition of beauty in *civ.* 22.19 as *partium congruentia*. Must this mean that *pulchritudo est solum in corporibus*? The *Tractatus* responds:

There is a congruence of parts, a congruence of *ratios*, and a congruence of order. The first is beauty in bodies; the second is beauty in creatures of spiritual substances, according to essential but not qualitative parts, which are matter and form, "*quod est*" and "*quo est*," but this is not in God. In God there is the highest congruence of order, the highest congruence of *ratios*, thus this is the highest beauty.[37]

This hardly forms a complete explanation, but it is a start. At the very least, the passage explains why the text invests beauty with a "synthesizing function." Beauty, the anonymous friar learns from Augustine, entails a harmony or congruence of parts. And not just in bodies. The angels too are beautiful precisely because they are composed. Of course God is not composed—divine simplicity proscribes it. But this need not subvert God's claim to beauty. For in God, anonymous writes, lives the highest congruence of order (*summa congruentia ordinis*), itself the highest beauty (*summa pulcritudinis*).

The text does not detail this order. Neither does it name the order's constitutive "parts." It teaches only that beauty arranges and orders its constituents—in bodies' parts, in angels' form and matter (or essence and existence). Beauty reprises this role among the transcendentals, or rather those *conditiones* which *addunt aliquam rationem supra ens*. Alexander illustrates this "certain reason" by appeal to Aristotle's immaterial causes. Each adds to the next. So too, each new transcendental performs a "progressive" or "cumulative" function.[38] And beauty comes last, sublating every and each transcendental—which is also every and each cause—within itself. So "beauty circulates through (*circuit*) all causes and is common to them."[39]

Aertsen thought that the *Tractatus*'s synthetic role for beauty was neither "explained" nor "grounded." We have seen it explained, if incompletely. Might it be grounded too?

BEAUTY AS SACRED ORDER OF THE TRINITY

I now mount a partial defense of the anonymous *Tractatus* author. The synthetic role with which he vests beauty among the transcendentals is not, I propose, a "surprising innovation." Attention to the *SH* shows that the *Tractatus* author writes a legitimate—if not finally exact—icon of Alexander's aesthetics. That Aertsen can so easily dismiss the nameless author's claim to legitimate interpretation of the *Summa*, that interpreters neglect beauty's synthetic presence among the transcendentals in the *Summa*, and that aesthetic interest in the *Summa* is wholly circumscribed by the transcendental question—all this follows from their neglect of a single passage in the *Summa*. Pity, since that passage rewards close readers with a rather different and, I think, more delicate pattern of Alexander's thought on aesthetics. His readers ignore that pattern, not least because they have dialed their scopes for the transcendental question alone.[40]

So far as I can tell, all of the *Summa*'s recent readers simply cease reading after its *respondeo*.[41] "This is all we find on beauty," Pouillon announces after reading it, "in the first part of the *Summa fratris Alexandri*."[42] This explains why his and others' interest begins and ends with how to construe beauty's relation or subordination to the good or the true. But there lingers below an important, tightly compressed argument interred in a response to the second objection. What escapes modern readers, however, rarely eludes those scholastics. The passage does not, of course, escape the *Tractatus* author's gaze. For this reason, I read in reverse: the forgotten reply to objection two first, the *respondeo* next.

Open curtains, then, on that forgotten scene. There, as in the *Tractatus*, the *Summa* meets an objection that the Augustinian definition of beauty renders the beautiful coterminous with the corporeal. Alexander responds, "There Augustine defines visible or bodily beauty, but the same is said of the beauty of fleshy, sensible things *just to the extent that it leads to* beauty intelligible or spiritual."[43] The created order thus constitutes what Bonaventure later calls a ladder whose parallel rungs chart the *itinerarium mentis in Deum*.[44] Here already in the *Summa* the beauty that flits across creation's surface discloses its transcendent depths.

All that is typical to any broadly Platonic aesthetics. But Alexander presses further still:

> For just as [Augustine says that] "the beauty of bodies is from a harmony of the composition of its parts," so also is the beauty of souls from a harmony of powers and the ordering of faculties (*ex convenientia virium et ordinatione potentiarum*). And beauty in the divine is from the sacred order of the divine persons (*ex ordine sacro divinarum personarum*), in such a manner that [there is] one person is not from another, [a person]

from whom another is by generation (*per generationem*), [and] from [these two persons] a third is by procession (*per processionem*).[45]

The passage proceeds in three steps. It first extends the Augustinian line on fleshy beauty to the beauty of souls. Next it extends the definition of beauty as "a harmony of parts" still more—it stretches even to God.[46] (A prima facie problem, again, given divine simplicity.) Third and most striking, the text submits an explicitly trinitarian canon for beauty. Notice how this trinitarian canon already resolves the problem of parts talk in God. Here, talk of "parts" issues negation. Unlike the body's limbs and the soul's powers, God's "parts" enjoy essential identity and personal difference. So God the trinity has and is God's "parts."

This introduces Alexander's peculiar grammar of divine beauty. For him it is not God as divine *essence* that makes God beautiful and indeed Beauty itself. This mostly characterizes what Dionysius and the long Neoplatonic tradition had taught.[47] No, it is rather God as *trinity*. From Augustine, Alexander adopts a grammar of beauty whose definition is harmonious, relational. Beauty on this view names a harmony of parts. From Dionysius, he adapts a Neoplatonic identification of the cause of beauty with beauty itself, or a grammar of beauty that is causal. So beauty is a name for the supremely simple God. Alexander commingles these: divine beauty is a harmony of God's persons, which are not really "parts." This synthesis, the coalescing of an Augustinian aesthetic with the Dionysian, becomes the style signature of the *Summa*'s aesthetics. Beauty is at once relational and causal exactly because God is at once trinity and creator. And this fits rather comfortably with what the *Tractatus* author writes, even if the latter does not reproduce all of Alexander's trinitarian precisions.

But if, as Alexander indeed argues, beauty names the sacred order that comprises the inner life of the trinity, and if it is this that serves as both canon and source of all beauty, then the implications of this forgotten passage are of deep promise. They are at least four. I arrange them in ascending order of importance before returning to the *respondeo*.

A first implication: this passage from Alexander establishes precedent for the *Tractatus*. Not that there exist no variations between them—there are some. The *Tractatus* only susurrates, for instance, the trinitarian connection that Alexander declares.[48] The former admits that beauty arranges parts in bodies and metaphysical elements in angels. It then locates beauty in God as *summa congruentia ordinis.*[49] But the text remains oracular about how this synthesizing feature of beauty works in—and presumably *as*—God. After all, what in God does beauty synthesize? On this point, Alexander's *Summa* completes the analogy. Beauty names the "sacred order" of the trinitarian persons (*ex ordine sacro divinarum personarum*), their mutual interpenetration, their taxic order. The "elements" of beauty's synthesis in God, put differently, must be the divine persons. Perhaps a spoor of this trinitarian logic lingers in the *Tractatus*. Anonymous writes of beauty that it *circuit omnem causam*. *Circuitio*, remember, often replaces *perichōrēsis* in Burgundio of Pisa's twelfth-century translation of *De fide orthodoxa*. So a trinitarian correlation is not unthinkable, however gossamer its thread.[50]

There runs another major variation between the texts. I mean, of course, anonymous's claim that beauty adds conceptually to being just as one, true, and good do—something absent Alexander's *Summa*.[51] These differences are no doubt deep and serious. But granting that point need not mean conceding with Aertsen that the "synthesizing function" the *Tractatus* accords to beauty proves nonnative to Alexander's text. The family resemblance between them, I think, seems conspicuous enough.

The forgotten passage also hints at an answer to the transcendentality question—this is the second implication. Which are Alexander's criteria for transcendentality? So far as it goes, Aertsen's canon for Thomas applies to the *SH*. To qualify as a transcendental, a term must add something to being that the other transcendental terms cannot and hence find its place among their order.[52] Alexander himself demands the first criterion at *SH* I, n. 72. There he announces that the *primae intentiones* adds something conceptually to being (*per rationem additam ad ens*). Alexander stipulates the second too in the three places he arranges an order for the transcendentals.[53] But to Aertsen's criteria I append a third item, one peculiar to Alexander, which I detailed in the last chapter. In the *Summa*, that is, transcendental determinations of being must be appropriable to one or another person of the trinity.[54] So again, the three criteria: a transcendental adds to being, finds its place among the others, and correlates a divine attribute to a personal property.

Beauty fails all three. Against the first, nowhere does Alexander say that beauty adds conceptually to being,[55] although he says this repeatedly of one, true, and good. Against the second, nowhere in the three places in which Alexander arranges the order of the transcendentals does he include beauty.[56] The intrinsic relation between one, true, and good does not obviously yield space for beauty.[57] And against the third, the case appears rather glaring. In fact, Hans Urs von Balthasar already flags the difficulty. The appropriative character of Franciscan transcendental thought, Balthasar notices—one to Father, true to Son, and good to Spirit—exacerbates "the difficulty of assigning to the beautiful its systematic place."[58] Given the criterion of appropriation, it seems impossible that Alexander could endow beauty with a transcendental status. Doing that would mean gifting transcendentality to a term that flutters free of trinitarian gravity in a way that no other transcendental does or can.[59] On Alexander's account, the *Tractatus's* claims that beauty both names a transcendental and that it synthesizes the others after a pattern analogous to trinitarian *ordo* prove incompatible.[60] In any case, this is not Alexander's way. Against Eco, then, I concede Aertsen's conclusion (though not always his premises). Beauty, it seems, is not a transcendental in the *SH*.

What to say then, to complete this second implication, about beauty's presence among the transcendentals in *SH* I–II, n. 75? Might beauty as sacred order redress the aporia? Ideally it would, since ruling against Eco on the transcendental question should not mean burying textual evidence to the contrary.[61] An easy option might chalk up the discrepancy between *SH* I, n. 103 and *SH* I–II, n. 75 to different authors. The *Summa* knew several, after all. Nevertheless I assume continuity before disruption, at least until continuity proves unlikely.[62] Its likelihood here is already destabilized by the second text listing true, good, and *beautiful*. Why not one, true, and good, as everywhere in *SH* I?

Again, attention to the text suggests an answer. There Alexander explains exactly *what* he lists—and it is not the "first determinations of being" (*primae determinationes entis*).[63] Instead, he is interested in "the condition of creatures (*conditiones creaturae*) concerning quality, which are true, good, and beautiful."[64] More, Alexander addresses the sudden absence of "one" from the index. He has already treated unity as a created condition in his questions on quantity.[65] So yes, this list of *conditiones creaturae* differs from the list of *primae determinationes entis*. But this does not—or need not—spell disruption—not, that is, if these passages connote different (if related) things.

Aertsen shows that the "first determinations of being" comprise three related spheres: divine attributes, *primae intentiones*, and *primae impressiones*.[66]

As divine attributes the transcendentals work theologically, as first intentions logically, as first impressions epistemically. *SH* I–II's talk of the *conditiones creaturae* reads otherwise. If the emphasis on the transcendentals in *SH* I has more to do with discerning the trinitarian source and shape of all being as such, the emphasis here on the "conditions of creatures as to quality" (*ex parte qualitatis*) concerns how concrete creatures exist. Whichever species of quality Alexander invokes—Aristotle catalogs four[67]— *qualitas* always concerns the determination of a subject. Or as the Philosopher has it: "that by which things are said to be such and such."[68] Thomas later advises that studies of *qualitas* consider "evil and good, and also changeableness."[69] These are precisely the sorts of questions that follow in *SH* I–II: whether evil is said to be beautiful; whether we should call monstrous things beautiful; whether beauty is able to increase or diminish in the world; whether mutable goods contribute beauty to the universe; and so on.[70] All this recommends a better solution to the textual aporia—better, at least, than the multiple-author solution. True, *SH* I speaks of one, true, and good; and *SH* I–II of true, good, and beautiful. But this difference is explained by the fact that each text treats of different things, or rather the same things under a different aspect.[71] So again, the second implication: beauty is not a transcendental in the *SH*.

There follows a third implication, vastly more important than the last. If the above passage meets the transcendental question, it also transfigures it. It follows from the *Summa*'s trinitarian account of beauty, I mean, that the transcendental question is not the only one to pose. Not that I oppose asking the question—no, I posed it above. In fact, posing the transcendental question to the *SH* forms the condition for the possibility of discovering beauty's expanded scope. In this way the narrow transcendental question reveals its own limits. Asking it first discloses Alexander's elegant peculiarities on both beauty and transcendentality.

The problem comes only when readers presume that it is the first and *final* question to ask. Nursing a fetish for the finality of the transcendental question leads Eco to exaggerate and Aertsen to understate. Doubtless Aertsen is right to challenge Eco on the question. But it does not follow that Aertsen himself is correct to banish beauty to the realm of epiphenomena. Beauty may not number among the determinations of being themselves. But that does not and need not render its significance epiphenomenal—far from it. On my reading, beauty's absence from the *Summa*'s transcendental index invites another explanation. Key to that explanation is the fact that Alexander identifies beauty with the sacred order of the trinitarian persons, not to a person specifically. The deep significance of beauty, then, lies precisely in its omission.[72] This is because there are three, and only three, persons who together constitute and individually comprise the trinity. Plainer still: if one belongs to the Father, true to the Son, and good to the Spirit, then beauty—as Brother Alexander writes—names the sacred order of the trinitarian persons. Beauty names nothing less than their taxis. And that, to put the point sharply, is no epiphenomenon.

The fourth and final implication of the above passage is that it yields a fresh and distinctively trinitarian account of beauty—a medieval supplement, perhaps, to recent theologies of beauty that revolve almost exclusively around Christology. Attending to and explicating Alexander's theology sounds a calling that I cannot answer in this chapter. That task, like that of the angels scaling Jacob's ladder, involves two directions—heavenward and earthbound. I would first, that is, relate Alexander's description of beauty as *ordo sacer divinarum personarum* to Alexander's mostly ignored trinitarian theology.[73] If divine beauty is the canon of all beauty, and if divine beauty is the order of the persons, then what exactly is that order?[74] Next and world-facing, it would then repair back to the *Summa's* delicate pattern of thought that threads beauty through all of the causes—not unlike what the *Tractatus* describes.[75] (I treat both of these questions at length anon.)

BEAUTY AS ORDER OF THE TRANSCENDENTALS

For now, I close by returning at long last to the *respondeo* in *SH* I, n. 103. Recall the question: Are beauty and good the same? Alexander begins by reinscribing a passage from Augustine's *div. qu.*[76] The passage draws a distinction, "since good is said in two ways (*dupliciter*)." If good as the excellent (*honestum*) names what is sought for its own sake, good as the useful (*utile*) names a waypoint toward another end.[77] Then Augustine indexes the excellent (*honestum*) to intelligible beauty (*intelligiblem pulcritudinem*) and the useful (*utile*) to providence. The former refers to something's intrinsic beauty and the latter to how providence invisibly works all things toward the good. On Augustine's authority Alexander identifies beauty with the good as the excellent (*honestum*), not as useful (*utile*). Why? Their difference arises from how beauty and good relate to final causality. As a "disposition of the good," beauty has its end in pleasing apprehension.[78] But the proper end of the good is to delight affection. And delighting affection seems to concern divine providence and so what is useful (*utile*). Pleasing apprehension concerns intrinsic beauty, and so what is excellent (*honestum*).[79]

Beauty's relation to the final cause, then, has to do with its intrinsic allure. Later the *Summa* names this allure "form" (*species*). The form of any given thing *t* connotes "that by virtue of which [*t*] gives pleasure and is appreciated."[80] So "form" (*species*) bears something that attracts. What is it? "Something is said to be beautiful in the world," Brother Alexander continues, "when it bears the proper measure (*modum*), form (*species*), and order (*ordinem*)."[81] Alexander learns from Augustine to read Wisdom 11's triad trinitarianly— as "a triple trace of the creator."[82] This every creature bears.[83] What enraptures us about something beautiful, then, is exactly its trace of trinitarian taxis. An appetite for this beauty, Alexander later argues, suffuses the ensemble of creation.[84] So much, altogether too briefly, on beauty's relation to the final cause.

Beauty and good differ too in their relation to the efficient cause.[85] The good concerns "what flows from a cause according to indistinction" (*quod fluit a causa secundum indistinctionem*), but beauty *secundum distinctionem*. Alexander invokes Dionysius to corroborate. "The good is called first beauty, since from it all things that exist are given the beauty proper to them." Alexander does not elaborate. He intimates only that beauty's relation to efficient causality concerns "distinction."

The mists that shroud this relation dissipate where Alexander details efficient causality later in *SH* I–II. There he notes that St. Paul's phrase "through whom" (*per ipsum*) typically denotes the Son's role in formal or exemplar causality.[86] But not always. Sometimes it describes the Son's efficient causality. As very God, the Son also causes efficiently—or he receives the power to cause efficiently from the Father. But aside from stressing the unity of causality in God,[87] why spotlight the Son's efficient causality? Because "through the Word was made everything that was made." Under that *ratio*, Alexander thinks it fitting to predicate efficient causality of the Son. When we do that, we name an intrinsic connection between "the source of all things and the most perfect beauty."[88] Since "the Maker of everything is wise through his own art," and since the Son is eternal Art of the Father (*ars Patri*), "the Father knows creatures to be through the Son."[89] This is fitting, again, since the Son names the locus of the divine ideas. In him they are one, in creation many.[90] The Son's work of distinction, then, describes beauty's relation to the efficient cause.

Beauty and good differ last in their relation to the exemplar cause. The good is called exemplar in relation to an end, "like an art or rule of operation to a goal."[91] Again Alexander summons Dionysius to testify. As intelligible light (*lux intelligibilis*), the good "collects and gathers all things" to itself. In this way, good relates to exemplar as final cause relates to formal. The final cause, Aristotle taught, holds explanatory priority over the others.[92] What a thing is for determines all else about it, including what it is. "For the final cause," Alexander writes, "is the *ratio* of the other causes."[93] Or so the good to the exemplar.

Beauty functions differently. Beauty does not gather and collect all things to itself like the good. Rather, as the *exemplar ipsum,* beauty names "distinction and harmony of difference." For this reason, beauty has less to do with beginnings or ends than it does with metaphysical structure—or order. According to Dionysius, beauty names "the exemplar according to which all things are distinguished."[94] Beauty relates to the exemplary cause, then, to the extent that beauty rules and norms all distinction.

It is a rather dense scholastic business, that—too dense for protracted commentary here. For now, my point is modest. I want only to point up beauty's presence across Aristotle's three immaterial causes. Given the *quaestio* under review, we might expect Alexander's notes on the relation between beauty and good as they concern the final cause. The good and the final cause share an intimate relation, of course—Alexander appropriates both to the Spirit.[95] Less expected, however, is Alexander's correlation of beauty to the exemplar and efficient causes. It is true that he continues to assay beauty's relation to the causes in light of the good. But in each case the good works like a heuristic.[96] Alexander does not mention the good across his explanations to remind the reader of beauty's subordination to it so much as he wields the good to contrast its relation to the causes from beauty's. Beauty, then, bears its own relation to the causes, different from and unmediated by the good's. The point, anyway, is that beauty runs across the causes in the *SH*—very like what the *Tractatus* describes.

And this raises a final question. Alexander discerns a tight braiding between the causes and the transcendentals: one to the efficient cause, true to the formal, good to the final.[97] Alexander also insists that both these transcendentals and their respective causes function as trinitarian appropriations. A crude visual might render those relations as shown in the accompanying table.

Transcendental	One	True	Good
Cause	Efficient	Formal	Final
Person	Father	Son	Holy Spirit

But where does beauty belong? How to depict its relations? I rebutted beauty's transcendentality above, so it is not clear how it belongs in the first row. And as I just showed, beauty runs across all the causes in a way the other transcendentals do not. So the second row also puzzles. Last, the reply to the second objection explicitly identifies divine beauty with the sacred order of the divine persons. But their order or taxis does not and cannot belong to one person to the exclusion of others. So again, the third row presents a difficulty. I ask again: Where and how does beauty belong?

I propose a solution. It begins by working backward from the trinitarian persons. If beauty describes the taxis among trinitarian persons, then it cannot bear content of its own. It is a structure, an *ordo*—one conditioned by a perichoretic relation. So much seems clear: conceiving taxis as subsisting somehow independently of the persons courts absurdity.[98] But suppose we extend this perichoretic line on beauty to the causes. On this picture, Beauty would neither belong to any particular cause nor subsist separately from them. There, like in the trinity, beauty would run across and under the causes as their structure. Alexander hints at exactly this connection when he elucidates the order of the causes.[99] The causes derive their order from the trinity, in whom they are one (à la divine attributes). But in creation they are many, and so appropriations of the persons. As appropriations, the causes are normed by trinitarian order. And again, if trinitarian order is identical to divine beauty, it follows that beauty structures and runs across the causes too—just as we see in the *respondeo* of *SH* I, n. 103. Thus beauty names both order among the persons and the causes.

And the first row? How does beauty fit among the transcendentals? Remember first the trinitarian peculiarities of the *Summa*'s transcendental thought. Alexander claims that one, good, and true "interpenetrate one another (*se circumincedunt*)."[100] Each presupposes the other—no one without true and good, no true without one and true, and so on. That Alexander applies perichoretic grammar to speak the relation between the transcendentals cannot be accidental. Indeed, here Alexander very nearly overtures the cadence of the Council of Florence's eleventh session: "the Father is wholly in the Son and the Spirit, the Son is wholly in the Father and the Spirit, the Spirit is wholly in the Father and the Son."[101]

What Alexander never claims, however, is that beauty "interpenetrates" one, true, and good. He constantly and consistently relates beauty to one, true, and good, yes. Still, beauty does not feature among them as another transcendental. How then does it relate? Beauty relates to the transcendentals, I submit, just as it relates to the trinitarian persons first and to the causes next. It names not a person, not a cause, not a transcendental term—it rather names a taxis, an order, a structure. In Alexander, then, beauty is the ordered interpenetration of the transcendentals.[102] Why? Because transcendentals in creation reflect their ground in divine attributes. And those divine attributes exist trinitarianly—they bear a fitting relation to a personal property.[103] They too, Alexander claims, "interpenetrate one another."[104]

To bring these points together: beauty, like one, true, and good, relates to all the causes. But beauty also names a "sacred order," the very structure of the trinitarian persons. Divine beauty, then, is trinitarian taxis. Yet trinitarian taxis bears no metaphysical content. Neither does it subsist as a cause separate or independent from the others. Neither again does it constitute a transcendental in its own right. Within this redrawn picture, beauty relates to each line on the first chart. But it does so curiously, inexactly, dimly. (See accompanying table.)

Transcendental	One	True	Good	Beauty*
Cause	Efficient	Formal	Final	All causes*
Person	Father	Son	Holy Spirit	Taxis*

Beauty, the scare asterisks mean to signal, is not a transcendental, not a cause, and not a specific trinitarian person. Yet beauty relates to the transcendentals, the causes, and the persons. Beauty endows their structure, their taxis, their "sacred order."

So Eco and Aertsen are not altogether wrongheaded to seek beauty's relation to the transcendentals. Asking after beauty's relation is not the question that needs transfiguring. I want rather to transfigure the question as posed, the one that assumes beauty might number among the transcendentals in the same way that one or true or good does. If the motifs I scrawled above reflect Alexander's, then beauty for him does not stand among the transcendentals as one among others. No, beauty is that by which the transcendentals relate one to another. It is their very principle, the means of their perichoresis. Or, in the *Summa*'s preferred idiom: *ipse ordo est pulcher,* order itself is beautiful.[105] Asking after beauty's transcendental content, to extend the trinitarian analogy, is like asking for the content of trinitarian taxis in abstraction from the persons. At best it indulges irrelevance, at worst heterodoxy. Blindness to the taxic dimension of beauty betrays a blindness to the trinitarian stimulus behind the *Summa*'s transcendental thought.[106] The extent to which this blindness is born of the limitations of the transcendental question is exactly the extent to which the question obscures more than it illumines, at least in the *SH*.

A final point: that beauty does not number among the transcendentals as typically conceived does not mean that beauty does not always and everywhere determine being.[107] Neither does it spell beauty's absence from some or another pitiable being in creation's ensemble.[108] It means only that beauty is present among creatures differently than are one and true and good. These, remember, are divine attributes appropriable to the persons and in which creatures participate. But Alexander conceives beauty otherwise. Beauty is not a divine attribute but a divine structure, a "sacred order." Determining exactly what this structure is and how it manifests across creation—these anticipate the desiderata of my next two chapters.

CONCLUSION

Scholarly evidence both for and against beauty's transcendentality in the *SH* has drawn no conclusions—only an aporia. Yet this same scholarship reads the *Summa* as a surrogate to Thomas Aquinas. Eco tenders a "yes" for exactly the reasons it finds in Thomas—and vice versa for Aertsen. Aertsen thinks transcendentalists on beauty betray undue influence by the *Tractatus de transcendentalibus*, probably a later gloss on *SH* I. Aertsen thinks the image of beauty sketched in the copy bears little relation to its archetype in the *SH*. I demur. The *Tractatus* and the *SH* share deep resemblances, even if not final identity. Among the most important of these resemblances is the *Tractatus*'s description of beauty as the highest congruence of order.[109] This description exhibits traces of the thicker trinitarian account of beauty in Alexander, who grounds beauty in the "sacred order of the divine persons." Implications immediately follow this peculiarly trinitarian account, one of which answers the transcendental question negatively only to transfigure it. Why? Because grounding beauty in trinitarian taxis invites questions deeper than the transcendental one. These are at least two: first, what exactly is beauty's relation to this taxis *ad intra*; and second, what is beauty's relation *ad extra*—to all of creation, say, through trinitarian beauty's presence across the causes?

These questions comprise the book's next two parts. Part II treats of the trinitarian question *ad intra*, or the taxic order of the divine persons that is beauty. And part III pivots *ad extra*. There I study the trinitarian grammar of causality and its traces across creation. Together these account for beauty's presence across orders both created and not.

PART II

THE TRINITY'S BEAUTY *AD INTRA*

If the source of all beauty is the "sacred order" of the trinitarian persons, then beauty must necessarily lack content. This is because the order of those persons is not ontologically other than the persons or the divine nature. No, their order names their relation one to another as very God. So instead of grounding beauty in the divine nature as the long tradition from Augustine and Dionysius had, Brother Alexander rules beauty according to the logic of trinitarian taxis. He grounds beauty, that is, in the order and perichoretic relation of the divine persons. This is Brother Alexander's peculiarly trinitarian grammar of beauty: for him beauty names not content but a structure—an order.

This means that beauty does not and cannot stand as one among other transcendentals. Instead beauty is that by which the transcendentals relate one to another. It is their very principle, the means of their circumincession. Asking after beauty's transcendental content, to extend the *Summa*'s trinitarian analogy, is like asking after the content of perichoresis abstracted from the persons.

Chapter 4, then, reroutes this study according to Brother Alexander's peculiar aesthetics. It moves thought away from transcendentals to attend instead to what he takes beauty to be: the order of the trinitarian persons. Predictably the question of order pervades Brother Alexander's trinitarian theology. Yet Alexander is hardly interested in order itself considered generally. Rather he is interested in order derived from the trinitarian processions: the Son from the Father and the Spirit from both. If this trinitarian order grounds all others, and if it is also beauty itself, then we must begin again with the trinity.

CHAPTER 4

THE BEAUTY THE TRINITY IS

W hen then we think the creator," Augustine once confessed, "we must think the trinity. For in that trinity is the highest origin of all things, the most perfect beauty, and the most blessed delight."[1] This chapter has as its topic the trinity that God is—or at least as Brother Alexander conceives that trinity. Narrower still: it treats what Augustine calls "the most perfect beauty" in that trinity. Brother Alexander, remember, identifies this beauty as the sacred order of the trinitarian persons. Beauty is not, as my last chapter argued, a divine attribute—not like one, true, and good. It names rather an order. For Alexander, seeking beauty means divining the very structure of God. And so it is to that structure that this chapter attends.

Brother Alexander doubts we can reckon the trinity without thinking its order.[2] That is his argument, anyway—I merely render it. First I offer general remarks on how Alexander contrives the persons and their processions. A second section dwells indulgently on his questions on trinitarian order, since it is exactly this that Alexander identifies with divine beauty. And last I consider and meet an objection. Does Alexander's filigree of beauty as trinitarian order clash with the typical scholastic habit of writing an icon of beauty patterned after the Son?

That is what this chapter promises, anyway. Among the many things this chapter cannot and will not offer, however, is an exhaustive doctrine of the trinity across the *Summa*. That task requires more devotion than a single chapter can promise.[3] Brother Alexander's questions on the trinity sprawl across nearly 300 bicolumned pages—more still if you include his questions on the trinitarian missions.[4] Another role I fail to perform here is that of historiographic cartographer. I do not draw, redraw, or burn maps of the vast literature on medieval trinitarian theology—not even those detailing the Victorine-Franciscan axis[5] of trinitarian thought. The extensive maps the literature drafts concern me only when they themselves concern the *SH*.

PERSONS AND PROCESSIONS

Distinction requires content. It needs, that is, something to distinguish. In trinitarian theology, the question of this something concerns "who," not "what."[6] Writing of the trinity means conceiving how those "whos" differ whose "what" does not. However raw Augustine wrung his hands over it,[7] the long Latin tradition had named these "whos" *personae*—persons.

Brother Alexander knows competing definitions of *persona*.[8] In one place he catalogs them. He lists Boethius's first: "an individual substance of a rational nature."[9] His next two come from Richard of St. Victor: "an incommunicable existence of an intellectual nature" and something "existing in itself alone by way of some mode of rational existence."[10] And his last one Alexander cribs from nameless "masters": "person is hypostasis, distinguished by a property pertaining to dignity."[11] Together these issue the standard thirteenth-century bill of fare. Its items, gathered and delicately curated over time, were selected by the schoolmen according to theological taste.

Which tempts Brother Alexander? He likes Richard's criticisms of the received Boethian definition. We should accept it, Alexander counsels, only under Richard's heavy revisions.[12] One of these demands that "incommunicable" displace "individual," at least if the persons in question are divine. Another suggests that "existence" depose "substance," for *substare* and *subsistere* are not God's.[13] Readers should accept Boethius's substance talk only under the stipulation that "substance" name hypostasis, not *ousia*. Alexander's obeisance hardly fools. It does not conceal his obvious and final shilling for Richard's definition.[14] Nevertheless, across his replies to objections, Alexander registers affinity for the "definition of the masters."[15] With it, he writes, we speak the different persons according to different dignities. We might (though Alexander does not explicitly) merge these two definitions into one. On this hybrid definition, a divine person is an incommunicable existence of an intellectual nature, distinguished by a property pertaining to dignity. And that—crudely put—is what there is three of in the trinity.[16]

All this operates at vertiginous heights of scholastic abstraction, almost too formal to mean much. Applying it means asking how this definition of person accounts for specific differences among the trinitarian persons. The second bit of Alexander's hybrid definition anticipates his answer. We ought to distinguish *this* divine person from *that* by his "property pertaining to dignity." In the scholastic idiom, this concept flies under the sign of *pro-prietates personalis*. "A personal property," Alexander explains, "is appropriate to one person only and what distinguishes that person from every other."[17] This means that there are precisely as many personal properties as there are persons.[18] And that is three.[19]

Why? Alexander explains:

> Order in the divine persons is according to the *ratio* of origin. But this is the first division of being: everything that exists is either from another or not from another. And this is the first *ratio* of distinguishing an essence from essence. So too there is a *ratio* of distinguishing persons in the divine. Again, 'being from another' is either through generation or spiration. So we already have three properties: for from "not being from another" follows the property of innascibility (*innascibilitas*), and from 'being from another through generation' follows filiation (*filiatio*), and, again, from "being from another through spiration" follows procession (*processio*).[20]

Brother Alexander begins by confessing one of his trinitarian presumptions, perhaps his most important. That presumption prefers origin over relation for distinguishing the trinitarian persons.[21] On this point Alexander reveals his debt to Richard of St. Victor, who wrote that in God, "it is solely in origin that one should seek the distinction of the persons or existents."[22] Little surprise that this locates the *SH* on the Franciscan side of the trinitarian turf war that divided rival mendicants. Brother Alexander, that is, prefers the emanationist account over the relational one burnished, cossetted, and defended by the Dominicans.[23]

Most basically the emanationist account grounds trinitarian difference in peculiar modes of emanation or personal origin.[24] Its emphasis falls upon the way a person bears divinity. So the Father is Father, Alexander says, just to the extent that he bears divinity "not from another" (*non ab alio*). His very lack of origin names his personal property. To be Father is just to be God innascibly, to be God the Unborn.[25] Not so with the Son, who is very God because the Father generates him. The property of the Son, then, is filiation (*filiatio*) because and to the extent that he bears divinity "from another through generation" (*ab alio per generationem*). And again, the Spirit bears divinity by proceeding from the Father and the Son. It is his and his only to be breathed. So "procession" means being God "from another through spiration" (*ab alio per spirationem*). On the emanation account, "three irreducibly distinct emanational properties account for the fact that the three divine persons are emanationally distinct, yet essentially identical."[26]

So construed, studying the trinity within the emanation account is always a kind of drawing, a tracing of intratrinitarian origins.[27] What remains of this section on general trinitarian business, then, provides a précis of Brother Alexander's accounts of the persons in particular.

Alexander's trinitarian theology begins where everything must—with God the Father.[28] The very name "God," Alexander argues, refers not to the divine essence but to the Father.[29] It is he who sires Son, Spirit, and creation,[30] he who is "first principle, whence comes all nature and all essence."[31] These descriptions already invoke the Father's personal property: innascibility (*innascibilitas*).[32] Its prefix suggests that its work is principally and mostly negative. To bear innascibility as the Father does is simply to be unbegotten, "being not from another" (*non ens ab alio*).[33] Brother Alexander collects and arranges various positions (*plures opiniones*) on innascibility's technical definition.[34] Innascibility names "a certain property that inheres in the Father by which he is from nothing," or "a universal authority or principle that's in the Father alone," or "a fontal plenitude that's in the Father," or a "notion . . . a privation of being from another from whom others come."[35] Recherché definitions aside, innascibility affirms that somehow the Father is "from himself." So affirming innascibility mostly means affirming a negation. How exactly someone might derive from himself, Alexander thinks, transcends reason's deliverances.

The Father bears another notion beyond his personal property:[36] his paternity (*paternitas*).[37] If innascibility suits the Father better in the order of being, paternity suits him in the order of knowing.[38] *This* invokes the Father's not being from another, *that* his being whence another comes through generation.[39] Thus paternity denotes a notion that belongs to the Father in virtue of his authoring the Son and Spirit *in actu*.[40]

Brother Alexander braids innascibility and paternity tightly with another conceit. I mean of course the scholastic law that *bonum est diffusivum sui*, the good diffuses itself. If its rootstock is Neoplatonic, its bough is Dionysian. Alexander applies it variously and extensively across his *Summa*. Nowhere, though, is the axiom's concentration denser than in the *Summa*'s trinitarian theology.

Alexander indexes the *bonum est diffusivum sui* axiom to the Father—not to the divine essence[41]—as "fontal plenitude." In this way the self-diffusive good becomes the *Grundlage* of Alexander's trinitarian thought.[42] He applies its logic first to the generation of Son and next to Spirit's spiration. In fact, each argument he recites in favor of the Son's generation turns on the logic of self-diffusion. It glows brightest in Alexander's second argument. If the good be self-diffusive, then the highest good will be the most self-diffusive—a self-diffusion greater than which cannot be thought. And what greater diremption exists than a diffusion of one's substance without remainder? It belongs to the good *naturaliter*, then, to pour itself out exhaustively. Hence the good generates something of its like from its substance.[43] But generation's power and act must also be eternal and necessary.[44] And not just necessary *ex consequenti*, but properly. God's perfection, that is, demands that God be who God is—the highest good. And so the Father generates his Son eternally and necessarily, and this because of the Father's hypostatic diremption.

As with the Son, so too with the Spirit. Of Alexander's five arguments for the Spirit's procession, only one appears original to him.[45] He draws it from the logic of self-diffusion. As "fontal plenitude" and "highest good," the Father gives all he is *naturaliter* to the Son. Is the Father therefore depleted? No, Brother Alexander counters—not if diffusion is of two kinds. Again, he distinguishes diffusion "through the mode of nature" (*per modum naturae*) from diffusion "through the mode of the will" (*per modum voluntatis*).[46] That the Father generates the Son meets and exhausts diffusion of the first sort, not the second. Diffusion *per modum voluntatis* belongs rather to the procession of Spirit. And this too must prove necessary. For Alexander, remember, self-diffusion is perfect if and only if the highest good diffuses itself in both ways.[47]

The Son's generation by the Father yields his personal property: filiation.[48] For Brother Alexander, the Father-Son conceit grounds the Son's identity. He knows other models for depicting their relation—Augustine's psychological model, for instance.[49] He knows too that every attempt to depict it must invariably fail.[50] But some fail more instructively than do others. For this reason Alexander insists that the Son is only Thought and Image and Word of the Father *because* he is first the Son.[51] Again—and this is typical of the emanation approach—Alexander draws dark underscores beneath the Son's trinitarian origin. The Son lives as God most fundamentally as *ens ab alio*, the one existing from another.[52]

Concomitant to the Son's *ente ab alio* is his *a quo alius,* his "whence another." That is, his being given entails his own giving. So Alexander often narrates the Son's life as a certain intermediacy, a divine in-between. The Son's, Alexander writes, is the *ratio* of the middle.[53] This means first that he is medium between and among the Father and the Spirit.[54] He middles the Father and the world too.[55] The last hangs on the first, since there is no essential diffusion of Spirit to creation without the Son's (and Father's) personal diffusion of the Spirit.[56]

This double diffusion forms the Spirit's personal property—procession.[57] And though the term applies to the Son, it is more properly the Spirit's. Alexander thinks this distinction an important one. The difference between procession *per generationem* and procession *per spirationem*[58] has mostly to do with the shared notion Alexander calls "common spiration" (*communis spiratio*).[59] Procession by generation confers a certain "dignity," here the power to spirate.[60] Father and Son, then, are active "breathers."[61] Not the Spirit, who is breather only passively. Another related difference concerns Alexander's distinction between production *per modum naturae* and *per modum voluntatis.*[62] That last, remember, exhausts and completes trinitarian production. The Spirit is *terminus* of the good's diffusion, of trinitarian order itself.[63] This culmination explains the Spirit's "being from another but whence no one" (*esse ab alio a quo nullus*).[64] For Alexander, no other divine person proceeds from the Spirit.[65]

The Spirit's procession as will or love invites other names.[66] He is Gift, Love, Bond. He is Gift (*donum*) because he is the emanation of generosity (*emanatio liberalitatis*) from Father and Son's mutual delight (*condilectio*).[67] He is Love too—or rather Love received (*amor debitus*). The Father is Love freely given (*amor gratuitus*), the Son their Love shared (*amor ex utroque permixtus*). But because love finds its depth in reception (*habet originem ab alio nec est origo alterius*), the Spirit is Love properly speaking.[68] And he is Bond (*nexus*), since his is the chain (*vinculum*) that shackles Father to Son and trinity to creation.[69]

The above depicts in thumbnail sketch the shape and several features of Brother Alexander's study on the trinity. Most characteristic among these features are distinction by origin, double procession by self-diffusion, and double production by nature and will. Distinguishing, proceeding, producing—each reruns the same logical sequence. Alexander's filigree of the persons, then, hews eternity's supernal pattern: not from another whence another (Father), from another whence another (Son), and from another whence no other (Spirit).[70]

If Alexander prefers the emanation account—discriminating the persons by origin—he will need to say more about the peculiarity of trinitarian origin. Or he will need to show how trinitarian emanation does not multiply *ad infinitum*. How does trinitarian order avoid infinite processions?

"Taxis or order," the long tradition held, "refers to the relationship that exists among the hypostases."[71] In patristic literature, this order refers to "the basis of origin." Or so it goes with the Cappadocians and Athanasius,[72] whose accounts of trinitarian order brandish scripture's baptismal formulation against the heterodox—principally Eunomius. Accounts of trinitarian order bear a twin purpose. The first is to say—or rather show—how the trinity lives as an intrinsic relation, not as a loose confederation of personalities. The structure of the persons, that is, cannot prove accidental or arbitrary. Their order reveals how God is the particular God that God is. The Father is God "not from another," the Son God "from another through generation," and so on. The other purpose aims to show how this order conditions consubstantiality among the persons. This too begins with the Cappadocians, since Eunomius imagined order to tell against consubstantiality.[73] Even so, the strategy of deriving unity in difference from trinitarian order lingered long after Eunomius's defeat.

Because Alexander has much to say about essential equality, I presume rather than defend the proposition that trinitarian order grounds consubstantiality.[74] Instead I assay trinitarian order's first task: to show that the divine persons bear an intrinsic relation one to another.[75] Like the Cappadocians, Alexander knows "many doubts about order." He arranges and treats them in dialectical cycles.

I. Does the Trinity Bear an Order?
The first cycle concerns the very idea of order itself. Can there be order in the trinity? Alexander begins with three objections. First, order belongs to time or position. But the Athanasian Symbol proscribes talk of time in God. "In the trinity," it states, "there is no before and after (*prius aut posterius*)." Neither is there simultaneity, which supposes presence together in time.

Order of position too seems impossible, at least if it implies an arrangement of parts in a whole.[76] But perhaps order is otherwise, a second objection muses. If so, it concerns essence or person or notion. After all, these categories exhaust speech about God.[77] Order cannot be of essence, since order entails distinction of origin. But the divine essence itself, Alexander concludes against Richard of St. Victor and Joachim of Fiore, neither generates nor is generated. So the essence itself cannot claim an origin or principle. It exists, in Alexander's idiom, "by indistinction" (*per indistinctionem*). Neither is order proper to the persons, it seems, if indeed order names the "habit of person to person." Nor is it proper to notions either, since notions or properties[78] distinguish the persons. Order has more to do with fittingness than distinction proper. Third, Alexander recites Augustine. His *De civitate dei* defines order as "the arrangement of things equal and unequal that assigns to each its due place."[79] There can be no disposition of place in the trinity, however, and so no order either.

Alexander's objections diagnose the trouble. "Order" proves too polyvalent a term, so capacious that it is almost entirely vacuous. We cannot know, then, if we should predicate "order" of the trinity until we know what it is we ask. So the question becomes: Order of which kind, of what acceptation?

Alexander takes inventory. There is order of place, of time, of cause, of *ratio*, of natural origin. He concedes that the orders of place and time fail the trinity. The trinity knows neither *superior, inferior, et iuxta* nor *prius, posterior, et simul*.[80] And the others? Order of cause fails because a cause is prior to its effect. And order of *ratio* actually turns out to bear two *rationes*. The first concerns differentiae to a genus, whose implied account of individuation renders it unsuitable for the divine persons. The persons are not differentiae of a common genus. Next Alexander proposes a second *ratio* for the order of *ratio*: "first, middle, and last (*primus, medius, et postremus*)." The "first," Alexander learns from Boethius's commentary on Porphyry's *Isagoge*, is most generic. It is first in the line of predication. "Last" is most determined. Suspended between these hangs a "middle," a subaltern genus.[81] This second line on the order of *ratio*, Alexander thinks, coheres comfortably with the order of origin. So construed, Boethius's model suits the divine persons. How? One is a person "from no one and from whom others," another "from whom no one but from others," and still another "as if a middle, both from another and from whom another." For this reason, Alexander admits both the order of origin and the second

order of *ratio* into the trinitarian life. That life, his readers recall, is constituted "according to these differences: not from another, from another, et
cetera." True, this does not name order in any obvious sense. "This," Alexander admits, "is not order *simpliciter*." Still, order belongs to the trinity
cum additione, or in the layering of the orders of *ratio* and origin. Hence
Alexander's conclusion: yes, there is an order in the trinity.[82]

The next question elaborates.[83] What might it mean to posit an order of
nature or origin[84] in the trinity? Alexander registers three difficulties. The
first suggests that order spells distinction. Does not an order of nature suggest a distinction of natures? Supposing that something cannot be ordered
to itself and that God is simple, it follows that there cannot be any order of
nature in the trinity. A second objection: there is a *ratio* of principle in the
order of nature that prescribes that the principle be first. Transposed into
the trinity, this would mean that the Father as "first principle" (*principium
principii*) precedes his Son by nature.[85] But that cannot be—at least according to Augustine and the Athanasian Symbol. And last: an order of nature
suggests an order of substance or essence. When we say "order of essence,"
Alexander notes, we mean either that essence is the principle of order or
that the essence is itself ordered. Essence cannot simply be the principle
of order—if essence is absolute, then order is relative. But again, essence
cannot be the principle of distinction. It neither generates nor spirates. Essence, then, cannot prove the principle of order. Neither is the essence ordered, since (again) something cannot be ordered to itself. Talk of person
does not much help either. Order entails difference, and the persons do not
essentially differ.

II. What Is the Trinity's Order?

These objections only sharpen Alexander's arguments for an *ordo naturae*
in the trinity. They also introduce the questions that comprise the next and
largest dialectical cycle on the distinction of persons. Alexander's cut against
the second objection runs deep and swift. There exists but one nature in
the divinity. And, as both the Philosopher and the Athanasian Symbol
agree, "before" and "after" cannot apply to an infinite God.[86] Next Alexander whets his blade against the first and third objections at once. That
which is ordered is not the *ordo naturae*, but the *ordo personarum*. As to the
ordo naturae, we can distinguish nature and essence. (Not *in re*, obviously—
these are identical in God—but in speech.) Nature names an essence "with

addition," Alexander writes—principally an essence with the power of producing something similar. So it goes in creation. For example: the nature of a peregrine entails among other things the power to produce more peregrines. But between peregrines and God gapes an analogical interval of infinite metric. So an *ordo naturae* in the divine persons cannot mean simply "natural order"—not if the persons are more than a tripled contraction of some deity genus. Alexander suggests rather a certain and analogous *ratio* of order. And that *ratio* concerns the principle of distinction among the persons, or the power to produce another similar.

So the order of the trinity issues in the distinction of persons. And that distinction has something to do with the power of production. Whose then is it to produce? If it is someone's, is there some person who remains unproduced? Must there be necessarily?[87] Here Brother Alexander's arguments excite negation. Extending the Father's "dignity" of being "without origin" to another person proves disastrous. First, it divests the trinity of "the highest connection and order to one another."[88] The Father, "principle without principle,"[89] inaugurates order exactly when and as he diffuses himself. "Hence," Alexander concludes, "this diffusion introduces order."[90] Without a singular principle, then, the trinity of persons would lack its intrinsic order and *ratio*. It would dissolve into an arbitrary cluster or ensemble. Second, surely everyone agrees that applying filiation to two persons invites redundancy into God. Who would abide two Sons? But the same holds, mutatis mutandis, for innascibility. For Alexander, "perfection of origin and order" demands that only one person be "without origin" (*sine origine*), which for him also means that only one person generates. Third, Alexander confesses a prima facie difficulty. Trinitarian order is "order according to origin (*secundum originem*)." But the Father has no origin. Alexander learns from Richard of St. Victor that origin applies to the Father. It does not "because he has origin from another person, but because he is the principle of origin of the other persons."[91]

Another question asks whether there must necessarily be only one person without origin. Alexander recycles the above arguments from "highest order," "highest connection," and "highest relatedness" to show why.[92] Mostly the arguments perform reconnaissance for the incursion that follows.

That incursion marches under a filioquist banner.[93] If only one of the divine persons lacks origin, do the others proceed immediately from him and not from one another?[94] Alexander's conclusion hardly surprises. "On this point," he writes, "the Greeks err by holding that the Holy Spirit proceeds immediately and only from the Father and in no way from the Son."[95] More interesting here (as everywhere) is not the conclusion, but rather the dialectical pressures that together fashion it. Alexander applies several.

First, differentiae follow from genera in the order of reason (*ordo rationis*). And if the order of the divine persons is both the exemplar of order and according to the *ordo rationis*, then divine order entails that two persons proceed from the Father as the differentiae do from a genus. And these differentiae proceed from a genus directly, not from other differentiae. It follows, then, that the second and third persons of the trinity proceed from the Father directly and not through each other. And whatever holds in the *ordo rationis*, it seems, should hold ever more perfectly in the *ordo* of the divine persons. After all, that order offers the archetype for all other orders. Yes and no, Alexander responds. Yes, the divine order grounds all and every other order. But no, the order of differentiae to genera cannot be projected in exemplary fashion in the divine persons. Why not? Because that order implies imperfection. Differentiae differ materially, not formally. In other words, that order depends for its coherence upon a potency that God lacks. Recall the Boethian line: first, last, and middle as most general, most specific, and in-between concerns an order of *forms*. In this way, Boethius's image approximates the order of the divine persons, which demands something most general, most specific, and something in-between. Or as Alexander has it: "a person having origin who proceeds from one without origin and yet another who proceeds from both."[96]

A second objection holds that the trinity comprises speaker, word, and breath. And words and breath issue directly from a speaker, not from one another. Why should it be otherwise in the trinity? Augustine sorts both words and breaths into inner and outer. The inner speaker is *mens*, Alexander thinks it obvious to say, while the inner word is *intelligentia*. Inner *spiritus* proceeds from both *mens* and *intelligentia*. Surely this is love or love-in-a-way, just as Augustine says. The trouble with "the Greeks," Alexander crows, is that they trade only in externals. A picture holds them captive. Yes, outer word and breath may proceed simultaneously and immediately. But it does not follow that it is so with *inner* word and breath.

Objection three throws down another glove. Hebrews 1:3 calls Christ "the splendor of glory." According to a twelfth-century *Glossa* on the same,

whatever is noblest of creatures should be attributed to God. What is nobler among creatures than the power of producing? And how much nobler
is the power to produce through one, not two? So it must be in the trinity
too. It is nobler, then, that the Spirit proceed from one alone.

Here again Brother Alexander reverts to his distinction between natural and voluntary production. Only in the first case is production from one
nobler. Alexander concedes that this argument applies to the generation
of the Son. It is not so, however, with the production of will. No, this kind of
production concerns what is enjoyable and delightful. It follows, in other
words, the logic of perfect charity, which per Richard of St. Victor "tends
toward the other."[97] Because it desires to love and be loved, perfect charity
cannot be solitary. If the perfection of the will is charity, the perfect production *per modum voluntatis* will require that "the production of the Holy
Spirit . . . is necessarily not from one alone but from many, according to the
rush of love from one into another."[98]

The trinitarian distinction Alexander innovates between natural and voluntary production raises as many questions as answers. In fact, difficulties flow
from it almost inexorably.[99] The most challenging of these wonders if there is
a way to interrupt diffusion. If not, why limit the number of divine persons to
three? Why not an infinity? Alexander makes quick work of the infinity
problem. An infinity of persons is impossible, at least if the good is known
only through and as order. On this account, being good means bearing an
order.[100] But no order spans an infinity. How could it?[101] Any God who lives
as infinite persons could be Lord only to "disorder and confusion."[102]

But remonstrating an infinity of persons is not yet positing a number,
much less three. Doing that requires argument, so Alexander offers several.
Some are external, issuing from a philosophic predilection for the number
three. One of these arguments reinscribes a Pythagorean presumption into
trinitarian logic. What number, the Philosopher remembers the ancients
arguing,[103] contains a higher order or concord than three?[104] Another argument conditions self-diffusion.[105] If the good be self-diffusive, then surely the
greater the communication, the higher the good. This is true, Alexander allows,
so long as that communication is also "ordered and distinct."

Other arguments are internal and issue from the deliverances of revelation. Some rehearse Richard of St. Victor's protestations against a quaternity. One argues that a doubling of personal properties confounds the
principle of divine proportion.[106] Another asserts that two persons "whence

no one" (*a quo nullus*) would mean that neither proceeds from the other.[107] These persons would lack fraternity (*germanitas*). They would not belong to each other immediately. Still another argument retrieves Richard's logic of *condilectio*.[108] The perfect community of the good demands the highest love. And love is deeper when it delights. Delight is possible with two persons. *Condilectio,* however, requires three but no more, not if the community of perfect love should hold fast to its erotic equipoise. A final argument holds that the twin modes of production render another divine person superfluous.[109] As self-diffusive good, the Father produces his Son by nature and both breathe the Spirit by will. Production's modes thus exhausted, introducing another person invites insidious repetition. "It is therefore superfluous and vain," Alexander concludes, "to posit more [persons]."[110]

Alexander completes this second cycle by defending Spirit's "whence no one" (*a quo nullus*) as a power rather than a lack.[111] Again, self-diffusion is good only when it is also ordered. Good's diffusion becomes confusion if it lacks an end term (*terminus diffusionis*). The nature of the highest good demands an end no less than it requires a beginning and a middle. That end is the Spirit, whose nonproduction (*non-productio*) names a dignity unique to him.[112] On this account, good's self-diffusion contains its own limit. Now the Spirit indeed diffuses, Alexander reassures, but he empties himself *essentialiter* (not *personaliter*) into creation's ensemble—not into a fourth person.

III. Can God Be without Order?
A third and final dialectical cycle ponders how much sense there is in predicating an order of God absent the persons.[113] Not much, Alexander thinks. Trinitarian order always and everywhere invokes the *ratio* of origin. And the *ratio* of origin entails different principles, since Anselm demands that neither reason nor nature allows us simply to identify without remainder what originates from another with its origin. Thus a Godhead somehow divested of the persons has no "this and that."[114] Still it may be possible to contrive an order in God according to understanding (if not in reality). We could, Alexander supposes, dream an order among God's mind and understanding and love. In that dream, mind precedes understanding and both proceed love. But we will need eventually to awaken to the truth that as divine attributes, these do not and cannot truly differ. Not to say so would mean courting Abelard's error of indexing divine attributes to divine persons too closely. So no, Alexander concludes, a God who is not persons cannot be a God of order.

This final point hides a massive implication under scholastic jargon. If a God robbed of persons describes a God without order, and if, according to Alexander, the "sacred order of the persons" just names divine beauty, then a God who is not three divine persons is a God without beauty. It is a God who is not Beauty itself.[115] This marks a major difference between Alexander's way of construing beauty and very nearly everyone else's. Take Thomas Aquinas's, if only because it is most familiar and ready to hand. The Thomas who comments Dionysius indexes God's beauty to the divine essence. If God is beauty qua essence, then beauty names a divine attribute.[116] True, Thomas does not imagine the divine essence to be somehow *other* than the persons. But he does not imagine the trinitarian persons or their order to form beauty's primary referent.[117] Even when he sometimes identifies beauty with the Son, Thomas does this according to the logic of appropriation. But this is not Alexander's way. For him, as we have seen, divine beauty is "from the sacred order of the divine persons."[118] And that "order itself is beautiful."[119]

Alexander's point is hardly reducible to a "scholastic disposition"—to a harried fetish for system that possessed medievals. It is not order in general and as such that Alexander styles beautiful. Rather he judges order considered abstractly and *per se* as an "indistinct and confused notion."[120] An objection specifies that beauty is rather *this* order, the trinitarian one that belongs to and among Father and Son and Spirit. It is the different concord and concordant difference of their properties that "exists mutually with one another in the divine plurality of persons that is supremely beautiful and the most ordered of all."[121] The relation of each person and his irreducibly personal property one to another accounts for the trinity's peculiar and unspeakable beauty. To threaten this delicate equipoise by doubling a personal property, say, would be to "confound rather than to extend the principle of proportion."[122] Beauty for Alexander is no more or less than God's being *non ab alio a quo alius, ab alio a quo alius,* and *ab alio a quo non alius*—equally, simultaneously, eternally.[123]

IS NOT THE SON BEAUTY, TOO?

That Brother Alexander so identifies beauty with the order of the trinity raises a question. The long theological tradition very often associates aesthetic terms with the Son.[124] In fact, naming the Son "beauty" (*species, pulchritudo*) and "image" (*imago*) forms an ancient Christian habit. Augustine does it, for example, as does Hilary before him.[125] Peter Lombard renews the practice by salvaging their passages from the sea floor and redisplaying them for comment.[126] Later scholastics appraise these passages. William of Auxerre, Albert the Great, Thomas Aquinas, Bonaventure, Ulrich of Strasburg, Duns Scotus—each employs the grammar of appropriation to identify beauty with the Son.[127] Or they discern, in Scotist patois, "a specific agreement between essential properties and the proper characteristic of some person."[128] In his early *Glossa*, Alexander of Hales himself relates aesthetic terms to the Son as well.[129]

How does this habit relate to Brother Alexander's in the later *SH*?[130] Does identifying beauty as trinitarian order clash with appropriating beauty to the Son? Are these claims noncompossible?

The answer presumes a history. When he comments on Dionysius's *De divinis nominibus* 4.7, Albert the Great makes a decisive move.[131] On Augustine's authority, Albert reads Dionysius to identify "form" (*species*) with "beauty" (*pulchritudo*). At length and elsewhere Albert repurposes each to appropriate the Son.[132] His student Ulrich remembers and repeats this identification.[133] So does Albert's earlier student in what is undoubtedly the most remembered and often-read passage on beauty in the long Middle Ages. "But form or beauty (*species autem sive pulchritudo*)," Thomas says, "bears a likeness to the personal properties of the Son. For three things are required for beauty: integrity or perfection first, then proportion or harmony, and also clarity."[134] Then Thomas details how each feature relates to the Son's personal property. Identifying and appropriating beauty to the Son also takes root among the little friars. "Though the Dominicans are not as interested in the idea of Christ-beauty as the Franciscans," Bychkov notes, "the Augustinian association between the Son and . . . *species* is best developed by Bonaventure."[135] And what Bonaventure limns of Christ-beauty[136] continues in Scotus.[137]

Brother Alexander knows this identification. Sometimes he writes of it, though not without rhetorical restraint.[138] He never hesitates, however, to describe the Son as "image" (*imago*) or "form" (*species*). Indeed, he devotes an article to the last and several to the first.[139] "Form" (*species*) names the Son to the extent that his generation by the Father enacts a knowing from a mind.[140] Both of Hilary's definitions of *imago* suit the Son too. The first correlates image with form, and thus with "cognition." But these appropriate the Son, who is "principle of knowing the Father" (*principium cognoscendi Patrem*).[141] The second definition describes both Son and Spirit, at least until the condition "imaged" (*imaginata*) is added. Only the Son figures the Father—only they share the notion of active spiration. For this reason and others, the Spirit cannot be *imago* proper. So if Son and Spirit both bear "being from another" (*esse ab alio*), they do so equivocally.[142] The Son alone images his Father "more expressly" (*expressior*).[143]

Brother Alexander never dithers, then, about appropriating "image" (*imago*) or "form" (*species*) to the Son. His hesitation has rather to do, it seems, with identifying "beauty" (*pulchritudo*) with *imago* and *species*. Not once across his massive *Summa* does Alexander appropriate the specific term *pulchritudo* to the Son. Neither does he—as will Albert and Thomas— identify *species* with *pulchritudo*. Why not? That *pulchritudo* should fail to function as an appropriation should hardly shock. Not, anyway, if my last chapter was right to argue that beauty names the trinitarian order instead of an essential attribute. Recall that appropriations—as chapter 3 showed— describe essential attributes somehow associated with one or another personal property. Such is appropriation's grammar: if *pulchritudo* does not number among the former, it cannot number among the latter either. However much Alexander allows aesthetic terms (*species, imago*) to orna- ment the Christ, he prefers to earmark *pulchritudo* for the trinity.

In fact, Alexander's trinitarian aesthetic bleeds through even his study of the Son as *imago*. As he reads and teaches Hilary's definitions of *imago*, he lapses back into trinity talk. We can, Alexander thinks, speak *imago* in different moods. Passively, *imago* names the Son as *imago Patris*, the Father's image. Relatively, *imago* names the divine essence itself. Its persons imitate it, and it imitates them, for they are it, and it is they. Actively, *imago* names "the divine essence in the persons" (*essentia divina in personis*). Trinity- God expresses the divine most totally and is imitated most sublimely in and as the image of the human (*imago hominis*). In this sense, even the trinity is called *imago hominis*, the human's image.[144] That seems scandalous enough. But now Alexander says more. The divinity in three persons, not just the Son, comprises the exemplar for express imitation (*exemplar ad imitatio- nem expressam*). The trinity alone, then, is the "full and precise *ratio* of image." And it is this that the rational soul imitates.[145]

So again, is Alexander's claim that beauty be trinitarian order noncom- possible with the claim that the Son too dons aesthetic names? Not finally.

As for "form" (*species*), Alexander consistently conceives it Christologically as an appropriation to the Son. "Image" (*imago*) invites more difficulty. It operates as both an appropriation and as a name for the essence in three persons. Yet Alexander quite explicitly teaches that "image is not taken univocally" (*non sumatur univoce*). Rather it applies variously to essence, essence in persons, the Son, and rational soul.[146] So *imago* picks out trinity like this, the Son like that, and so on. Bychkov notes a tendency in the Franciscan tradition to conceive "beauty in application to the trinity . . . equivocally."[147] That seems right, I think, so far as his claim goes. But let us allow that analogy belongs to equivocity as a species to its genus.[148] We could then ask how the Son's beauty relates analogously to the trinity's and the soul's to both. The relation between the first two seems clear enough in the text. The Son images the Father to the Spirit, and it is this order among them that Alexander thinks divine beauty just is.

CONCLUSION

The principal argument of this book holds that Alexander conceives and patterns beauty after the order of the trinity. After surveying the transcendentals and articulating beauty's relation among them, we arrive at length at the very thing. After some loose remarks about persons and processions in general, I argued that distinguishing the trinity's persons by origin entails an order. It must, at least if it is to yield a trinity and not a quaternity, say, or a quinternity or an infinity. Close attention to Alexander's several questions on order traced three dialectical cycles. First, origin conditions order—Alexander very often simply names this the *ordo originis*. Second, trinitarian order prescribes a highly specific procedure for depicting intratrinitarian life. That life, Alexander insists, comprises a Son from a Father and a Spirit from both. Its depiction must therefore positively vibrate with filioquist logic—Alexander's does. And third, Alexander insists that there can be no order in God without persons. No order, no beauty—not if order is beauty. But order there is, and so Alexander hymns the divine plurality of persons as "the most beautiful and most ordered."[149] And Alexander's preference for beauty's trinitarian filigree is not finally incompatible with its sometime Christological associations. Yes, Alexander sometimes appropriates aesthetic terms (*species*, *imago*) to the trinity's second person. But no, this mounts no final opposition to his stricter identification of "beauty" (*pulchritudo*) with trinitarian order.

So much, then, on the beauty of the trinity. Does creation too suffer it? When the Spirit pours himself into creation, he endows what is not trinity by nature with its order.[150] As Alexander says, "hence that diffusion introduces order."[151] Still, how exactly Alexander imagines creation to bear traces of trinitarian order awaits Part III.[152]

PART III

THE TRINITY'S BEAUTY *AD EXTRA*

Part II admired the beauty of the trinity. That beauty is just its "sacred or-der": one from no other (Father), another from him and from whom an-other (Son), and still another from them and whence no other (Spirit). But does creation also suffer this beauty? Alexander thinks so. When the Spirit pours himself into creation, he endows what is not trinity by nature with trinitarian order.[1] As Alexander says, "that diffusion introduces order."[2] Creation's beauty, too, will bear a trinitarian order. How?

Alexander grounds trinitarian acts *ad extra* within acts *ad intra*. The act of creation, then, finds the condition of its possibility within the eter-nal act of trinitarian procession. Indeed, Alexander thinks that causality itself can be appropriated to the persons. This connection yields an effect: it signs all of creation with trinitarian traces (*vestigia*). Chapter 5 assays these traces and their varieties. Together these account for creation's beauty. A creature is beautiful because it reflects the order of its trinitarian creator. Most beautiful among creatures, Brother Alexander thinks, are human beings, whose resplendence among creation has to do with their being *imago trinitatis*, the image of the trinity. So chapter 6 maps that image, particu-larly the perichoretic relation of its powers—remembering, understand-ing, and willing.

Sin damages this image. In so doing, it parodies and inverts trinitarian relations. For Alexander, that is, sin proves fundamentally and principally antitrinitarian. Chapter 7 shows that if grace heals this damage, it does so by rendering souls trinitarian again. Among grace's effects, then, is a shared delight (*fructus*) between God and creature. If God delights in the trinity God is, God also revels in the soul whose trinitarian image grace has restored.

CHAPTER 5

THE BEAUTY CREATION IS

B elieving in one God who is trinitarian communion," Pope Francis writes in *Laudato Si'*, "suggests that the trinity has left its mark on all creation."[1] He continues, "The Franciscan saint teaches us that each creature bears in itself a specifically trinitarian structure."[2] Francis invokes Bonaventure, not Alexander of Hales. But much of Bonaventure's theory of creation as trinitarian theophany owes to the *Summa*, where that trinitarian showing intimates more than just a maker who just-so-happens-to-be trinity. If the order of the trinity accounts for divine beauty in the *Summa*, traces of that trinity will account for creation's beauty. For Alexander, then, creatures not only bear beauty as created. They bear beauty as created and thus marked by the trinity.

In English the word *creation* labels both act (God's) and effect (also God's, however different in nature). I allow this double acceptation to provide this chapter's structure. So my first section below reads creation under its first aspect—as act. It studies what God the trinity did and does and will do to bring about what God is not, namely the ensemble of creatures. Within this first section, I show how Alexander teaches the trinitarian processions *ad intra* to ground creation *ad extra*. Next I outline his theory of trinitarian causality. My second section reads creation under the second acceptation, or what it is that God's act effects. If a cause remains in its effect, a trinitarian cause ought to linger in its effect trinitarianly. So I trawl Alexander's doctrine of trinitarian traces before I sift through his long questions on the beauty of creation. My proposal throughout is simple: for Brother Alexander creation's beauty derives from and points back to the trinity's.

CREATION AND THE TRINITARIAN PROCESSIONS

In his scriptum on the *Sentences*, Thomas Aquinas writes that "the eternal processions are the cause and *ratio* of the making of creatures."[3] The *Summa Halensis* lacks Thomas's programmatic statement, but it shares a logic. Studying that logic in full—holding it up to the light as the jeweler holds a gemstone to her loupe—is not possible here. Instead, this brief section hazards only a conspectus of how Alexander grounds creation in the trinity.

Trinitarian patterns already texture Alexander's answer to who exactly it is who creates. "God"—yes, very well. But who is that? Here again, Alexander figures God trinitarianly. For him, the God of Christian confession scarcely acts as divine essence only.[4] He insists instead that "the term 'God' supposits for diverse *persons*."[5] St. Paul divined the same, Alexander thinks, when he praised the God "from whom and through whom and in whom are all things" (Rom. 11:36). These prepositions hint at the divine acts of origin, work, and conservation. And each in turn appropriates a trinitarian person.[6] Thus Christian grammar demands that "the Father and Son and Holy Spirit are one principle of creatures."[7] Only the God *who is trinity* creates.

More, it is exactly *as trinity* that God creates. Alexander here tautens the hitch between trinity and creation by securing creation to personal properties. He begins with the Father's: paternity (*paternitas*).[8] Alexander tethers creation to paternity by applying his grammar of appropriation. Among other things, the Father's personal property reveals the divine attribute "power" to be an *appropriated* personal attribute. Or it is a divine attribute with special reference to one or another member person of the trinity. "The work of creation (*opus creationis*)," Alexander writes, "belongs more to power." By the same score, the very name "Father" betrays not only a "personal property or the relation of Father to Son." It also names a "relation to creatures according to creation or a relation of the Father to humankind according to re-creation." And precisely as the unbegotten Father (*esse non ab alio*), he sires Son and Spirit and creation. He is "principle" (*principium*) to all—and in that logical order.[9] The Father alone lives as "first principle from whom all nature and all essence comes."[10]

The Son's property also roots creation. Filiation, remember, characterizes the Son's particular "being from another" (*esse ab alio*). But particular to the Son is the *ratio* of the middle.[11] In the *Summa*, this middling between Father and Spirit forms the condition for the possibility of the Spirit's spiration[12] and the world's making.[13] How exactly? The Son's eternal reception of the divine essence from the Father models all forms of being from another—creation's too.[14] "To receive a nature," Basil of Caesarea said, "is common to the Son and to all creatures."[15]

Alexander says more still of the exemplary role the Son plays for creation when he studies the name "Word" (*verbum*). It is "by the Word that God speaks to creatures" and "by the Word that everything is spoken."[16] In this sense the Son is "not the Word of creatures, but the Word by which the creature is made."[17] I say more about the Son's exemplarism below. But the point here is how the Son's generation *ad intra* proves a necessary condition for each and every act of divine diffusion *ad extra*.[18]

Which brings us to the Spirit, in whose spiration trinitarian diffusion climaxes.[19] As *completio trinitatis*, the Spirit is *esse ab alio a quo nullus*.[20] Or the Spirit is "being from another but from whom no one [comes]"—no divine person anyway. Only here Brother Alexander reminds readers that *ad intra* does not exhaust the trinity's modes of diffusion: "the Spirit diffuses himself not to other persons, but to *creatures*."[21] On Alexander's account, then, the Spirit is also exemplar. The Spirit is called "Gift," for example, because his life is given without remainder by Father and Son.[22] And he models this reception by offering himself to creatures.[23]

TRINITARIAN CAUSALITY

For Alexander it seems clear that creation is a trinitarian act *ad extra* sheltered within trinitarian acts *ad intra*. The very act of creation is less clear. Accenting the trinitarian cannot mean overriding the singularity of creation's act. Neither can it threaten the ineliminable simplicity of God. And so the question becomes: How to affirm both the singularity and trinitarian shape of creation's act at once? To answer, Alexander plies his grammar of trinitarian appropriation. Properly appropriated, causality itself exhibits a trinitarian structure.

Already at *SH* I, n. 73 Brother Alexander announces,

> The divine cause is a cause in a triple genus of cause: efficient, exemplar or formal, and final. Which causality, though it be common to the whole trinity, is indeed appropriated (*appropriatur*) as the efficient cause to the Father, the exemplar to the Son, and the final to the Holy Spirit.[24]

Readers must wait until *SH* I–II for further instruction. There and at last, Alexander relates creatures in general (*de creatura in communi*) to their cause (*de creatura secundum causam*). Doing that means studying the "divine cause" within its "triple genus."

After worrying at the causes' eternity and essentiality, Alexander regards their order. Like the *ordo trinitatis*, the order of the causes entails eternity and essential identity. The *rationes* of immaterial causes only seem to differ because they happen here below. A sculptor (efficient) hews stone (material) to her model (exemplar or formal) to yield an effigy whose end is ornamenting an imperial palace (final).[25] In God things are otherwise. First, divine simplicity means God's persons, attributes, and activities belong to one essence. Second, God's causal act cannot be serial—the Athanasian Symbol forbids any "before and after" in God.[26] So the order the philosopher attributes to the causes applies only as they appear in creation (*secundum quod sunt in creatis*).[27]

In God all immaterial causes are one. Indeed they must be to the extent that their *rationes* name divine attributes. But even here Alexander displays his trinitarian preoccupation. Richard of St. Victor had taught him to appropriate divine attributes. So he does:

> Allowing that they are common to the three persons, these reasons [of the causes] are nevertheless appropriated to those persons. Hence in the book *City of God* 11, "Since it is said *God said, let there be light and light was made*, and *God saw the light, that it was good*, it is understood who made it and through what it was made and on account of what it was made" . . . It is clear that he who spoke *fiat* is called by the name efficient [cause], since the speaking of God is his making; but the means by which he made belong to the exemplar cause; but for what [it is made], [this belongs] to the final [cause].[28]

Here Alexander follows predictable exegetical patterns. To the Father belongs creation's *fiat*, to the Son its means, and to the Spirit its purpose. Augustine taught the same, even if he had not yet correlated the persons with Aristotle's immaterial causes.[29] Eriugena pressed further still, binding intratrinitarian acts to the eternal causes.[30] Distinctive to Brother Alexander, however, is a thorough study of the immaterial causes *from within* this trinitarian frame.

How does God cause efficiently? And what has this to do with the Father? Whatever else divine causality entails, it cannot involve necessity from without. It is only "by God's gratuitous will" that God "creates creatures."[31] If Alexander allows that creation bears a necessity of fittingness (*necessitas congruitatis*), he forbids any natural necessity (*necessitas naturae*).[32] He extends this ban to internal necessity. Neither the self-diffusive good nor justice—the two strongest candidates for internal necessity—can compel creation. Alexander's arguments against the first option counter an unnamed *haereticus*.[33] Against him, Brother Alexander relocates the self-diffusion axiom from efficient to final causality.[34] Neither can justice demand creation's making. What exists only in absence cannot yet make any claim upon God.[35] But even if not strictly necessary, God's efficient act of creating displays an intimate likeness to the Father's generation of the Son.[36] The latter already meets the scholastic principles of self-diffusion, of the *ab uno unum,* and of both volitional and natural communication *ad intra.* The result is that Alexander has relieved creation of these axiomatic pressures. His God remains free to create "according to the freedom of God's will."[37]

Another major difference between the Father's siring of the Son and creation concerns the divine essence. The Son's life just is the divine essence—creation's remains borrowed. Neither is creation somehow spun from the divine essence. Creatures exist in God as efficient cause only *potentialiter,* Alexander insists, not *essentialiter.*[38] "But I say 'efficient,'" he clarifies, "not by act, but by habit."[39] Otherwise God "might be understood to depend upon the essence of creatures."[40]

Alexander explains how creatures exist in God when he explains exemplar-formal causality. The hyphen carves a razor-thin distinction, one Alexander inherits from Seneca.[41] If exemplar refers more properly to God, form speaks to "forms in matter."[42] The latter locates its ground and cause in the former, in whom all forms are finally indivisible.[43] The need for Alexander's distinction seems translucent enough. God cannot act as a formal cause somehow intrinsic to a creature.[44] Professing God as "the universal form" (*forma universi*) had been Amalric of Bena's mistake.[45] But that God's—or the Word's—exemplarity should stand at a remove from typical formal causality does not mean that Alexander fastened some fifth cause to Aristotle's four. Hence the hyphen. It is best, Alexander seems to think, to conceive the exemplar as an *extrinsic* mode of formal causality.[46]

Exemplar-formal causality is appropriated to the Son. The linchpin here is St. Paul's talk of Christ as "the wisdom of God" (1 Cor. 1:24). For the long Christian tradition, wisdom names the Son as God's self-knowledge. Where Platonism knew a distinction between divine knowing (*Nous*) and the One, Christianity advocated consubstantiality.[47] Gilles Emery judges that

"Christian Platonism finds its ultimate expression" in its transposition of the world of ideas into the Son.[48] Perhaps.[49] But suppose for a moment we leave aside the lexical connection between Pauline "wisdom" and God's knowledge. Why else appropriate exemplar-formal causality to the Son?

Alexander submits two reasons. The first has to do with the mode of the Son's procession. Alexander does not, it is true, set much store by the psychological model for the trinity.[50] But he often keys the Son's generation to the divine intellect.[51] Alexander's further hesitance to describe divine attributes without trinitarian grammar leads him to appropriate God's knowledge to the Son.[52] To the extent that exemplar-formal causality moves within the atmosphere of divine intellect, it will belong to the Son. The second reason concerns likeness. Obviously the Son bears a singular likeness to his Father.[53] And it is in his likeness, too, that all others participate.[54] A question follows hotfoot: What distinguishes the Son's likeness from creation's participation in it? Alexander illustrates his point. An idea in the soul bears some likeness to an intelligible form. But that idea is not thereby consubstantial with the soul.[55] So too with God's exemplar-formal causality: its formal act works externally and at an essential remove from what it causes.

Both efficient and exemplar-formal causality find their end in the final cause. For Aristotle the latter wields explanatory power over the former.[56] It does because "the final cause," Alexander teaches, "is the *ratio* of the other causes."[57] Where he enlarges upon the claim, he writes,

> The end takes up (*induit*) the *ratio* of the other causes, which are principally these: the efficient cause, insofar as it moves an agent; the formal [cause], insofar as it is the agent's measure (*regula*) according to which he does his work; and the final [cause], insofar as the work is completed . . . So since the end is good—the good itself—insofar as it moves, it takes up the *ratio* of the agent; insofar as it measures (*regulat*), it [takes up the *ratio*] of the art or exemplar; and insofar as it completes, it is in its proper mode of final cause.[58]

Here final causality takes up, puts on, and dons the *rationes* of efficient and exemplar causality. But how? Its consummating force issues from its relation to the good. If the good orders all (even nonrational) desire, then the final cause structures all activity here below.[59] Somehow, then, the good causes causality itself.[60] On Alexander's view the good and its final cause arpeggiate creation's composition, preservation, and end.

Brother Alexander is not the first to discern the Spirit's diatonic play. But he is among its most devoted enthusiasts. Take his celebration of Spirit as *completio trinitatis*.[61] This "pneumatic finality"[62] features prominently across Alexander's texts. Those texts often extend this pneumatic emphasis to the Spirit's appropriations: efficient–exemplar–formal–*final*; one–true–*good*. Across these triplets, the last term seems always to sublate and consummate the others. Onto these Alexander tacks another triplet: power–wisdom–will.[63] Will's appropriation to Spirit recalls his manner of procession (*per modum voluntatis*).[64] Still again, the final term proves decisive: "the divine will is the principal cause of [creation's] production."[65] But Alexander avoids a free fall into voluntarism by cleaving the divine will to the good. "The divine will never moves itself to act by reason of will," he teaches. And it does so only "by reason of divine goodness." It is precisely as divine will and goodness, then, that the Spirit enacts the final cause. He is end, climax, *a quo nullus alius*—he who draws every creature to its term in God.

TRINITARIAN TRACES

If a cause remains in its effect,[66] then a triple cause lingers in its effect triply.[67] As Bonaventure later wrote, all creation witnesses its "trinity-maker" (*trinitas fabricatrix*).[68] Bonaventure's expansive teaching on creation's trinitarian traces remains justly familiar. But in this section I regard Alexander and his school, who first develop what Bonaventure later refines. Like Bonaventure, Brother Alexander sorts trinitarian likeness (*similitudo*) by degrees of intensity.[69] Trace (*vestigium*), image (*imago*), and likeness—let us call these grades.[70] Each grade comprises certain triplets of properties, dispositions, or habits—let us call these modes. Every and each triplet hews to the logic of appropriation, since "the divine works of power and wisdom and goodness are indivisible, although they may be so appropriated."[71] I offer a brief word on the trace and its attendant triplet(s) before showing how they account for creation's beauty.

At the first grade of likeness stands the trace (*vestigium*).[72] Because every creature carries the trinity's trace, its boundary is coextensive with creation's. For Brother Alexander, in other words, being created means necessarily bearing the trace.[73] In this sense, the trace comprises what is most general—a genus under which the whole ensemble of creation falls. However general, "trace" is said variously according to different modes.[74] Each mode comprises a found triplet. Like other scholastics, Brother Alexander collects these triplets, mostly from Augustine and the canon of scripture. How do they relate? How do they differ?

First to consider is measure-number-weight (*mensura-numerus-pondus*). "You, O Lord," Wisdom 11:21 prays, "have disposed all things in measure, number, and weight."[75] Scholastics learned to brandish this scripture from Augustine's *De genesi ad litteram*.[76] Alexander argues that this triplet *stricto sensu* describes bodies. But he extends it to spiritual things "through a certain likeness" (*per quamdam similitudinem*).[77] In spirits the triplet names not properties but rather certain "dispositions." So measure names a disposition by which something is in itself and whose being and power remain finite. Number is a disposition by which something bears a species and form on whose account it is discerned from everything else. And weight names a disposition by which something is ordered to its end. Under these stipulated definitions, measure–number–weight appropriates the trinitarian persons.[78] This triplet, however, predicates created dispositions more in becoming (*in fieri*) than in being (*in esse*).[79] As such, it claims only a remote relation to its cause.[80] We can speak of divine measure, number, and weight only obliquely. After all, God is measure without measure, number without number, and so on.[81] Unlike unity-truth-goodness (*unitas-veritas-bonitas*),[82] then, measure-number-weight belongs to the creator only "equivocally."[83]

The trace comprises other modes too. These stand as "diverse dispositions," each appropriating the persons under different *rationes*. One derives from Augustine's *De diversis quaestionibus*: *quo constat-quo discernitur-quo congruit*.[84] This triplet signals God's reign over created being as its source. Another from Dionysius names God's efficient causality, mostly as it relates to the angels.[85] This is essence–power–operation (*essential-virtus-operatio*).[86] These triplets "indwell creatures" too, each bearing nearly as loose a connection to the trinity as measure–number–weight.[87]

Mode-form-order (*modus-species-ordo*) proves different. This triplet rather evokes creation's diffusion from its trinitarian source[88] or its triadic source, at least: "these three are taken on account of the *rationes* of the three causes: for *modus* belongs to the efficient cause, *species* to the formal cause, and *ordo* to the final."[89] But what exactly *is* this triplet? Does it name *essentialia, accidentalia*, or something else besides? Alexander thinks this triplet proves essential, though it is not obvious how. It does not describe metaphysical properties constitutive of a creature's essence.[90] Rather it names "dispositions" or "relations to its causes." Nevertheless, to the extent that this or that creature cannot be without her essential causes, these "relations" remain essential to the creature.[91] Her relations to her causes reveal the conditions under which a creature is God-like (*deiforme*).[92] This is the very stuff of theology, Alexander writes. So much so that "if things are known without those [three], they are not known by theological knowledge. For that, those [three] are necessary."[93] Theology's knowledge, Alexander concludes, belongs less to some thing's proper *ratio* and more to what accounts for its God-likeness.

These three relations, like those considered above, belong to all creatures, though not in the selfsame way. According to nature, all creatures feature mode-form-order as their deiform relation to God. Thus in nature the triplet is fixed, which is only to say it is incapable of corruption or gain.[94] It suffers change only under the direction of a rational will—and not just the change inherent to creation's *ex nihilo* fragility. Above volitional creatures under sin's damage there looms a darker *vertibilitas*, not "in nonbeing simply" but "in the nonbeing of death." This is evil.[95] In this shadow, mode-form-order suffers diminution "through sin" (*per peccatum*). Yet however damaging the rational creature's choices, she approaches "the nonbeing of death" only asymptotically. She cannot, Alexander thinks, deliver herself finally and irredeemably to the *nihil* whence she came. Should she try, she will find the traces of her *deiformitas* inscribed too deeply upon herself.[96] She is capable of corruption, yes, but not self-annihilation.[97] "There is no vice," Alexander recalls Augustine saying, "so contrary to nature that it destroys the traces (*vestigia*) of nature."[98]

Together these triplets gather under the trace (*vestigium*). The trace and its modes occupy the lowest rung on the "ladder of nature" (*scala naturae*). Higher still rise image (*imago*) and likeness (*similitudo*), though these await study in later chapters. Here I want only to underline how creation's trinitarian traces account for its beauty. Before addressing their aesthetic quality, though, I offer a brief word on the practice of locating trinitarian triplets across creation.

Whatever its scriptural warrant, the venerable practice of mapping triplets cannot claim a purely Christian bloodline. Neoplatonists knew many, for example. Their principle of predominance even allowed them to predicate each of God. "For we say that life is triadic," Proclus says, "and also that these three things . . . are everywhere."[99] And, as Hegel is altogether too eager to point out, triplets have featured across divergent religious systems since the Pythagoreans. Of course, on Hegel's view, Christianity represents a culmination of these systems. But this, some brood, edges uncomfortably close to natural knowledge of the trinity—a collapse of grace into nature. It is exactly this collapse that critics of the *vestigia trinitatis* traditions find so execrable. What is the trace doctrine, Karl Barth asks, but an attempt to discern "an essential trinitarian disposition supposedly immanent in some created realities *quite apart* from their possible conscription by God's revelation"?[100]

But Barth and his like are not the first to moot the problem. Medievals knew it too.[101] Alexander confesses that natural reason alone cannot know the trinity "according to its properties" (*secundum propria*).[102] This is visible only under grace's soft glow, since "our intellect is rendered dark by original sin."[103] True, pagans may and did discern Aristotle's three immaterial causes. Some even learned to correlate them with divine unity, goodness, and truth.[104] But outside a trinitarian frame these represent divine attributes— not appropriations proper.[105] To appropriate, according to Alexander, is to link a divine attribute to a person with special reference to his personal property. Hence an essential attribute differs from an *appropriated* essential attribute. The latter offers a thicker description exactly to the extent that divine attributes as such differ only conceptually but personal properties really. "Power appropriated to the Father vis-à-vis his *innascibilitas*" says more than sheer "divine power."[106] Pagan, Jewish, and Muslim philosophers may know the latter. But they could not derive the former from it.

An aside: Assuming only Christians know triplets to point up their trinitarian source, traces still lack what is peculiar to the trinity.[107] The trace still traffics more in the realm of the "triadic" than the "trinitarian" proper. Peculiarly and properly trinitarian dimensions await its higher levels— image and likeness. I will say more on these in later chapters.

Knowing the trace as trinitarian, Alexander argues, remains a necessary condition for admiring creation's beauty. Why? Because objectively speaking, the trace accounts metaphysically for a creature's beauty. With and because of it the volcano and the giant sequoia and the pterodactyl bear God's beauty—without it, not. Alexander writes with dispatch and precision:

> Beauty and good accompany one another. Thus since goodness is determined by mode and form and order in the universe, it follows that beauty is

determined [by them too]. This seems so, for a thing is called beautiful in the world when it holds its own mode and form and order . . . The beauty of the world descends from the first beauty . . . Therefore, the beauty of creatures is a certain vestige stretching toward uncreated beauty through thought (*per cognitionem*) . . . It ought to be said that beauty rises in the world from the three aforesaid things [mode, form, order].[108]

The passage is compressed but clear. The beauty the world features derives from God's beauty. And because that beauty lives as trinity, so too will beauty here below—however analogously. The trace, then—mode, form, and order—together comprises and guarantees created beauty. And this is simply to say that the set of created beauties that does not feature this trace is null. Every creature is beautiful, and that beauty will be entirely explicable by the trace.

Subjectively, however, the trace remains fragile. Its objective conditions cannot mitigate against its possible misconstrual. On Alexander's view it is possible to get the trace wrong. Doing that means reading creation's triplets under the aspect of beauty or delectability *non referendo illam ad deum*, without referring them to God. Conjuring Kierkegaard's Johannes, we might call this the gaze of the aesthete.[109] The aesthete "prefers the poem to the art of confecting poetry, since he sets more store by the ears than by intellect."[110] Gazing at the trinity's traces like that courts error, Alexander warns. This is because the aesthete confines himself to the immanent frame. He is blind to or uninterested in transcendent causes. Like Johannes, the aesthete's fate is tragedy. He fixes himself to *temporalia* without regard for providence, "not wanting the things he loves to pass away."

Is another gaze possible? Alexander tropes Aristotle: our vision may construe the ensemble of creatures "as picture" (*ut picturam*) or "as image" (*ut imago*).[111] The first treats creation as "in itself according to itself" (*in ipsa re secundum se*), the last "as it leads to the that whose image it is" (*secundum hoc ducit ad aliud cuius est imago*). Unlike the gaze of the aesthete, this gaze remains open to being led-by-the-hand (*manuducari*) to the cause whose trace creation is. Call this the iconic gaze, for it reads the world as icon—as window, that is, from surface beauties to their depth. Nurturing the iconic gaze, then, renders the world as it really is, "as bearing beauty from the highest beauty and delectability from the most delectable." In this way, "the traces attend us (*manuducunt*) to him whose traces they are."[112]

THE BEAUTY OF CREATION

An aesthetic manuduction is exactly what the *Summa* charts. Its second book opens with a long sequence of questions on beauty, among the first of its kind and certainly of its length.[113] We might sort these questions by kind or category. A first dialectical cycle assays matters of quality. It asks, that is, about the nature of beauty and with what it agrees. Is beauty simply identical with agreeability, for instance? And how (if at all) does it cohere with evil? A second dialectical cycle considers matters of quantity. It poses questions in order to scout the limits of beauty's quality. In this dialectical exercise Brother Alexander examines whether beauty can be increased (and by what) or decreased (and by what). How much change is too much? Below I consider both dialectical cycles in their turn: beauty's quality and quantity.

Before that I tender a warning. Across these texts Brother Alexander picks up new uses for "beauty" (and with it, "order"), related but distinct from the trinitarian acceptation considered until now.[114] I distinguish at least three uses: the trinitarian, the providential, and the hierarchical. The first figures beauty and order according to the canon already studied in previous chapters, which is to say according to trinitarian taxis. That beauty and its order almost always serve metaphysical purposes. Typically it accounts for the kind of beauty a creature bears *qua* creature of the trinity. A second acceptation—the providential—conceives beauty or order as God's providential activity across time. On this use and for example, Alexander thinks it possible to name evil beautiful just to the extent that divine providence elicits good from it.[115] Still a third use denotes the universe's natural hierarchy of created being—angels above humans, humans above spotted-necked otters, and so on.[116] I say these three ways of speaking "beauty" are distinct but related (and thus analogous) for two reasons. First, because each does its work within an Augustinian definition of order.[117] And second, both the providential and the hierarchic derive from the trinitarian.[118]

I am most interested in the trinitarian, the acceptation under investigation across this book and least in play throughout Brother Alexander's questions *de pulchritudine creati*. So why treat these long questions *in toto*? I do so because Alexander's readers have not often distinguished analytically among beauty's variant uses. Most often those readers neglect the trinitarian for the providential or the hierarchic.[119] When they do, they abstract the questions on creation's beauty from Brother Alexander's trinitarian aesthetics. Careful attention to the text reveals that Brother Alexander embroiders the trinitarian across these questions, however much more needlework he pays the trinitarian and the hierarchic.

I. Beauty's Quality

Alexander begins his investigation of beauty's quality by repeating the definitional question. I already considered this passage and its comparison with *SH* I, n. 103 above. Yet I flag again how Alexander here surveys beauty within a perusal of "the conditions of creature." He speaks then of *created* beauty. Then again the trinitarian account of beauty in book 1 lingers at *SH* I–II, n. 75. There Alexander again indexes created beauty to mode-form-order.[120] Such accounts for the natural appetite for beauty native to all creatures.

Like many scholastics, Alexander next probes the distinction between the beautiful (*pulcher*) and fittingness (*aptitudo*). They and he ask because an authority first did—this time Isidore of Seville.[121] A quotation from Isidore trusses beauty to the inner and fittingness to the outer.[122] A villager exists beautifully in body and soul, but fittingly in her garments. Both are differently necessary: beauty evinces metaphysical necessity, fittingness only existential. Then Alexander generalizes the point. "Beauty is said in itself," he writes, "but fittingness is said according to what is accommodated to people or other things with which a person agrees." The division between beauty and fitness rests upon the deeper one between substantial and accidental form.[123] This article, like a modern preface, forms a rhetorical paraleipsis—mostly it confesses what its author will not do. Alexander will feature only what concerns beauty said "properly."

Next comes a set of questions whose force Alexander feels. Or so his rhetorical arrangement suggests—he dedicates three separate articles to it. What about evil? Can beauty abide its hideous face? Alexander sorts evil under three different theological headings: evil done (*malum culpae*), evil suffered (*malum poenae*), and hideous things (*res monstruosae*). He reserves an article for each.

He learns from Augustine to call the first *malum culpae*, the evil of fault or evil done.[124] This cannot be judged beautiful for at least two reasons. First, sin fails the principle of created beauty. Unlike the creature, sin is not a trace of God (*vestigium dei*). Second, not only does sin fail to number among creation's beautiful things. It actively defaces and deforms them.

And since "whatever deforms beauty opposes beauty," the evil of sin cannot be beautiful. Alexander concedes the objections. "Evil of any type whatever, along with wicked deformity, is deformed (*deforme*)."[125]

But sometimes good is elicited from evil (*ex malo elicitur bonum*). When that happens—when bodies once cut down by blade or time rise again, say—evil appears beautiful within a certain order (*in hoc ordine dicitur pulcrum*).

The Augustinian bite of Alexander's argument is deep. It cuts deeper when Alexander concludes the article with a protracted quotation from Augustine's *De civitate dei*. That quotation yields two clues for understanding Alexander's aesthetics of evil. The first clue is that Alexander endorses (or at least very attentively entertains) Augustine's chiaroscuro theodicy. An attentive listen to creation's full movement, Augustine says, displays how God resolves even sin's sour notes into *pulcherrimum carmen*, the most beautiful song. The quotation also reveals that the "order" under which evil becomes beautiful by eliciting good cannot be the order of the trinity. It is rather *ordo saeculorum*, the order of the ages. In Augustine's idiom, *saeculum* describes *this* age—the order wrought from nothing, damaged by sin, superintended by death, healed by Christ, and inextricably tangled between two cities. In that order, Alexander glosses, we call the evil of sin beautiful not "absolutely" (*absolute*) but "within [this] order" (*in ordine*). Sin is and has no beauty because it is and has nothing. It appears beautiful only in its providential reprise. Or recalling my distinctions above: evil is beautiful only in its providential acceptation, not its trinitarian one.

So much, Alexander thinks, for evil done (*malum culpae*). He wonders next about evil suffered (*malum poenae*). Is this beautiful? Admitting this seems to imperil the Christian claim that "death or any evils suffered (*mala poenae*) are neither goods nor beauties."[126] Yet however bitter the *malum poenae* seems to those who taste it, "it is nevertheless good and beautiful all the same."[127] How? One objection notices how Augustine lauds death—the very form of *malum poenae*—as *instrumentum virtutis*, an instrument of virtue. That does not or should not be taken to mean that death is good or beautiful *per se*. No, death as "lack of life" (*defectus vitae*) remains always and everywhere evil. But "death" may also describe the state of a dying man, in which case it describes a "corruption of life" (*corruptio vitae*). Death and her other corruptions sting creation only to the extent that they are "gathered in the universe by order." Again, only through providence's prism can *malum poenae* refract a "certain beauty of order."

Last among the evils Alexander appraises are *res monstruosae*, hideous things.[128] The Latin *monstra* points vaguely to the preternatural or aberrational. For Alexander the term encircles two different sets. The first set hosts physical irregularities (a man with six fingers or two heads, to use his examples). The other set encircles imagined creatures.[129] Alexander dismisses the last from scrutiny. As imagined, God is not their author. So the *monstra* under consideration must be those "imperfect on account of nature's curse." Are these beautiful? Not obviously, not if *monstra* lack the mode-form-order constitutive of creaturely beauty.[130] But this lack, recalling Alexander's argument above, can asymptotically approach but never achieve erasure. No creature can lack beauty without remainder. "Nothing can be made by God the author," Alexander writes, "which is not beautiful."[131] Lesser beauties of various kinds issue *a summe pulcro*, from the supreme beauty. Here again Alexander repairs back to Augustine's aesthetic argument from providence. God alone contrives the beauty of the cosmos. He alone braids its beauty together through likeness and difference.[132] Thus to recoil from a creature's ugliness is already to betray one's tightly constricted vantage of salvation history's arc. Still, we ought not conflate providence with will. If God stitches irregular patterns into the cosmic fabric, he does not first will those irregularities. Irregularities among creatures cannot owe to their author or first cause. They must be instead wholly explicable by proximate causes.[133]

II. Beauty's Quantity

Alexander now shifts the question. He asked first about beauty's quality—what was it and what belonged to it? He asks now after its quantity—what contributes or detracts from it? Is beauty even the sort of thing that can be contributed to or detracted from? A first question poses the latter puzzle, but everything following it poses the former.

Alexander thinks it an empirical truism that beauty fades.[134] It is a cliché, even for him. The sunflower's petals wilt, the youth's skin creases and gathers, the canvas fades.[135] So too with spiritual beauty, since surely sin cheats souls of their luster.[136] The most pressing difficulty Alexander raises concerns mereology, the relation of parts to wholes. An objection supposes that a decrease of a particular creature's beauty spells a decrease in the general inventory of created beauty. His response to this objection distinguishes essential beauty (*pulcritudo essentialis*) from the accidental (*quae erat ex accidenti proveniens*).[137] If the former is not subject to change, the latter is. In Aristotelian metaphysics the essential whole is always more than the sum of its parts. Accidental parts do not together constitute an essential whole. So individual losses of beauty—autumn's kiss freezing the sunflower, say—do not spell an essential loss of beauty.[138] Not, anyway, if the world's essence can do with or without the sunflower.

What is true of the macrocosm holds for the microcosm. The soul too, that is, is engraved with immutable, essential beauty (*substantiae sive essentiae*). That immutability protects against sin's vandalism.[139] Its incursions cannot breach essential beauty, which inheres by mode-form-order—or trinitarian beauty. Not even Adam's sin threatened that.[140] Yet sin may and does deface the beauty of the soul's will (*voluntatis actualis*). This raises difficult and immediate questions: how does this distinction between essential and volitional beauty in the soul map onto Alexander's distinction between essential and accidental beauty in the universe? Alexander does not here elaborate. It suffices now to note a distinction between essential and accidental beauty. If the latter is fragile, the former is inviolable.

Because the dialectical cycle of questions on beauty stands some distance from that on trinitarian traces, Alexander reminds readers whence creation's beauty derives. What accounts for this essential beauty that creation bears so indelibly? For creation to be beautiful, it must bear a relation to the canon and source of beauty—the trinity God is. "The beauty of the world," Alexander writes, "descends from the first beauty." Alexander marshals arguments from Augustine and Isidore. Each grounds created beauty in the trinitarian trace. "A thing in the world is called beautiful (*pulchra*) when it holds its own mode and form and order." In this way, to repeat a passage treated above, "the beauty of creatures is a certain trace stretching toward uncreated beauty through thought ... but the vestige is applied principally according to mode and form and order."[141] Alexander thinks this triplet can be thought to exist in two ways: ideally (*secundum quod sunt in generibus et speciebus quae permanent*) or really (*secundum quod sunt in rebus transeuntibus*). Alexander further thinks the triplet exists really in two different ways: in something insofar as it passes over according to itself or insofar as it is compared to another that succeeds it. Here below creatures exist beautifully as both ideally and insofar as they really exist according to their metaphysical determinations.

Alexander's next question stoked controversy. Albert the Great, Thomas Aquinas, and Bonaventure receive Alexander's arguments with tensed rhetorical muscles. As we might expect of feuding posses, Bonaventure defends his confrère. And the Dominicans in turn and predictably constellate against him. The feud between them centered on the aesthetics of evil. In fact, it restages an earlier feud between the twelfth-century masters Peter Lombard and Hugh of St. Victor.[142] The Lombard had bristled against Hugh's suggestion that "it is good for evil to exist" (*bonum est malum esse*) and that, further, God even wills it (*malum esse vult*). His polemics ignore the aesthetic shape of Hugh's arguments,[143] though it is hardly lost on Alexander.[144] Alexander's *Glossa* rehearses many of them. The *Summa* and Bonaventure remember these arguments to commend them. Albert, Thomas, and Ulrich recall them for rejection.[145]

I flag this thirteenth-century controversy only to call attention to its source in Alexander's texts.[146] I read it without comment upon its scholastic commentators. Evil may be said to contribute to the universe's beauty in two ways only. The first way is to the extent that evil done (*malum culpae*) demands penalty; the second is to the extent to which goods shine the more radiantly when collocated with evil's dark.[147] The first exception struggles with Dionysius's claim that evil contributes to the completion of the whole.[148] Better, Alexander thinks, to read Dionysius to say that evil contributes to beauty only *per occasionem*—that is, in the event of sin's rupture and grace's healing.[149] The second exception derives authority from Latin writers. Augustine and Isidore both variously advance a chiaroscuro aesthetic. As in Caravaggio's canvasses, the high contrast between dark and light fixes the gaze upon the latter.[150] But again Alexander allows this only under the stipulation that it describes the beauty of the universe as it now is and not essentially.

And what of mutable goods?[151] Do they contribute to the world's beauty? Surely the contrast between mutable and immutable establishes order.[152] And is not order beautiful, after all? Yes, though change here below often tends heavily and quickly *ad non-esse*, in the direction of nonbeing.[153] But even that—the serial appearance and dissolution of creatures—thrums rhythmically. So it sounds to Alexander's ear—at least as Augustine trained it.[154] If admiring life's cyclical patterns is one thing, discovering beauty in the soul's fall is quite another. This happens when *mutabilia* unnaturally superintend *immutabilia*.[155] Or when, in Brother's Alexander's preferred idiom, "the sinning soul is posited because the body preserved its own modus, form, and order."[156] Remember, Alexander asks, the beauty found in evil's punishment, which elicits good from evil. "If [the soul] suffers justly or usefully, beauty is in the universe."[157]

Salvation history proves decisive for Alexander's final two questions.[158] His first question asks after *mirabilia*, "wonders," which pose two prima facie difficulties. If wonders are "things which run against nature" (*contra naturam*), then they "deform beauty" (*pulchritudinem*).[159] More, if God truly pronounced "good" everything created in Gen. 1:31, then nature cannot want for anything.[160] It seems, then, that saying wonders add to creation's beauty amounts to confessing creation's incompleteness without them.

Alexander solves this by narrating salvation history with Augustine's epochs: before the fall (*ante lapsum*), after the fall (*post lapsum*), and under grace (*sub gratiam*).[161] The first epoch and its beauty knew no miracles (*miracula*). The second saw a proliferation of miracles, aimed to meet and restore the "various modes of defects." After and under grace, third, the world and its beauty know wonders (*mirabilia*) but no miracles (*miracula*). Alexander does not detail this distinction. But he does promise that the "renewal of the world" (*innovatio mundi*) will occur above nature, hence miraculously.[162] If wonders operate *supra naturam*, miracles run *contra naturam*. A response to the first objection specifies that *contra naturam* need not mean destructive of nature (*destructivum naturae*). Clearly this could not add to the world's beauty. But *contra naturam* may also intimate a restoration of nature by surprise—by a mode that exceeds or disobeys expectations.[163] So the distinction comes to this: if miracles work *contra naturam* after sin damages it, wonders work *supra naturam* after Christ has defeated sin.[164] But both in their time confer beauty upon the universe.

The denouement of Alexander's dialectical cycle on beauty's quantity considers the incarnation and its attendant sacraments.[165] Here again salvation history figures heavily in Alexander's response. Christ's incarnation would not have conferred beauty before the fall. Why not? After all, a hypostatic union between God and creature harmonizes extremes "so that the beauty of the universe would shine forth" and permits the highest grace to "give beauty to nature."[166] Alexander reminds his objector that Gen. 1:31 proclaimed creation good before the incarnation. Creation in its first state had beauty enough without the incarnation.[167] But it is hardly so in the second state.[168] Yet even there incarnation adds beauty not solely because of the restoration of fallen nature, but rather because of its mode. Salvation may have come by other means.[169] The beauty of the incarnation belongs instead to its manner—most fitting (*optimum*), most graceful (*decentissime*). Alexander catalogs six reasons for the peculiar appropriateness of the hypostatic union.[170] For these reasons and more, the incarnation ornaments the universe with its beauty.[171]

As noted, the vast majority of Alexander's *de pulchritudine creati* labors with the providential account of beauty. Some little of it operates inside the hierarchical account. But these shifts in emphasis do not remove the trinitarian account from view. In fact, both the providential and the hierarchic depend upon the trinitarian for their coherence. "Order in the divine persons," Alexander writes, "is the exemplar of every order."[172]

CONCLUSION

In the *Summa* Brother Alexander refuses to offer an exhaustive account of creation without trinitarian grammar. He prefers instead to depict creation as an ensemble of trinitarian traces. If these traces display trinitarian order, they also somehow glister with divine beauty. Somehow, that is, creation's beauty issues from God's. This chapter articulated the logic interred beneath that "somehow." For Alexander the way the trinity underwrites creation's beauty begins with the intratrinitarian life. This is because the act of creation, he thinks, flows freely from trinitarian activity *ad intra*. This means too that the trinity structures causality as such. In Alexander's hands Aristotle's immaterial causes become trinitarian appropriations. The act of creation thus inks creatures with the Trinity's style-signature—the trace (*vestigium*) and its iterations. Whatever scholasticism's dialectical sequence asks of Alexander—on beauty's quality and quantity—the trace abides as the inviolate ground of creation's beauty.

For all my talk of traces, I have said vanishingly little about creation's highest trace of the trinity: the human. Here Alexander's schema anticipates Bonaventure's. As created, the human is trace (*vestigium*); as rational, she is image (*imago*); as graced, she is likeness (*similitudo*). The last of these comprise my final chapters.

CHAPTER 6

THE BEAUTY THE SOUL IS

Consider again Brother Alexander's depiction of trinitarian beauty. Only notice now what is hidden there about the soul. "Just as the beauty of bodies follows from the harmony of the composition of its parts, so too the beauty of souls (*pulchritudo animarum*) follows from the harmony of the composition of its powers."[1] Alexander adduces these examples to illustrate what he writes next. "Beauty in the divine is from the sacred order of the divine persons." Chapters 3 and 4 elaborate what that last clause compresses. I read now in the reverse— this chapter seeks clarity on how exactly Alexander conceives the *pulchritudo animarum*, the beauty of souls. How does the harmony of the soul's powers mirror the order of the trinity, Alexander's canon for beauty? What is it to think the harmony of those powers?

That question invokes scholastic controversy. It restokes debates over the relation of the soul to its powers that smoldered beneath the first half of the thirteenth century.[2] This was scarcely the only controversy whose flames refined scholastic psychology.[3] Others burned too, some much hotter: over monopsychism, for instance, or the soul's union with the body, its number of substantial forms, its being the site of personality, its bond with sensitive and vegetative powers. Still, the question of the soul's relation to its powers figured prominently across the early Franciscan school inaugurated when Alexander took the habit. Why? At stake was nothing less than the posterity of Augustine's trinitarian psychology. Could it brave the heat of fresh philosophical learning? Would it emerge refined or scorched? Stepping back into this debate illumines what the later *Summa* imagines the beauty of souls to be.

The structure of what follows is of necessity Janus-faced. It looks backward first—to the two dominant theories over the relation of the soul to its powers in the early scholastic idiom. Next it curates texts from the Halensian school to trace how its response to the controversy eventually met and sublated those of its two opponents. The chapter's other face looks ahead. There I show how the Halensian answer to the soul-powers question prepares the panel on which Brother Alexander styles his icon of the *pulchritudo animarum*. Most of that section lingers over Alexander's icon of the soul to comment its trinitarian gilding.

THE SOUL AND ITS POWERS: A DISPUTED QUESTION

In his *Archéologie du sujet*, Alain de Libera vivisects Heidegger's *Bildungsroman* of the modern subject.[4] De Libera is precise, his scalpel sharp. The decisive scene occurs far earlier than did Descartes's *cogito*, he argues. It arrives instead with Peter of John Olivi—a fourteenth-century Franciscan whose apocalypticism earned him censure. Olivi's innovation, de Libera claims, lies in his fusion of two models of subjectivity: the Aristotelian and the Augustinian. The former keyed subjectivity principally to *hypokeimenon*—or *subiectum* in Latin. Against this, Augustine forged a "perichoretic model" of subjectivity from "mutual immanence or mutual indwelling of the divine persons . . . borrowed from his trinitarian theology and firmly based on the rejection of the Aristotelian *hypokeimenon*."[5] As Augustine knew, the latter would not do for Christians. Christian grammar proscribes talk of God as some *hypokeimenon-subiectum* who "stands under" accidental properties.[6] And if the rational soul is *imago dei*—or indeed *imago trinitatis*—then neither can it bear its faculties accidentally.

I am not here interested in disinterring the modern subject or else assaying whether de Libera gets Olivi right. Rather I am interested in how Brother Alexander anticipates teachings de Libera locates in later Franciscans.[7] Whether or not he invents the modern subject, Olivi reconciles the perichoretic account with the peripatetic in studied imitation of maneuvers made by his earlier Franciscan confrères.[8] It is those maneuvers this section remembers and admires. First I offer a thumbnail sketch of the scholastic contest over the soul's relation to its powers. Doing that means summoning the polemical heat within which the early Franciscans forge their own psychology.

I. The Identity Thesis

The more popular early thirteenth-century account of how the soul relates to its powers simply equates them. Call this the "identity thesis."[9] This thesis and its apologists claim common parentage in Augustine.[10] His fevered search for a created trinity across his *De trinitate* supplied medieval thinkers a deposit of psychological speculation. Across books 8–15, Augustine discovers lesser trinities—the object, the perceiver, and the perception; lover, beloved, and love itself; and so on. Then he lights upon the highest created trinity. Because it is sheltered in the highest part of the human soul (*mens*), it alone merits the laurel *imago trinitatis*. That trinity comprises the soul's faculties: memory, understanding, and will. This yields a near perfect analogue to the *trinitas quae deus est*, Augustine thinks. Each of these faculties indwells a single substance while each presupposes the other. Some passages even suggest identity between these powers and the soul itself, perhaps none more than *trin.* 10.11.18. "These three then," Augustine writes, "memory, understanding, and will, are not three lives but one life (*una vita*), nor three minds but one mind (*una mens*)."[11]

Medieval readers hardly encounter a pristine Augustine. Like scripture or Dionysius, Augustine spoke to medievals across centuries—often through interpretive aids. *Trin.* 10.11.18 is no exception. This passage elicits glosses first by Isidore of Seville and next by near-obsessive attempts of twelfth-century compilers systematically to order and arrange psychological sources into textbooks.[12] Two among the twelfth-century psychological treatises of this period stand out: Peter Lombard's *Sentences* and the anonymous *De spiritu et anima*.[13] Master Peter studies the *imago trinitatis* in Book 1, distinction 3. Most of it rewrites texts from Augustine's *De trinitate*. Peter does not explicitly address the question over the soul's relation to its powers. But he proves evocative enough. Most often the Lombard speaks about the faculties' presence "in" the soul.[14] But in at least one place, the Lombard (with Augustine) omits the preposition. "This," Master Peter writes, "is the sense from which those three *are said to be one* or one substance."[15] Master Peter's claim reflects Augustine's at *trin.* 10.11.18 that memory, understanding, and will "are one mind, one life, and one essence." Together with Peter Lombard's interpretation, this text weighs the presentation of Augustine heavily toward the identity thesis.

Omnipresent across thirteenth-century psychologies is the Augustinian *De spiritu et anima*. Whatever its authorial provenance, the text gathers and harmonizes authorities on psychology. The result hosts an old-growth forest of opinions, impenetrable because untended.[16] Across and beneath its pinewood, the text takes a hard line in favor of the identity thesis.[17] Scholastics most often draw from its thirteenth chapter. After arguing for the simplicity of the soul, the text announces that its powers "are natural to it and are nothing other than the soul itself."[18] This only approximates divine simplicity, however, since while "God is *all* that he has (*omnia sua*), the soul is *some* of the things it has (*quaedam sua*)." After all, the soul has but is not virtue. The text concludes that "the soul's whole essence consists in these powers." In fact, "we may even speak of these as the soul's 'trinity.' This trinity is the very unity of the soul and the soul itself (*ipsa anima*)."

Philip the Chancellor advocates the strongest iteration of the identity thesis.[19] The question crops up at three sites across his corpus. I consider only the first, since his argument there remains materially consistent elsewhere.[20] That first site is fenced in by an overarching question: How is the human said to bear the image of the trinity in memory, understanding, and will? By the time Philip poses the question about the soul's relation to its powers, he has already made the *imago trinitatis* the fundamental conceit around which to arrange Christian psychology.

Philip begins his answer as all scholastics did: by burnishing fine-tuned distinctions. Psychological powers are of three kinds, he writes.[21] The first are accidental (*accidentalis*), whose absence does not affect the essence of their subject whatever. Think, on this point and for example, of the power to receive color proper to hair or skin or vellum. Other powers are natural (*naturalis*) and issue directly from their essence, forming its properties (as in the power of fire to heat). A third kind of power is essential (*essentialis*), which is to say identical to and coextensive with its essence. Here too Philip tenders an example, one his thirteenth-century readers do not much like. Just as the power to receive form belongs to the essence of prime matter, so too the powers of memory, understanding, and will belong to the essence of the human soul. True: distinct act belongs properly and discretely to each power. But these powers are "perichoretic"—the word is Philip's—just to the extent that they "posit a likeness to the divine persons indwelling themselves (*sese circumincedentes*), just as the Damascene says."[22] Philip ties off the argument with a reference to Augustine that suggests the *imago* indwells the soul *essentialiter*.

II. The Difference Thesis
That Augustine sounds Philip's final note typifies the former's centrality for the identity thesis. But Augustine's *auctoritas* might have been equally marshaled by the opposition—defenders of what I call the "difference thesis."[23] Proponents of this view, it seems obvious to say, do not think the soul ontologically

coextensive with its powers. Portions of Augustine's *trin.* lend themselves to this thesis. At *trin.* 15.17.28, for instance, Augustine denies that his favorite created trinity (memory, understanding, and will) is adequate to the simplicity of trinity-God. At *ep.* 169 the contrast is stronger still.[24] It seems curious that scholastic boosters of the difference thesis rarely counter identity-leaning texts with these. But then scholastics were not particuarly anxious to uncover Augustine's authentic teaching—or even always to read him in context. Scholastic habit locates *auctoritas* less in the historical Augustine than in excerpted passages, here in the "one life" text of *trin.* 10.[25] Advocates of the difference thesis did not seek to oppose this passage with counterevidence from other of Augustine's texts. They sought instead a more persuasive reading of it.

Defenders of the difference thesis knew other authorities. We might expect one of these to be Aristotle's *De anima.* But from John Blund through the *Summa*, psychologists privileged another *De anima.* If early thirteenth-century texts capture classroom pedagogy, then the *De anima* under scrutiny was not Aristotle's—it was Avicenna's.[26]

Avicenna appealed to defenders of both theses alike, if differently. His rigorous defense of the soul's simplicity fits comfortably with the identity thesis, which feared a division between the soul and its powers would spell irreparable fissure within the soul itself. Still, Avicenna proved more important to the opposition for at least two reasons. First he explicitly announces that the soul is not coextensive with its powers.[27] But difference-thesis defenders recruited Avicenna for another reason—for his innovative ontological distinction between essence and existence. That distinction describes everything below God, whose essence just *is* his existence. For Avicenna, then, God and God alone bears *necessary* existence. As *necesse esse*, God's is the only essence that *must* exist. All others exist contingently.[28] Medieval authors found in Avicenna's distinction a parallel with an older, Christian distinction between *quo est* and *quod est* drawn by Boethius. Only in the first (*primum*) were these things one—in all else they remained distinct.[29] That God alone bears truly metaphysical simplicity, it seems fair to say, remains the motive force for defenders of the difference thesis.

The difference thesis found a zealous advocate in William of Auxerre.[30] The identity thesis is "against philosophy" (*contra philosophiam*), William hissed in his *Summa Aurea*—even "against God" (*contra deum*).[31] Why? *Contra deum*, because the identity defenders afford a level of simplicity to the soul that is proper to God alone. Neither is William persuaded by Philip's argument from prime matter. Saying that the power to receive form belongs to prime matter *essentialiter* risks incoherence. Prime matter is necessarily and definitionally prior to all form. And surely formlessness itself cannot be a form. So nothing can belong to prime matter *essentialiter*, William concludes. That courts nonsense.

How is the identity thesis also *contra philosophiam*? Here William enlists Porphyry.[32] In the third chapter of his *Isagoge*, Porphyry names rationality a quality.[33] But to the extent that qualities are accidents, they cannot prove essential to the soul. William's rhetoric is quick and hot. He reads Porphyry aslant, never explaining what *qualitas* here means. Neither does he learn from Porphyry's next chapter to distinguish different senses of the term. Unlike Bonaventure and Thomas,[34] William stops reading where Porphyry supplies what (William thinks) he needs: a philosophical authority calling rationality an accident. "Thus 'rational' is a quality," he concludes, "and thus it is not the same as the soul."[35] The same follows for Augustine's other two powers: memory and will. For William they too relate to the soul as accidents—nothing more.[36]

So rise the hammer and anvil of early thirteenth-century psychology. The identity thesis affirms that the soul simply *is* its trinity of powers. This was the majority report despite its difficulties, principally the near-divine simplicity it indulges to the human soul as *imago trinitatis*. Counter to this ran the difference thesis, whose concerns fall squarely on the uniqueness of God's simplicity. But is it then somehow accidental to the soul that it be a created trinity? Or is it safer to gamble the identity thesis? Whose steel to suffer, hammer or anvil?

THE SOUL AND ITS POWERS IN THE
EARLY HALENSIAN SCHOOL

So much by way of a mise en scène. How does the Halensian school weigh in? By "Halensian school,"[37] I summon at least Alexander of Hales and John of La Rochelle.[38] Each in his way refines and burnishes the question on the soul's relation to its powers. I regard both—but Alexander's *Glossa* most[39]—before reading the *Summa*, whose account leans heavily on theirs.[40]

To Alexander's *Glossa* first.[41] Our question sits within a cluster of explanatory notes on the third distinction in the Lombard's first book.

Neither the Lombard's text nor Alexander's gloss on it comprises a standalone treatise. Book I, distinction 3 itself curates quotations in a series of dialectical rhythms on a theme—here the relation between trinity and creation. Alexander riffs on pieces of the Lombard's text almost spontaneously like improvisations layered over a progression. Already Alexander has woven beauty and creation's triadic structure together.[42] He indexes eight created triplets, but all remain at the level of the trace.[43] Layers stratify when Alexander turns to the triplet of the soul. After cataloguing Augustine's various triplets across *De trinitate*, Alexander concedes that only one wins the title *imago*: memory, understanding, and will.[44]

Then he poses the question. How are these three powers said to be one substance? He registers both opinions before reinscribing a large section from *De spiritu et anima* in support of the identity thesis.[45] This he throws into dialectical relief with a selection from Boethius's *De trinitate*. Only in God are *quod est* and *esse* the same.[46] Then Alexander adjudicates among authorities. He begins by drawing an analogy. Just as bodies comprise a quantity of parts (*quantitas partium*), so too souls comprise a quantity of powers (*quantitas virium*).[47] True, these powers differ according to act. But it does not follow that they differ ontologically. Their relation one to another and to their essence is more integral.

So, are the powers of the soul identical to the soul itself? Identity is said in two ways. Here Alexander innovates—or borrows from Gilbert of Poitiers—a distinction between *essentia* and *substantia*: "for a subject differs in essence and substance."[48] Next Alexander defines his terms. An essence names "that by which a thing is what it is," a substance "that by which a thing subsists inseparably," and a subject "that to which things are added."[49] I take them in reverse. To grant that the identity of the soul and its powers obtains only at the level of subject would be to posit an accidental and so tenuous relation. This is because "the soul," Alexander learns from Avicenna, "is said to be a subject with respect to its accidents."[50] But if the subject affords only accidental identity, then the soul's powers will bear the same relation to it that eye color or skin pigment does. This is little more than William's difference thesis.

Not that Alexander prefers its opposite. No, in Philip's identity thesis Alexander spies a pious but pernicious overcorrection. Surely no created essence simply *is* its powers without remainder—not if being a creature means being composed, as the long tradition taught. We ought rather to confess that "the three persons alone agree in essence." Divine simplicity stipulates that essential identity belong to God alone. However admirable its attempt to spotlight the *imago trinitatis*, Philip's identity thesis cannot hold.

Alexander has very nearly written himself into a stalemate. Against Philip, Alexander denies identity at the level of essence. This inordinately divinizes what is created by according it a simplicity that is God's. Then again and against William, he denies identity at the level of subject. William got it wrong, Alexander thinks, just to the extent that he makes of the relation between the *imago trinitatis* and the soul something arbitrary. So Alexander counsels a third way. He identifies the soul and its powers at the level of substance, for him that by which a thing subsists inseparably. "These three powers are, then," he writes, "distinguished in terms of essence (*secundum essentiam*) but agree in substance (*in substantia*), because the soul is not a complete substance without its powers."[51]

At first this distinction seems mere prestidigitation. Can Alexander explain it, or is he an illusionist? He advises that we view the soul as a single *res* refracted through a triple-lensed stereoscope. Each lens yields a particular and discreet frame of composition. A look through the first affords a glimpse of essence and *essentialium*. The composition depicted here draws together *quo est* and *quod est*.[52] *Quo est* or essence is, Alexander says, whatever makes the soul to be the kind of thing it is. A second lens cuts a clearer image. In the *substantia* frame we see an essence and its native (if nonaccidental) properties. If these latter do not constitute an essence, they follow from it inexorably. With and only with these properties may an essence exist as "a complete substance subsisting independently."[53] And so substance appears identical to its properties—here the powers of the soul.[54] The third and last lens frames the *subiectum*, the *res* now constituted as a complete substance. So constituted, the *subiectum* may now support—or "stand under" (*substare*)—accidents.[55]

The undertow of scholastic distinction threatens to swallow readers who do not ask how all that bears on the soul-powers question. The soul's powers cannot be joined to it at the level of essence. This would render them *essentialia*—the essence of the soul would *be* its powers without remainder. Only God enjoys simplicity like that. The soul, like all creatures, remains composed *essentialiter*. Neither can the soul's powers be joined at the level of subject, since subjects trade in accidents. These powers cannot be accidents, not if Augustine is right to say that the soul's "being an image, then, will not perish, nor is it accidental."[56] The soul's powers find identity at the level of substance (*substantia*). Substance, remember, names an essence with concomitant properties. And these, at least in the case of the rational soul, are the powers of remembering, understanding, and willing. So Alexander's conclusion is this: it is true that these powers are neither essential nor accidental to the human soul. But it is also true that no soul may exist concretely "without its powers" in substance, "that by which a thing subsists inseparably."

So configured, Alexander's solution meets the theological anxieties of both Philip and William. It also transcends them. The soul's powers are not accidental to it—that is Philip's claim. But neither does it follow that that by which a soul is what it is—that is, a human essence—claims quasi-divine simplicity. Against Philip, Alexander preserves an analogical interval between God and creature. And against William, he does the same without rendering the *imago trinitatis* somehow accidental to the soul.

John of La Rochelle variously adopts, rewrites, and assimilates Alexander's position into his psychology. His *Summa de anima* (1235–1236) compiles a refined and near encyclopedic index of psychology.[57] It also proves an invaluable source for the *Summa*, once (erroneously) thought to antecede the *Summa de anima*.[58] For this reason lines often blur between John and the *Summa Halensis*, and not only because John likely wrote as Brother Alexander in *SH* I and III.[59] Even the spectral author who penned *SH* I–II and II–II cribs thick passages from John's *Summa*.[60] The *Summa Halensis's* study of the relation between soul and its powers hardly proves an exception. The two summae read almost identically on the question.[61] But only almost—the minor differences prove significant.

John of La Rochelle frames the question within broader studies of the *imago dei*. He begins by surveying three arguments in favor of the identity thesis.[62] Two resurrect the *De spiritu et anima*. First the difference between the soul's powers is nominal, not ontological.[63] Second, neither does this grant near-divine simplicity to the soul, since the *De spiritu* insists that the soul "is only some of what it has."[64] The soul lacks virtue—hence the soul remains composed. A third argument rehearses Philip's curious argument from prime matter.[65]

John's response is measured, reluctant, and ambiguous. He seems to prefer reporting to adjudicating. Some, he reports, distinguish soul as substance from soul as substance disposed to habits. The first posits identity between the soul and its essence, the second not.[66] Other masters think the soul entirely identical to its powers and that they differ only by *ratio*.[67] Still others divine a distinction between substance and essence—this is Alexander's *Glossa* position. I set John's version beside the *Summa*'s for comparison:

Alii dicunt quod in nullo alio a Primo est idem in essentia quod sua potentia. Unde dicunt quod anima non est idem in substantia; sicut enim non est idem esse et operari, ita nec essentia anima et potentia. Essentia enim animae est id per quod anima ad aliquid est efficiendum vel recipiendum. Dicunt tamen quod idem est in substantia, eo quod anima non subsistat sine suis potentiis, nec etiam intelligatur, nec ipsa potentia sine anima. Identitas ergo quam ponit Augustinus referenda est ad substantiam, non ad essentiam.[68]	*Dicunt quidam quod in nullo a Primo est idem essentia rei quod sua potentia; unde dicunt quod anima non est idem in essentia quod sua potentia, dicunt tamen quod sunt idem in substantia. Sicut enim non est idem esse et operari, ita nec essentia et potentia: essentia enim animae est id per quod anima est absolute essentia; potentia est id per quod animae ad aliud est efficiendum vel recipiendum. Dicunt tamen quod idem est in substantia, eo quod anima non subsistat sine suis potentiis nec etiam intelligatur nec ipsa potentiae sine anima. Identitas ergo, quam ponit Augustinus, referenda est ad substantiam, non ad essentiam.*[69]

This last position glosses Alexander's. So much seems clear from its upshot: identity between the soul and its powers occurs at the level of substance (*substantia*), not essence (*essentia*). Less clear, however, is whether Alexander here plays Socrates to John's Plato. Is this last position the one John endorses? Or is it one among others? Critical consensus escapes his (very) few commentators.[70] The question is sharpened also by a textual discrepancy. One manuscript appends another argument to the above passage, one that tips John's rhetoric in the direction of advocating Alexander's thesis.[71] Yet most manuscripts lack it. To the extent that they do, the question of which position earns John's approval remains unanswered.

What is oracular in John's *Summa* emerges with crystal clarity in Brother Alexander's. To be sure, most of the question at *SH* I–II, n. 349 recites John's *Summa* by rote. Only now Brother Alexander rearranges bits from John's question into a fresh form. New rhetorical form conditions content—or transforms it. In scholastic form relocating arguments means changing them. So arguments that in John only countered initial objections now comprise the *Summa Halensis*'s solution. In fact, Brother Alexander abandons the customary *solutio* that prefaces counterarguments. Instead he allows replies to objections to form his own *solutio*. William of Auxerre's protest against Philip's argument from prime matter now forms half of the *solutio*. John's précis of Alexander's *Glossa*—reproduced in full above—forms the other. Together this yields a decisive endorsement of Alexander's position. The soul does not bear essential identity with its powers, not as prime matter bears the power to receive forms.[72] But neither does it stand at a remove from its powers, not as William let on. Instead "identity—as Augustine has it—ought to refer to substance, not essence."

And that, to close the narrative fable, is how the *Summa* came to argue that the soul is its powers substantially, not essentially. But why write fables? Why linger over the question? Why trace it across the Halensian school? And what, finally, has any of this to do with beauty?

Nothing yet. But consider for a moment Alexander's achievement. Consider, that is, the pose he strikes between metaphysical subtlety on the one hand and his strong trinitarian psychology on the other. Consider how Alexander refuses to court Philip's identity thesis even as he commends his trinitarian psychology. Consider how Alexander and his school take seriously and handle with metaphysical rigor the peculiar analogical relation between the *trinitas quae deus est* and the *imago trinitatis quae anima est*. What this yields, at least for our purposes and in the *Summa*, is a guarantee. The guarantee promises against William of Auxerre's threat that the human being remains a uniquely and irreducibly trinitarian creature. "The theological interest at stake," Gilson explains, "was that for a true Augustinian it could not be 'accidental' to the human soul to be a created trinity, that is, an image of God."[73]

Even so, the arguments above do mostly negative work. They only forfend the threat of stripping the soul of its trinitarian structure. I relate the above principally to show the dialectical efforts that support Brother Alexander's account of *pulchritudo animarum*. If the triple powers of remembering, understanding, and loving prove somehow identical to the soul, then the soul is underwritten by trinitarian order. And if trinitarian order is just beauty, then the soul too will be beautiful. Or it might be, at least. So far Alexander has shown only that this is not impossible. His question now asks not how the soul relates to its powers, but rather how both relate to the trinity.

BROTHER ALEXANDER ON THE *IMAGO TRINITATIS*

If Alexander has preserved the soul's identity as *imago trinitatis*, he will need now to articulate it. So he does: he studies the soul in his long cycle "on the human" (*de homine*), which concludes a study of creation arranged after hexamerous patterns. There Alexander worries first at the soul's being, its relation to its causes, and its properties. That last terminates in a cycle of questions *de imagine*—on the image.[74]

The first article poses a grammatical question.[75] Is the soul "image" (*imago*) or rather "to the image" (*ad imaginem*)?[76] Some authorities—Hilary, for instance—prefer the latter. If *imago* means "an indifferent and indistinct likeness," it applies to the Son alone.[77] "Express likeness (*expressissima simili-tudo*)" invites the same difficulty. To bear express likeness is to share a form—even a unity of nature.[78] But these intimacies seem proper to the Son alone. So Alexander brokers. We can, he writes, take *imago* in its narrower or broader acceptation. With Hilary, Alexander restricts the former to the Son. More broadly, however, *imago* applies to the human as the "most express likeness among creatures."[79] Though Alexander denies formal or natural identity between God and creatures, he holds fast to an analogical interval between them. "Still," he writes, "there is some fittingness according to proportion."[80] Little surprise that the analogy is trinitarian: "just as God remembers, understands, and loves, so too [does] the soul according to its mode."[81]

Creatures too, then, boast the "image" honorific. But a question issues immediately: Which creatures?[82] Alexander canvasses three answers, each with tighter specification than the last. *Imago* may, he thinks, describe all creatures, all rational creatures, or all rational human creatures. Against the first, Alexander reminds his readers that the key lies in the definition of image as "*express* likeness."[83] The trinity signs all creatures with the trace (*vestigium*), remember. Anything brought into being by God reflects divine unity, truth, and goodness.[84] But the trace is not the image, whose dignity only rational creatures enjoy.[85] They and their like have what sensitive souls lack: the power of knowing themselves.[86] This makes the rational soul singularly God-like, though not without remainder. Its exercise of those powers lacks the simplicity proper to God, whose performance of them just *is* the divine life.

But angels too are rational.[87] What prevents us from extending the logic above to include the angels? Nothing so far. Alexander allows that the angel is image "according to simplicity of essence and a trinity of powers (*trinitatem virium*) by which it remembers, understands, and loves."[88] Still, this relation feels rather spindly. The angel, after all, naturally lacks a body.[89] It cannot therefore naturally press his image into service the way a human might—by moving and governing her body, that is, as God moves and governs the universe. Alexander adds a second reason the image belongs only commonly to angels and properly to humans. This concerns the relations *ad intra* among the triplet of powers. True, angelic simplicity better imitates God's own. But the acts of these powers run serially in humans, who remember and know and love discursively and in that order. And this renders the distinction among powers rather clear—clearer, perhaps, than in the angels.[90] Here again, Alexander underlines the peculiarly trinitarian order: knowing presumes understanding, and loving both.[91] A third and final reason Alexander adduces in support of the image belonging more properly to the human concerns procreation. Simply put, humans may and do reproduce their own like—angels cannot and do not. Alexander summarizes his arguments by grouping them as essential and personal. On the level of essence, humans image God better by a "cycle of governance and living." And on the level of person, they exceed the angels in "in acts of power evincing procession" and "the power of production."[92]

Alexander continues on, stropping his thought razor-sharp. Some of his questions assay the image at the level of nature: that the *ratio* of image pertains more to the soul than to the body it animates;[93] that it further suits the upper reaches of that soul;[94] that it belongs to the soul not abstractly construed, but only as it is turned toward God;[95] and so on. The questions grow more intricate as they proceed, edging closer to the recherché. His point throughout, however, runs rather simply. At base it reruns Augustine's. If God created the human after God's image, then the human will necessarily be somehow trinitarian. And the higher and so more God-like the human element—soul over body, say—the more trinitarian.

Other questions scrutinize the image in grace—or at its borders. Most important here is the structural distinction between image (*imago*) and likeness (*similitudo*). Likeness names either a general class of fittingness between two things or the degree of qualitative intimacy between them.[96] To the former belongs the *Glossa Ordinaria*: "where the image is, so also is the likeness." But the latter provides the logic for another of the *Glossa's* claims: "image is taken for natural things, likeness for grace."[97] Atop these distinctions Alexander layers another. If the image suits cognition (*in cognitione*), likeness trades in love (*in dilectione*).[98] Yet again the logic is trinitarian: knowing precedes loving as Son does Spirit. Thus the image "adheres more to nature . . . it is naturally prior to the likeness superimposed (*superinducta*) onto the image."[99] These distinctions mostly ornament a single point: image is not likeness, and that it is not has something to do with nature and grace.

Alexander's Augustinianism demands scrupulous policing of the border wall that cordons nature from grace. But so far he has said little about how distinction actually functions. How does grace confer likeness—along an Aristotelian spectrum from potency to act?[100] And what has all this to do with the Augustinian claim that the image follows the powers?[101] Image figures in both the orders of creation and grace, only differently (*sed differenter*). The *imago creationis* comprises the soul's natural powers (*potentias naturales*)—memory, understanding, and will. We can think the likeness as an *imago recreationis*, however, according to the "grace that reforms those powers" (*gratiam reformantem illas potentias*).[102] If the latter crowns only the just, the former features across the just and sinner alike. Both of these in their turn reflect the intratrinitarian life.

Just how they do, however, raises a special problem. Augustine speaks of the soul's trinity of *powers*, each following the other. But powers cannot produce powers. Acts produce other acts.[103] So though "image" is received "on account of [the soul's] powers," "powers" here work as synecdoche for the acts elicited from them. Alexander explains:

> A power in itself, absolutely considered, is not from a power. Still, in the eliciting of act one power depends on another and so is in a sense from it. So in the eliciting of act, memory is presumed before understanding: thus to that extent the [soul] imitates the trinity of persons on account of procession.[104]

This heavy and precise emphasis on act should not surprise Brother Alexander's readers. It is among his deepest trinitarian presumptions. His trinitarian theology, remember, advocates the emanation account for distinguishing among persons. That account locates trinitarian difference not in oppositional relations but in the acts of emanation in virtue of which the person bears divinity differently.[105] Here, the trinitarian emphasis on act *ad intra* shades into Alexander's psychology. The Son's act depends upon the Father's "prior" act of generation—just so, understanding presupposes a "prior" act of remembering.

This trinitiarian connection prepares readers to appreciate maneuvers in Alexander's final question. This question wonders how exactly the soul represents the divine image. Two difficulties loom, though Alexander drives the first away with ease.[106] But a second threatens immediately and irreparably to unravel the intricate embroidery Alexander has stitched above. "Some," Alexander reports, "will doubt what Augustine says . . . that the acts of remembering, understanding, and will indwell one another (*sese sunt circumincedentes*) as a likeness of powers to the divine persons."[107] Perichoretic relations among and within the trinity are, of course, "necessarily concomitant."[108] There is no Father without his Son, for instance, and no Spirit without both. But then I can remember and understand something— evil, say—without willing it. Am I not willing evil precisely to the extent that I fail to understand it?[109] So the soul's powers hardly cut an adequate likeness of intratrinitarian perichoresis. And since the soul's powers and their reflection of the trinitarian order constitute the soul's beauty, that too hangs in the balance. Alexander concedes the objection but holds fast to the main. Disorder of the soul's perichoresis menaces its lower levels, where the soul directs its gaze to "temporary things" (*temporalia*) or "workings of the will" (*operationes voluntariae*). Only at its highest reaches—"when the superior parts of reason consider first truth"—do the soul's powers indwell one another (*sese circumincedunt*).[110] When they do, the human soul "determines the beauty of the universe."[111]

CONCLUSION

By the time Brother Alexander wrote on the soul, trinitarian psychology was already a cliché. Augustine's experiments across *De trinitate* regulated study of the trinity and the soul. In Augustine's West, thinking the soul meant thinking the trinity. His scholastic readers asked not whether the soul is trinity, but rather how. The *Summa* shifts these habits by reinscription. If the order of the trinitarian persons forms divine beauty, the harmony of the soul's three powers account for it. Alexander and his school fight to secure this harmony against illicit identity or incidence. Securing it means finding sanctuary for the soul's powers in its substance, where powers are concomitant but not essential or accidental. Having secured its trinity of powers, Brother Alexander speculates over the soul's structure. He finds there not merely the trinity's trace, but also its logic. The soul too thrums with perichoretic movement—remembering, understanding, and willing indwell one another in a single soul like Father, Son, and Spirit in one nature. To that extent the soul imitates the trinity's beauty. It is to that extent too that the soul is beautiful.

Yet that beauty is not the trinity's—not by nature. No, it is *ex nihilo* and so more fragile, more vulnerable to sin's disorder. The disorder the soul invites here below in the devastation disfigures its will. The *imago creationis*, Alexander says, awaits restoration. Or it awaits its conversion into *imago recreationis*, whose passage only grace provides.

CHAPTER 7

THE BEAUTY GRACE GIVES

L ike other thirteenth-century theologians, Brother Alexander understood grace to effect an ontological change.[1] Being justified, they thought, signals a real transformation of the soul. Most often, thinking grace ontologically meant accounting for its created presence in souls. Theologians debated the exact nature of this presence.[2] But all agreed with John of La Rochelle that unless grace names a "change on their part, they are not any closer to their eternal good than before."[3] So construed, an infusion of grace (*gratiae infusio*) logically precedes divine acceptance (*acceptatio divina*). God accepts a sinner as just because and to the extent that grace is present within her soul.[4]

Later medievals began to conceive grace differently. If none among them denies grace's created presence,[5] it becomes slowly cleaved from the ontological change it effects.[6] For example: Scotus argues that a created habit of grace is only necessary for justification under *this* order—it might have been otherwise. Later, Ockham and Gregory of Rimini suggest that God may accept a person as *gratus* even absent the habit of grace.[7] Thus the late-medieval "covenantal" account of grace becomes "wholly forensic."[8] It denies, that is, any and every absolute link between justification and the soul's ontological change. In near perfect counterpoise to their earlier confreres, later Franciscans insist that *acceptatio divina* logically antecedes *gratiae infusio*.[9] God's eternal decision to justify always already accounts for grace's presence in the soul.

This chapter neither endorses nor rewrites declension narratives. It aims only to wonder at and about the early Franciscan commitment to the ontological change grace effects. My account here aims at coherence, not causation. I do not ask what *causes* Brother Alexander to champion grace as an ontological change. I ask instead what else doing so entails—or about how that commitment hangs together with others.

This chapter reads Brother Alexander's teaching on grace within his beauty doctrine. Doing that, I propose, yields hints at to how he defends grace as ontological change. For Alexander grace "assimilates us to the whole trinity."[10] Grace making pleasing (*gratia gratum faciens*) is for the *Summa* a grace that makes trinitarian. It is a grace too that begins in the incarnation, that removes the palimpsest of sin that obscures the soul's *imago trinitatis*, and that restores the soul as God-like (*deiformis*) and assimilated to God (*assimilatus deo*).[11] So graced, the soul becomes a site for "enjoyment" (*fructus*) of trinitarian beauty.[12] There and through the trinitarian missions, God the trinity delights in the renewed image even as the soul delights in God the trinity.

SIN AS ANTITRINITY

For Brother Alexander the beauty of the soul follows from the harmony of its powers. Disordering that harmony, it follows, blotches its beauty. Thus to the extent that sin damages the soul's beauty, its deformations are antitrinitarian. And when sin damages the images our souls are, it attempts a palimpsest over them. For this reason Alexander conceives sin principally and primarily as "disorder" (*inordinatio*). Its corruption of the will subverts the harmony of the soul's powers and so defaces its beauty.

Alexander intimates the antitrinitarian structure of sin already where he defines it.[13] Indeed, his definition forms a pastiche of four different definitions. Each are indexed to and subversive of one of Aristotle's causes.[14] The first associates sin with "an evil of the will" (*peccatum est malum voluntarium*). That, Alexander learns from Augustine, curiously accounts for sin's efficient cause.[15] As privation, sin lacks a *ratio*. So its efficient cause owes to a confused act of the will.[16] A similar inversion works beneath the second definition. It conceives sin as "a lack of owed justice" (*peccatum est carentia debitae iustitiae*).[17] But lacking justice means lacking the will's formal perfection—love. Lacking justice, then, defines sin against its formal cause: "a defect of form" (*defectum formae*).[18] Next Alexander learns his third definition from Augustine: "sin is the privation of the good" (*peccatum est privatio boni*).[19] This definition mostly ornaments the tight connection he has already forged between the good and final causality (and both with the Spirit). To lack the good is just to lack an end.[20] And a fourth definition recycles an Augustinian idiom. "Sin," the old saw goes, "is an excess of concupiscence" (*peccatum est superfluitas concupiscentiae*).[21] This excess issues from the flesh, which St. Paul says "lusts against the spirit" (Gal. 5:17). The flesh overwritten by illicit and garish desire for ephemera—this is sin's material cause.

The antitrinitarian structure here is so subtle that it is nearly imperceptible—only ears trained by Brother Alexander may discern it. Even so, his readers will know by now that invoking Aristotelian causes already means speaking trinity. Remember: already in *SH* I he showed how immaterial causes work as trinitarian appropriations: efficient to Father, exemplar to Son, final to Spirit.[22] Remember too that appropriating causality invests creation with a trinitarian shape.

Sin distorts this shape by inversion. It inverts the efficient cause by *failing* to cause according to any *ratio*. Like the Father, sin too is unbegotten; unlike Him, sin's innascibility proves barren. Sin inverts the formal cause by lacking form. This lack follows from a failure to issue love—if the Son breathes Spirit, sin breathes nothing. Sin inverts the final cause by lacking the good. And this means lacking any end whatever, since the good is that toward which all things tend. Absent an end, sin lacks the *completio* the Spirit is. Last, sin inverts the material cause by overestimating matter. Sin reroutes desire proper to God alone toward what is lowest. When excessive concupiscence usurps reason, body rules soul. The *imago trinitatis* now serves what it should by rights lord over. On Alexander's account, then, sin not only counters appropriated causes. It also apes their logic. In so doing sin attempts a palimpsest—erasure and displacement of the trinitarian icon written into creation.

Sin's antitrinitarian icon glows brighter where Alexander considers sin as the *privatio modi, speciei, et ordinis*—a privation of the trace.[23] Here again, Alexander insists that sin cannot damage or delete the trinity's trace without remainder—not ontologically anyway. Then he adds something puzzling. Mode, form, and order *can* be diminished "insofar as they indwell (*insunt*) wills capable of being ordered to the good."[24] What could this proviso mean? The passage introduces a fresh distinction—or recycles it. Alexander conceives the trinitarian processions as either natural (the Son's) or volitional (the Spirit's). He considers the trinitarian trace's relation to the soul along the same division. At the level of nature, the trace is fixed. But at the level of will?

First he explains how the triplet "indwells" a rational will. "Mode" (*modus*) calculates the extent to which the will "conforms [itself] to the will of the divine." "Form" (*species*) describes the will's natural (though not original) rectitude, which—following evil done (*malum culpae*)—suffers lingering trauma. And "order" (*ordo*) belongs to the will as its end (*ad finem*), that toward which it orders its collective efforts. Then Alexander associates the three elements of the trace with sin's causal distortions—efficient, formal, and final.[25] So if by nature the trace subsists indomitably, by will "it is able to be diminished but not totally destroyed."[26]

Evil done (*malum culpae*), Alexander writes, mangles each element of the trace simultaneously and equally. It must, if indeed mode, form, and order "represent the highest trinity"[27] whose persons also live simultaneously and equally. Sin damages simultaneously because the act of loving a creature as or more than the trinity is itself (anti)trinitarian. That act of the will inverts its *mode* by miscalculating, its *form* by sundering rectitude and preferring extremes to "the middle," and its *order* by inclining to extremes.[28] Sin damages equally because of the trace's peculiar perichoretic relation. A confused and imagined objector demurs: virtue—fortitude, say—may and often does "indwell" the soul without other virtues.[29] Alexander responds that it is otherwise for the elements of the trace. "One is not able to indwell (*inesse*) without the others or vice versa," he explains. "And for this reason, when one is intended, the other two are also; when one is diminished, the other two are also."[30] Given the logic of perichoresis, damage to one power spells damage to all.

Not only does sin simultaneously and equally damage the trace's elements in perichoretic relation, but it also parodies that relation. Sometimes, that is, Alexander imagines sin to parody even the logic of perichoresis. How? As evil, sin remains vampiric upon the good. Alexander's commitment to the *privatio* account explains his teaching that "evil is good *secundum quid*."[31] Thus as almost-not-but-somehow-still good, sin bears an *ordo*. Only sin attempts (and fails) a total inversion, explaining its classical definition as "disorder."[32] Even as disorder sin mimics trinitarian order.

And so Brother Alexander will say, for example, that negligence is not one sin among many. Negligence rather "circulates through (*circueat*) all sin," or it features across the triple vice of *invidia, superbia,* and *avaritia*. Negligence is always the neglect of "the elements circulating sin itself."[33] In another place Alexander calls vainglory the "mother of all sin [that] circulates (*circuit*) all evil."[34] True, *circumire* is not *circumincedere*. But then it cannot be: sin cannot attain a perfect photo negative of trinitarian perichoresis. If it could, sin or evil would emerge as another principle opposite good. Brother Alexander is no Manichaean. If sin parodies trinity, sin also must remain parasitically enslaved to it.

Thus sin deals in antitrinitarian corrosion. To the extent that it does, it forms a palimpsest over the trinity the soul is—or attempts to. The point here is not to detail how and everywhere Alexander depicts sin as antitrinity. Instead the point is rather *that* he does. Sin inverts the causes appropriated to the trinity. It also simultaneously and equally defaces the trinitarian trace written into the human will. It even parodies perichoresis. But if sin thus writes a palimpsest, restoring the soul's trinitarian icon belongs to grace's work.

GRACE'S TRINITARIAN CONDITION

If restoring the soul's trinitarian icon belongs to grace, then its work must also be trinitarian first and last. For Alexander that work begins where the trinity appears in history: the incarnation of the Word. So before he inventories grace's kinds and sorts their tangled relations one to another, Alexander asks after grace's condition. If we are justified by the faithfulness of Christ (Gal. 2:16), then we shall first need to assay that faithfulness. What then shall we say about Christ's grace? And how anyway does Christ communicate it to us?

These questions summon Christology proper according to Alexander, who treats them directly after Christ's conception and nativity.[35] Across these questions Alexander appraises Christ's grace under three headings: the grace of union (*gratia unionis*), the grace of the man Jesus of Nazareth (*gratia singularis sanctitatis*), and capital grace (*gratia in ipso secundum quam esset caput*).[36] Alexander voices each with trinitarian grammar, though I consider only the last and first. And since the hypostatic union itself generates Christ's human nature,[37] Alexander treats the first first.[38]

I. The Grace of Union

Talk of "the grace of union" sounds baroque, even garish—still another of the harlequin shades with which the schoolmen depict graces. For one reason or another, we (post)moderns do not typically describe the hypostatic union itself as a grace.[39] Alexander does. Indeed he must, at least to the extent that he teaches a humankind not naturally capable of union with God.[40] Not even original justice, Alexander contends against some Dominicans, renders Adam so capable.[41] No: salvation requires the grace of union because "it is not possible for the human creature to be elevated and disposed to divine union through the gift of created nature." "It is necessary for her to have grace," Alexander continues, "that elevates and disposes her to divine union. And this grace we call the grace of union."[42] By uniting humanity and divinity in his person, Christ traverses the interval yawning between God and cosmos.[43] Only in Christ, then, does humanity become supernaturally capable of the grace of union (*gratiae unionis capax*).

Having discussed the need for union's grace, Alexander must now explain what it is. He begins by drawing a distinction innovated already in Alexander's early texts.[44] "The grace of union," he writes, "is double": both *disponens* and *complens*.[45] As disposing, the grace of union connotes a "disposition that is nothing other than God-likeness (*deiformitas*) or divine assimilation."[46] If the grace of union *disponens* belongs properly to Christ's human nature, then its disposition is created grace (*gratia creata*). But as completing and perfecting, the grace of union works otherwise. The grace of union *complens* and *perficiens* just is "the Holy Spirit himself." As uncreated grace (*gratia increata*), the Spirit does not accord a disposition. Rather the Spirit lives as the Gift itself—"not by appropriation but by his property [as] love proceeding from the Father and the Son."[47] Here Brother Alexander restates his pneumatology by abridging it. As he argued already in book I,[48] love names the *ratio* of gift. And love—if love it be—derives gifts from pure liberality. So if the Spirit is Love, the Spirit is also Gift, and if Gift then also uncreated grace.[49] These judgments erect crossbeams on which Alexander hangs the grace of union: created grace as disposition, uncreated grace as Spirit.

Perhaps Alexander's distinction deals more wounds than it dresses. After all, he has allowed two questions to linger. The first wonders why the grace of union must proffer a double medium. Some Dominicans bridled at the very idea of grace as medium at all.[50] Alexander compounds their worry by positing not one but *two* media. Here again his reasons lay with his denial that the soul is naturally *gratiae unionis capax*. The soul cannot unite itself to God. Its nature and God's are "maximally distant."[51] And so the grace of union must mediate. When it does, it operates under two *rationes*. Under the first the grace of union disposes human nature for union by endowing it with a created disposition. Under the second the grace of union "completes and perfects" that union as Spirit. Thus "it is necessary that the grace of union [of the natures] is uncreated and created grace."[52] Only a single grace—Alexander asserts rather than argues—cannot be at once created and not. So the grace of union must prove "a double medium . . . namely created and uncreated grace, which is the Holy Spirit."

His solution only raises another question: Why identify the uncreated grace of union with the Spirit? Surely it was the Son and not the Spirit who assumed Mary's flesh. Other scholastics taught that imagining the Spirit as formal medium of the Son's hypostatic union was at best gratuitous and at worst blasphemous. Why does Alexander insist otherwise?

The question he asks is whether the Holy Spirit is better thought as the medium of union than are the other divine persons. In the Spirit's defense Alexander marshalls three arguments. The first and strangest derives from the psychology of the *De spiritu et anima*. There a tangle of logic associates the union between body and soul with spirit's mediation. The way spirit disposes body and soul to unite mirrors the double gift of the Spirit. *Ad intra* the Spirit is love "essentially and personally in the trinity itself." *Ad extra* the Spirit is love "through which the whole trinity is communicated" to humanity. But what higher communication of the trinity is there than its personal unity with humanity in Christ? Thus the "Spirit is more suitably called a medium of that union than are the other persons."[53] Alexander scrounges another argument from Dionysius. Love is unitive, Dionysius writes. And if that is so, the highest union ought to involve the highest Love—which must in turn be the Spirit. A final argument arrives from Augustine: the Spirit forms the nexus and chain and communion of Father and Son. If the Spirit unites the divine persons in the divine nature, why not also the natures in the person of the Son?[54]

Alexander concludes his study of union's grace by plotting its relation to capital grace.[55] Which is their relation, which their difference? Alexander teaches that as uncreated, these graces are the selfsame Spirit.[56] As created, the grace of union and capital grace differ in the order of knowing (*secundum rationem*), if not in the order of being (*secundum substantiam*). Here Alexander illustrates.[57] A single luminary illumines a dimmer one by its own light. The moon emits no light of its own—it shines only light borrowed from the sun. So it is with the grace of union and capital grace, Alexander proposes. Obviously light glows brightest in Christ, who as *lux mundi* (John 8:12) alone possesses power to illumine others. Christ's source light—the one uniting natures hypostatically—is thus the grace of union. And the borrowed light reflected in the *membra* of his Church is capital grace. But as with the moon and the sun, the difference here is one of appearance rather than being. The Gift is always and everywhere the one Spirit.

Next Alexander charts grace's sequence. Christ, he writes, is head of his members by faith. And in metronomic time the gift of faith antecedes the incarnation of the Word in first-century Palestine. But Abraham and the "holy fathers" (*sancti patres*) nursed faith too. Does capital grace thus somehow antecede the grace of union? If so, how so? To answer, Alexander rewrites Augustine. Time's metronome, he argues, never changes faith's object. And the object and content of faith cannot be other than the incarnation. The patriarchs foreknow it, the disciples witness it, and we now confess it. Whatever the age, faith always means faith in the God-man and so the grace of union. True, the order of knowing (*ratio intelligentiae*) privileges union's grace to capital grace.[58] Christ's incarnation forms the condition for grace's mediation to the members of his body. But here again Alexander posits identity in the order of being. Only now he explains why. Alexander cautions readers against neat distinctions between incarnation and the grace it imparts. He does so mostly to limn the unity of their singular mystery. If faith takes as its object the grace of union, the grace of union is the very cause of faith. And to the extent that both name the Christ's one Spirit, incarnation and salvation cannot be riven.[59]

II. Capital Grace

Scripture tropes the church as Christ's body (Col. 1:15–20, 2:9–15; Eph. 1:15–23). As his body the church garners salvation from Christ its head. Scholastics study this trope under the title capital grace—"the grace by which Christ is head"[60]—a scholastic term of art for the process by which Christ's grace of union reaches his church. The doctrine proves especially influential in Franciscan circles.[61] Like other masters Brother Alexander composes a cycle of questions on capital grace. But as we might expect, in Alexander's arrangement the trinity recurs like a refrain. Let us gloss Brother Alexander's long teaching on capital grace by accenting its trinitarian qualities.

First Alexander wonders aloud about the work St. Paul's body-image does. Why think about grace through this metaphor? Alexander adduces two reasons: one political (*ratio dignissimae et providentis ecclesiae*), another organic (*ratio influentiae*).[62] Politically, Christ plays head to the church as a sovereign plays head to her vassals. But organically—and more properly, Alexander thinks—Christ is head to the church as a brain to its body. Here expositing St. Paul commits Alexander to consulting Avicenna's physiology. Avicenna halved the brain: movement "flows" from one part, and sensory nerves "flow" from the other.[63] The Pauline image functions on analogy. As head, Christ's movement of love and sense of faith "inflow" the church. Thus the *ratio* of this particular metaphor is to render the church's dependence upon Christ. It is also to typify how Christ's grace of union mediates saving grace to his church.

Then Alexander adds a trinitarian proviso. True enough, Christ in two natures forms the church's head *sensu stricto*. But the trinity too is "head of the church" (*caput ecclesiae*), if more generally. "The whole trinity moves and rules and infuses the church with grace," Alexander instructs his readers, "by which it senses by faith and is moved by love."[64]

Accommodating the trinity as *caput* means multiplying distinctions.[65] So Alexander discriminates strict and general senses of the term even within the trinity. There and generally, "head" (*caput*) connotes a principle. And "principle" in the trinity supposits for something by turns personal or essential.[66] As head to the divine persons, the Father generates his Son personally and in substantial identity. As head to creatures *ex nihilo*, the "creator trinity" (*trinitas creatrix*) causes creatures in substantial difference. Stricter still, *caput* suggests "the inflow of spiritual sense and movement."[67] This strict acceptation itself spans two meanings: the *ratio* of inflowing alone (*ratio influentiae tantum*) and the *ratio* of inflowing and the conformity of nature (*ratio influentiae et conformitas naturae*). On the first supposition the head of the church is the trinity and so Christ *secundum divinitatem*. And on the second the head of the church names Christ *secundum humanitatem*. The latter suits Brother Alexander best. He teaches that if Christian grammar allows the confession of the trinity as head of the church, its precision demands that we crown as head Christ *secundum humanitatem*. Why? Alexander explains that in the economy of salvation, the church knows the trinity's grace only through Christ incarnate, crucified, and resurrected. And that arrives only *secundum humanitatem*.

For Alexander, Christ *secundum humanitatem* prevails as head over the angels, the elect, indeed every soul—even over the reprobate.[68] Mostly Christ prevails over his body, the church. Alexander wonders how and whether that body is a singular one. The Spirit, he teaches, gathers Christ's members into a single body by perfecting and disposing. The perfection of the Spirit unites

Christ to "the holy believers and his lovers," or so Hugh of St. Victor and 1 Cor. 12:4. The Spirit's, remember, is the work of uncreated grace—even the Spirit herself, who communicates the trinity to us. The same Spirit also binds Christ's body together by granting his members a *dispositio consimilis*, a consimilar disposition. Attendant upon this disposition—or created grace—are four features: rational cognition, concupiscible desire, irascible expectation, and the work of imitation. The first three features baptize Platonic tripartism into the Pauline idiom.[69] Faith transfigures the *logistikon*, love the *epithymetikon*, and hope the *thumoeides*.[70] Each severally and all together imitate the Lord, whose human life exhibits the same. And so the Spirit guarantees unity among Christ's body by perfecting and disposing.

If the Spirit unites Christ's members, how do they relate to their head? Presumably, Alexander learns from Hugh, as John 17:11 recommends.[71] There Christ implores the Father to fasten his disciples together just as he and "the Father are one." Only not just—the unity of Father and Son traffics in identity of substance (*consubstantialitas*). So Alexander parses and declines three modes of unity: substantial identity, personal identity, and identity of will.[72] Only the trinity possesses the first mode of unity and only Christ the second. A third sort locates unity in a shared will, a community of "justice in present and future glory." Common among the saints and their head, this unity is not the trinity's or Christ's—not exactly. The church only attains unity *secundum analogiam*. But it is a unity unthinkable apart from Christ's incarnation, death, and resurrection. Only that, Alexander concludes, restores the will to justice and glory which will be the saints'.[73]

Alexander closes his cycle of questions on capital grace by assaying *influentia*, his fundamental conceit for grace. If *caput* properly picks out Christ *secundum humanitatem*, then his human nature somehow "inflows grace to the church" (the English calque "influence" hardly renders the sense).[74] How? In three ways: by merit, by example, and as head. The first mode names how Christ, per Rom. 5:11, mediates the grace he merits to us. The second mode names how, per Rev. 20:12, Christ lives the book of life "according to which our book should be written."[75] The third mode names how Christ, as head of his members, suffers a natural desire for them.[76] Just as senses from the head collect in the body's wounds, so too does Christ "inflow" to his. Only the appetite of which Christ is possessed is the Spirit, "through whom the whole trinity is communicated to us." So possessed of the Spirit, Christ issues his senses and movement as head to his members *ut participemus suum Spiritum,* so that we too might participate in his Spirit. In this sense and for Alexander, the Spirit "completes" Christ's work in us. Just as a soul animates a head descending into its members, the Spirit fills Christ descending into his church.[77]

Let me now step back to ask what to make of all this. What important patterns stand out amid so much detail?

On its surface Alexander's doctrine of capital grace seems boilerplate. It holds that capital grace distributes Christ's grace of union to his members. Indeed, Brother Alexander neither begins nor innovates the subject. Distinctive and peculiar to him, however, is the trinitarian intensity that hums across his study. In fact, that intensity sounds mostly pneumatic. Alexander routinely and frequently conceives the Spirit as grace's formal cause. Leo XIII's *Divinum Illud Munus* offers a near perfect paraphrase of Alexander's account: "as Christ is head of the church, so is the Holy Ghost her soul."[78] The Spirit disposes created grace to both head and member— to the head as union of divine and human and to his members as a consimilar disposition.[79] As uncreated grace the Spirit perfects and completes the hypostatic union and its sequelae. Notice too how all this riffs the strophic chorus Alexander chants with liturgical repetition: the Spirit is "he through whom the communion of the whole trinity is ours."[80] That this refrain should figure at such a pitch and with such frequency should hardly surprise Alexander's readers. The Spirit, remember, lives as *communio* of the trinity *ad intra.*[81] Now Alexander extends the logic *ad extra.* The Paraclete not only unites Christ's two natures, but he also adjoins the church to Christ.

THE TRINITARIAN STRUCTURE OF GRACE

So the grace of union and capital grace—these mostly announce grace's conditions. Alexander turns now to address the very idea of grace. Of his enormous repository of questions *de gratia,* two sets stand out.[82] The first poses the definitional question: What *is* grace, after all? A second question asks after its work: What does grace do anyway? Which are its effects? Where Brother Alexander answers these questions, his "comprehensive trinitarianism" yet again bleeds through. Let us again follow Alexander's pedagogy through grace's definition first and through its effects next.

I. The Definition of Grace

Alexander begins his study of grace's ontology (*secundum rem*) by advocating its presence within the soul.[83] Sanctifying grace makes pleasing to God (*gratus deo*). And what pleases God but what is like God? Sanctifying grace, then, must also make similar to God. Thus grace's work renders the soul God-like (*deiformis*) and assimilated to God (*assimilatus deo*). Only restoring the soul's image from sins's palimpsest means that grace must really *ponere aliquid in ipso*, place something in the soul. Alexander draws these threads together: grace involves not just a real presence but also a real transformation of the soul. Only something real, he concludes, assimilates the soul to God.[84]

What exactly is this something (*aliquid*) in the soul? Asking the definitional question invokes controversy. Its cause célèbre is the Lombard's notorious line on charity in Book I, distinction 17,[85] which kindled "theological dynamite."[86] Already in the twelfth century Simon of Tournai had crowed that Master Peter conflated efficient and formal causality.[87] Bonaventure and Thomas would imitate Simon's rejection.[88] Some strategy was needed to disarm the Lombard's explosive, it seemed.

That strategy developed alongside early thirteenth-century theologies of "created grace" (*gratia creata*). Among its inventors was Alexander of Hales.[89] His early *Glossa* and *Quaestiones disputatae 'antequam esset frater,'* alongside his recently edited and later *Quaestiones disputatae de gratia*, mark the phrase.[90] The concept is refined further by John of La Rochelle, Alexander's cochair at Paris.[91] But early Franciscan distinction between uncreated and created grace (*gratia increata et creata*) awaits its fullest expression in the *Summa Halensis*.[92]

In his *Summa*, Brother Alexander repeats his line on grace both created and not. His definitions rehearse those he gave earlier in his questions on the grace of union.[93] Only here he issues readers a pithy summary, complete now with a mnemonic:

> On the one hand, we ought to understand created grace as a likeness or disposition on the part of the rational soul, from which it has what is accepted and assimilated to God, since here there is a transforming form (*forma transformans*)—this is uncreated grace. Similarly there is a transformed form (*forma transformata*) which is left behind in the one transformed—in the soul, that is—by transformation, and this is created grace.[94]

Why the grace of union must be both created and not seems obvious—it is a union of natures both created and not. But why does Alexander imagine that sanctifying grace hews to a similar logic? Why must there be a transforming form and a transformed form?

Again Brother Alexander nurtures Augustine's pessimism about the human condition. Not even prelapsarian Adam was capable of the grace of union (*capax gratiae unionis*), let alone his children after the devastation.[95] So devastated, we require divine succor—a transforming form to assimilate us to God.[96] And this, Alexander often repeats for his readers, is just the Holy Spirit. Now the Spirit as grace is necessary and sufficient *per se*, not *ex parte recipientis*. (Note how Alexander shifts the Spirit from formal cause—Master Peter's position—to efficient cause of grace.) Our "defect" is so deep and our "insufficiency" so grave that we cannot abide immediate contact with the Spirit's *forma transformans*. To receive it we must first suffer conditioning.[97] We require a "likeness or disposition" in the soul that disposes us to union with the Spirit and so assimilates us to God. This is sanctifying grace's *forma transformata*—created grace.

What sort of "form" is this? Aristotle catalogued two kinds: substantial and accidental.[98] But Alexander cuts a distinction so fine it is nearly invisible.[99] Created grace is an accident to the extent that it concerns *primum esse animae*, the first being of the soul. Were it not, the soul could not be metaphysically "complete" before grace's infusion. Yet created grace is a "substantial disposition" (*dispositio substantialis*)—and not a substance proper—considered *secundum esse*, or in light of *bene esse* or *esse ordinis*. What exactly this means grows clearer (if never finally transparent) where Alexander compares created grace to virtue.[100] Grace and virtue share a substance but not *rationes*. Again, Brother Alexander teaches through the analogy of light. Rays perfect the air severally, their source light singly. So grace perfects the essence of the soul, virtue its separate powers. However hazy his light metaphor, Alexander's point here is that though accidental *per se*, created grace works *substantialiter* on the soul and virtue on its powers. All of which should remind his readers of how the soul in its triple powers "is the image of the trinity of persons."[101] Not essentially, not accidentally, but substantially—this prescribes how grace transforms the soul too (on which more later).

Alexander finishes his teaching on sanctifying grace with a peroration. His dialectical rhythms have already taught his readers how sanctifying grace works. But in almost Socratic fashion, he pesters them again for a precise definition. Most properly and according to name, "grace" signals a "gift given by God without merits that makes its bearer pleasing to God."[102] But according to definition, "grace is a habit of the soul, universally ordering [literally: ordinative of] the whole of life."[103] Fortunately Alexander elaborates: less a natural power than a "habit" or disposition, sanctifying grace is a quality of a peculiar sort. More, it is a habit written less upon the body than upon the soul. Yet unlike other habits of the soul that condition certain faculties, grace orders the "whole of life." If political virtues too order the whole of life, grace does so "universally"—without reference to or regard for local custom or jurisprudence.[104]

I pause here to appreciate what Alexander has just taught and why it matters. Grace, he wrote, "assimilates us to the whole trinity." And its work consists in "universally ordering the whole of life." What is this order but the trinity's? And what is the trinity's order but Alexander's rubric for beauty itself? Here Alexander only whispers this connection between grace and his trinitarian beauty doctrine. It grows louder and more explicit where Alexander treats grace's effects.

II. The Effects of Grace

If grace is "nothing other than a likeness of the soul to God," then it must somehow assimilate the soul to God. Alexander arranges grace's effects into three triplets. The first triplet recalls Dionysius, who imagines the angels purifying and illuminating and perfecting.[105] So too grace, whose "proper and essential effects" imitate the angels.[106] Assimilation of the soul to God comprises these three works, which "necessarily run together (*concurrunt*)." How exactly do grace's works move the soul from dissimilarity to likeness? Purifying, Dionysius says, shrives the soul of dissimilarity. It does so as natural forms do—by first removing what prohibits. And as the introduction of form illumines matter, so grace's consimilar disposition (*dispositio consimilis*) illumines the soul. Last the form perfects matter, just like grace in the soul.

So transfiguring the soul comprises a triple process.[107] By it the soul is purified of dissimilarity and illumined by likeness and perfected to assimilation. These first works, Alexander says, belong to the order of becoming (*respectu fieri*). Only the eschaton perfects the soul, for only there is the soul "totally completed" (*totum completum est*). Then light shall at length swallow the dark. We see it now too (1 Cor. 13:12), if only in glimpses. The Christian life is thus directed to attain grace's spiritual light (*lux spiritualis*), where there glooms no darkness at all.

The second triplet of grace's effects collects three other verbs, here vivifying and assimilating and making-pleasing. John 1:4–5 calls the Word "the life and light of man." Likeness to him, grace, must then be the soul's light and life. As light, grace suffuses the soul according to the triple process already detailed: by purifying and illumining and perfecting.[108] As life grace operates differently.[109] Here Alexander's arguments apply the logic of love divined by the Victorines.[110] "I know, my soul," Hugh had sung, "that love is your life." Thus the first effect of grace as life is to vivify. Next comes love's work: "I know, my soul," Hugh sang again, "that when you love something, the power of love transforms into likeness."[111] Thus the second effect is to assimilate lover into beloved. So assimilated, the soul pleases God. At Prov. 8:17, Wisdom says "I love those who love me." Grace's third effect as life, then, makes pleasing (*gratus*). And all this from the logic of love, Alexander argues. Love imprinted on the soul vivifies, the imprint made alive assimilates, and the soul assimilated makes pleasing.

Alexander tacks on a third triplet: justifying and exciting and eliciting the motion of merit. If, as Alexander will say later, the first triplet considers truth and the next good, this one concerns free choice (*liberum arbitrium*) or power. Like divine power, free choice eschews coercion. So grace works on the will through consent. When it does—Bernard of Clairvaux writes—grace moves the will through justification.[112] With the will so moved, grace now offers reason excitation. This process terminates in the conversion of the whole faculty of free choice. Transfigured by grace, free choice directs its acts to merit.[113] And so grace's work on free choice: justifying and exciting and eliciting the motion of merit.[114]

Or so Alexander's teaching on the three triplets of grace's effects. Still, the triplets seem arbitrary, unnecessarily intricate—as if Brother Alexander has foraged as many triplets from authorities as he could find only to flaunt his collection. But just here Alexander rewards close readers. After displaying his triplets, he reveals their logic:

> We should understand that grace relates to the soul as life and as mover and as light, since grace is a likeness of the highest truth, and so it relates to light; and [grace] is also a likeness of the highest good, and so it

relates to life; and [grace] is also a likeness of power or virtue, and so it relates to the soul as a mover of choice. But power is attributed to the Father, truth to the Son, and good to the Holy Spirit. And thus grace is a likeness of the whole trinity and assimilates us to the whole trinity. But as it relates to light—to that which is a likeness of the first truth—three effects of grace are assumed. And as it relates to life—to that which is a likeness of the highest good—three other effects are assumed. And as it relates to mover—namely as that which is a likeness of the highest power or virtue, there are its three effects, namely to justify, to excite, and to elicit the motion of merit.[115]

The logic of grace's effects hews to the logic of trinity, or at least trinitarian appropriation. A first triplet considers grace's effects from light and so truth; a second from life and so good; and still a third from power and so as mover. Power, truth or wisdom, and good—these, his readers remember, name appropriations for Father, Son, and Spirit.

That Brother Alexander should revert to trinity talk here makes good sense. Whatever exactly grace does, Alexander repeatedly teaches that it assimilates souls to God. Now, here, he weaves several strands of his thought together. Remember that at its highest level, the soul comprises a trinity—its powers circumincess according to trinitarian patterns.[116] Sin's depredations invert and distort that perichoretic order. Restoring its damage means that grace assimilates souls not just to God, but to the *trinity* God is. For Alexander grace yields nothing less than a likeness to the whole trinity (*similitudo totius trinitatis*)—one that assimilates us to the whole trinity (*assimilat nos toti trinitati*). In grace the soul reflects the Son's truth or wisdom, the Spirit's goodness, and the Father's power. This comes only by grace's triple triplet. The soul conforms to the Son as truth in light by grace's purifying, illumining, and perfecting; to the Spirit as good in life by grace's vivifying, assimilating, and making-pleasing; and to the Father as power in motion by grace's justifying, exciting, and eliciting to merit.

All of which culminates in Alexander's claim that "since the Holy Spirit is love, he transforms us into a divine form (*divinam speciem*) in order that the soul itself might be assimilated to God."[117] Alexander does not elaborate.[118] Neither does he explicitly connect his claims about grace's effects to the trinity of the soul or sin's antitrinitarian palimpsest. Likeness to the trinity, it seems, involves fixing sin's damage to the soul's three perichoretic powers somehow. But how? Perhaps Brother Alexander fails to finish his thought. Or perhaps he assumes that the invocation of trinitarian logic is sufficient for his readers to complete it for themselves. Either way, he narrates each epoch of salvation history with trinitarian discipline. Creation, fall, grace—Alexander explains each to relate (or distort) the trinitarian structure of the cosmos and all of its contents.

What has the above to do with beauty? Recall that Alexander thinks the soul beautiful because of the "harmony of its virtues and the ordering of its powers."[119] If sin's palimpsest distorts this beauty, grace restores it. But notice the logic: bearing grace just means being assimilated to the whole trinity. It means possessing *deiformitas*. And if the trinitarian order is just beauty, what is bearing its likeness but being beautiful?

So much seems clear: for Alexander grace's shape is trinitarian, and its result—to the extent that it assimilates the soul to the beauty the trinity is— is beautiful. But now a final question presses in, the one with which I framed this chapter: Why does Alexander insist that grace names something real in the soul? Or better: What does grace's beauty or trinitarian shape have to do with the something (*aliquid*) it is, anyway? Why does this *aliquid* need to be a trinitarian one?

GRACE AS TRINITARIAN ENJOYMENT

Fragments of an answer rest in Alexander's doctrine of the trinitarian missions.[120] Alexander's readers sometimes notice how his *Summa* develops the scholastic teaching of trinitarian missions in both precision and abstraction.[121] Indeed, the *Summa* sets thought on the trinitarian missions moving along several tracks. Among these tracks one depicts the effect of grace as an aesthetic "enjoyment" (*fructus*) of the trinity. Grace making pleasing makes of the soul a "temple or dwelling of the Son and Holy Spirit, disposing the soul that they might exist in it by *ratio* of enjoyment."[122] Brother Alexander explains:

> Given in the missions of [the Son and the Spirit] are not only their gifts, but indeed [the persons] themselves. And they inhabit the soul and exist there in a way more particular than they were before. So "mission" is said only by reason of those gifts, for which reason they are said to inhabit the soul and to exist there according to a mode different than

before in order that not only their gifts are with us in their mission, but even [the persons] themselves. This is only through grace making pleasing (*gratiam gratum facientem*), according to which they are in the soul under the logic of enjoyment (*in ratione fructus*).[123]

Grace making pleasing steels the soul for its suffusion by *gratia increata*, the Spirit. Alexander now couples this account with the trinitarian missions of Spirit and Son. The invisible missions of both disclose knowledge of the trinitarian processions.[124] But they also gift the soul "dispositions for enjoying" (*dispositiones mentis ad fruendum*) the intimate, personal presence of the Son and Spirit.[125] That Alexander now runs grace through the trinitarian missions spotlights another aspect of grace's economy. From this angle of vision, the problem grace solves is not only the "maximal distance" between our nature and God's.[126] Neither does grace work only to efface sin's palimpsest. For Alexander grace also suffuses the soul with the power of enjoying the uncreated good (*virtutem fruendi bono increato*), possible only *per gratiam et virtutes*.[127]

The language of enjoyment (*fructus*) recurs throughout Alexander's study of the trinitarian missions.[128] Other scholastics also use it to figure the trinitarian missions.[129] All, however, arrogate the term and its use from Augustine.[130] "To enjoy," Augustine writes in *De doctrina christiana*, "is to hold fast to [something] in love for its own sake."[131] He elaborates the relation between *fructus* and love in *De civitate dei*: "love, then, longing to have what is loved, is desire; but having and enjoying (*fruens*) it is joy."[132] For Augustine, then, *fructus* depicts "love reposing,"[133] the delicious pleasure of possessing what one loves.

Alexander thinks this is what grace making pleasing gives. The Spirit gifts a created *habitus* that "assimilates to" and renders a "likeness of God."[134] And this, Alexander writes, is "salvation itself."[135] But grace making pleasing renders not some abstract *similitudo animae ad deum*. To be sure, likeness to God remains an ancient and ubiquitous trope for grace.[136] But Alexander's trinitarian commitments require more. For him the very shape and effects of grace transform the soul into the trinity God made it to be. So the soul is not abstractly deiform. Rather the soul bears within it the "internal *ab alio* structure" of the trinity it mirrors.[137] Here Alexander recruits the likeness trope to a different end. What he seeks is not just likeness but likeness that invites (or signals) divine presence.

For Alexander the life of grace comes to this: that we might enjoy the trinity, "the highest beauty and highest delectable"[138] whose image we boast. But the trinity in turn revels also in its likeness. The soul pleases the trinity, Alexander writes, precisely by assimilating and reflecting its own peculiar beauty.[139] Or God adores what is God-like. And this means that grace saves exactly to the extent that it makes beautiful. Alexander's theology of grace very nearly glosses Psalm 149:4: "For the Lord takes pleasure in his people; he will beautify the meek with salvation."

CONCLUSION

Walk past the portrait of Alexander of Hales at St. Isidore's in Rome and pass into its great aula. Notice there the large fresco that gazes out over the lectern. It depicts two friars, their hands raised in adoration of an ascending Blessed Virgin. "Without stain (*absque macula*)," whispers the brother on the right—Anthony of Padua, if iconographic convention holds. Directly opposite him stands Francis, discalced and punctured by stigmata. He too darlings the Virgin with words. She, he says, is "total beauty" (*tota pulchra*). The inscription above the Virgin explains Francis's approbation. *Toti[us] es trinitatis nobile tabernaculum*—you are the celebrated tabernacle of the whole trinity.

Notice that the Virgin is *tota pulchra* exactly to the extent that she is also *trinitatis tabernaculum*. This image forms a *tableau vivant* of grace according to the *Summa*. Because beauty is trinitarian for him, Alexander studies grace as a trinitarian exercise: as a solvent for sin's antitrinitarian palimpsest, as a self-gift of the trinity to the church through Christ and his Spirit, as the trinitarian shape of and condition for enjoying the trinity's indwelling. Together these features of grace illumine Alexander's insistence that grace posit something real in the soul. Without it, Alexander might ask, how might we enjoy the personal presence of the trinity? And what renders us beautiful to the trinity itself if not our real reflection of God's own trinitarian beauty? As David Bentley Hart has it, the "beauty of the trinity, this orderliness of God's *perichoresis*, is the very moment of delight . . . the analogy that lies between worldly and divine beauty is a kind of *analogia delectationis*."[140]

Such is Alexander's teaching on grace's beauties. Refined of sin's palimpsest and burnished by grace, the saint becomes again what she always was: an icon of the trinity.

CONCLUSION

Pope Alexander IV was first to admire beauty in the *Summa Halensis*. But he was scarcely last. Medieval readers like Albert the Great, Bonaventure, Ulrich of Strasburg, and Denys the Carthusian did too. And since Leo XIII kindled the "fourth scholasticism,"[1] some modern readers have admired beauty in the *Summa* too. But recent aesthetic admiration, it turns out, betrays finicky and faddish tastes. Narrow interest in beauty's transcendentality or subjective disclosure discourages attention to beauty's presence elsewhere—indeed, everywhere. This narrow interest causes some readers to malign Alexander as an aesthetic pretender.[2] Sometimes even those with subtler theological tastes fail to discern beauty's theological and trinitarian profile across the text.

I too have admired beauty in the *Summa*. But I admire its beauty theologically—as a teaching about God's beauty and ours. My proposal, the one this book defended, holds that Brother Alexander thinks beauty trinitarianly. Or does he think the trinity aesthetically? Either way, the *Summa Halensis* grounds beauty in the structure of the trinity. Alexander says exactly this: *pulcritudo in divinis ex ordine sacro divinarum personarum.*[3] Beauty, that is to say, just is the order of the persons.

There follow by entailment two concomitants to this claim: first, that beauty hews to the logic of perichoresis. This idea pushes thought about beauty fast and far away from thought about divine attributes. For Alexander beauty is unlike the transcendentals one, good, or true. It names not an attribute of the divine essence, but rather a mode of relation. So it goes, too, in creation. Alexander constantly and consistently depicts beauty in creatures as a *vestigium trinitatis*—as a triplet of some kind or another. A second concomitant sharpens this one. It requires that beauty obey not just perichoretic logic but perichoretic logic of a particular order. Beauty's order, then, reflects trinity's taxis: *qua una persona non ab alia, a qua alia per generationem, a quibus tertia per processionem.*

Why have Alexander's claim and its entailments eluded so many of his readers? Part I attempted diagnosis and correction. Chapter 1 presents Brother Alexander's peculiarly trinitarian preoccupation within his doctrine of the transcendentals. Chapter 2 shows that Alexander's account of the transcendentals betrays not just a "trinitarian motive" but even trinitarian theology proper. The transcendentals, that is—one, true, and good—form trinitarian appropriations. For Alexander, speaking the transcendentals already means speaking trinity.

Chapter 3 extends this argument to beauty. Beauty does not number among Alexander's transcendentals. But this exclusion scarcely renders it epiphenomenal. Instead, and because it names the trinitarian order, beauty describes the way in which the transcendentals interpenetrate one another. If beauty is not one among the transcendentals, it does name their order. Moreover, the transcendental question is not the only or even the most interesting one to pose to beauty in the *Summa*. Its correlation of beauty to *congruentia compositionis partium*—whose archetype is the *ordo sacer divinarum personarum*—awakens still deeper questions. Brother Alexander flags some: about *pulcritudo animarum*, for instance.

Parts II and III consider these and other questions. Responsive to Alexander's own canon for beauty, chapter 4 reroutes my study. We began again, then, with the trinity. There and after brief comment on personal properties, I focus attention on the how "order" forms a lodestone around which all things trinitarian orbit. Order magnetically attracts and disciplines thought about the trinity in three ways. First, order for Alexander is always conditioned by origin—order is always an *ordo originis*. Second and concomitantly, order follows a particular and filioquist sequence. And third this trinitarian order establishes divine order itself: without it God is disorder. Alexander concludes that the trinity's plurality of persons is "most beautiful and most ordered."[4] And if this is God's order, it is also God's beauty.

In creation the trinity diffuses divine order.[5] Chapter 5 traces creation's order back to the trinitarian processions. And because the cause remains in its effect, trinity inscribes its order (and so beauty) into creation. Detailing the style signature of the trinity upon creatures produces Alexander's doctrine of the *vestigia trinitatis* and their kinds. Much of this, I show, underwrites Alexander's extended speculations *de pulchritudine creati*, on the beauty of creation. Highest among the trinity's traces, however, is the human person. So chapter 6 lingers over *pulcritudo animarum*—the beauty of (human) souls. Alexander thinks their beauty imitates the trinity's more than any other triplet, not least because rational souls evince a peculiarly trinitarian order. Remembering, understanding, willing—these powers perform and reveal the order of the trinitarian life. Articulating just how the soul's trinity of powers imitates the *trinitas quae deus est* engages the collective efforts of early Franciscan psychology. The Franciscan solution eventually features across the *Summa*, where Brother Alexander ornaments it with his trinitarian aesthetics.

So far, so schematic. Chapter 7 embeds Alexander's theology of beauty into salvation history. The effect is striking. Brother Alexander depicts sin as *disorder*, a palimpsest that attempts erasure of the soul's *imago trinitatis*. Its restoration comes only when the trinity interrupts history in the incarnation. In the incarnation the trinity donates its native graces to the church. Created grace, then—that which orders the soul and assimilates it to the trinity[6]—describes both a trinitarian process and its correlate effect. Alexander narrates grace's work as a making trinitarian, a progressive assimilation to Father, Son, and Spirit. The result of grace's work is, *inter alia*, shared delight. *In ratione fructus* the saint delights in the trinity's personal presence. And the trinity in turn enjoys the saint, in whose renewed *imago trinitatis* God revels. For Alexander salvation itself consists in becoming trinitarian. And what is this but becoming beautiful?

Such anyway is the structure of this book's proposal. The basic contention it tests and defends and refines is, however, much simpler: that beauty has something to do with the trinity and that neither proves finally insignificant or epiphenomenal to the *Summa*. I present this not as the correct or only view on beauty Alexander's readers must hold. I submit it only as one that Alexander's readers have not yet (so far as I can tell) entertained. But they should: I entertain it myself above, taking it to have interpretive advantages over its alternatives.

Like all argument, mine is not without its difficulties. In celebration of scholastic disputation and *in imitatione fratris Alexandri*, I close by voicing and responding to some of them.

1. *Your argument traces beauty across different topics in the* Summa
   Halensis. *But on your own confession, Alexander rarely uses*
   pulchritudo *or its like to describe the soul or grace. At best your
   aesthetic interpretation of psychology or soteriology courts anachronism.
   At worst it indulges an aesthetic rage with Balthasarian abandon.*

Conceditur: *pulcritudo* and its like do not feature everywhere across the *Summa*.[7] Neither does the language of *circumincessio*. Alexander's long section on grace, for example, runs without mention of either term. But we should not confuse the absence of a word for the absence of its logic. After all, Alexander's teaching on the trinity lacks the term *circumincessio* too. Does it therefore lack its logic? My argument allows Brother Alexander to unsettle and reconstruct expectations of what theologies of beauty ought to entail. He associates beauty principally with *trinitas* and *ordo*, and not (as we might) with the definition and analysis of artistic production. So the very objection betrays a presumption against deriving the meaning of concepts from their rhetorical performance within the text. Presuming a theory of aesthetics, smuggling a lexicon proper to it, and then ruling out my interpretation by that rubric—surely this indulges a deeper anachronism. It is better, on my view, to try (even to fail) to trace Brother Alexander's own patterns of thought on beauty.

As to the aesthetic rage, I agree that it often possesses a thinker like Balthasar to steamroll subtleties and blunt finer points. I agree too that in his paragraph on the *Summa*,[8] Balthasar applies too heavy an interpretive hand; his Thomist pieties are too strong, and his Christic framework is too comprehensive. But whatever Balthasar's foibles as a historian (and they are many), he reads the *Summa* as a theologian. True, my more historical rendering of the *Summa* sometimes amends Balthasar's more constructive take. Even so, I present my reading to theologians like him—to adopt if helpful, to adapt or ignore if not.

> 2. *You claim that Brother Alexander construes beauty differently than other scholastics did. It is clear enough that most conceive beauty as a divine attribute—as a description, that is, proper to the divine essence. But then you never proffer an alternative definition of "beauty." If Alexander's account is different, what exactly is it?*

Yes, beauty escapes definition in the *Summa Halensis*. Neither of Brother Alexander's two descriptions are definitions proper. The first associates beauty with a "harmony of the composition of parts" (*congruentia compositionis partium*).[9] In God this harmony identifies the *ordo sacer divinarum personarum*, the sacred order of the divine persons. A second and more subjective description names beauty a *dispositio boni secundum quod est placitum apprehensioni*, a disposition of the good that pleases apprehension.[10] Neither of these forms a definition—not on a strict Aristotelian view, anyway. On that view, defining a thing means identifying its genus and specific difference.[11] I define a human being as an animal (genus) with reason (difference). And so on. Obviously the *ordo sacer divinarum personarum* neither bears nor is a genus. It denotes mode or relation, not nature. The second description fares little better. There Brother Alexander teaches not that something is beautiful *if* it pleases. Quite the opposite: something pleases exactly *because* it is beautiful.[12] So this description does not stipulate beauty's subjective condition so much as it determines beauty from its proper effect. At best, then, this second description yields a definition *per posteriora*. Or, as Alexander has it, a definition *per positionem effectus consequentis*.[13] It "defines" only how beauty appears to souls, not what beauty is. Alexander takes care here not to confuse the order of seeming with the order of being. His readers should too.

If the *Summa*'s trinitarian line on beauty compounds the problem, it hardly invents it. Precise definition will elude even transcendentalists on the beauty question. It must: *primae ergo intentiones*, Alexander writes, *non erunt definibiles per priora*.[14] For Alexander transcendentals necessarily exceed genus and difference. That, after all, is what they "transcend." I should add here that beauty's lack of definition is something of a scholastic epidemic. To the extent that other scholastics also think beauty somehow transcendental, they too deny it proper definition.[15]

So no, I do not proffer an alternative definition of beauty. But I do not because Alexander denies that one is possible. What is, however, is an alternative pattern of thought on beauty. And that is what I have attempted to sketch here.

3. *Your argument claims that Brother Alexander's theology of beauty is "peculiar." But you fail to show how it is unique among scholastics. And you say almost nothing about how Alexander's aesthetics is received. How can you assert its peculiarity?*

I use "peculiar" advisedly. To claim a teaching is "unique" among scholastics is nearly always reckless and indefensible. Defending a claim like that would mean poring over thousands of volumes. It would also mean consulting many more manuscripts that await editing—perhaps even discovery. By deeming Brother Alexander's theology of beauty "peculiar," I mean only that it is so relative to theories more commonly held among scholastics. Albert the Great, for instance, rejects Alexander's way as incompatible with divine simplicity.[16] Other scholastics like Thomas largely agree—to say nothing of Plato and Plotinus and Proclus and Augustine and Boethius and Dionysius before them. Among these, then, Brother Alexander's perichoretic line on beauty appears peculiar.

Not that other scholastics do not know Alexander's way. Albert knows enough about it to chart another. His profligate borrowings from the *Summa* in general and on beauty in particular have not run unnoticed.[17] And through Albert's instruction, Brother Alexander's aesthetics reaches others—Thomas Aquinas and Ulrich of Strasburg, for instance.[18] Bonaventure also knows and uses Alexander,[19] as does Bonaventure's brood.[20] Even Scotus's aesthetics cuts a "remarkable similarity" to Alexander's.[21] Less predictable but more interesting still is Alexander's return in the fifteenth-century aesthetics of Denys the Carthusian.[22] But none, so far as I can tell, endorses *in toto* the trinitarian line on beauty here traced.

Still, these judgments about peculiarity and influence remain incomplete, provisional, and suggestive. Their function here aims at titillation rather than demonstration. Substantiating them falls wide of this study, but it also roughs out further research.

> 4. *Your argument does not adequately address the difference between uncreated and created beauty. If beauty in the trinity is "the sacred order" of the persons, then what exactly accounts for creaturely beauty? Triplets in creatures may mirror trinitarian order. But they do not possess it as theirs.*

This is a deep and important objection. Indeed, its force can be strengthened. Let me explain. Alexander is clear enough about the infinite interval that yawns between God and creation—they are "maximally distant."[23] So distant, in fact, that between them there passes neither likeness nor fittingness.[24] Alexander is clear too that there exists no univocal predication between God and creatures. God talk, he insists, labors strictly "according to analogy" (*secundum analogiam*). Taken together, these points typify a doctrine of participation—a logic Alexander explicitly promotes. "The good," he writes, "is said of God by nature and of the creature by participation."[25] This proposition reclines comfortably within a broadly Platonist horizon whose law is participation.

I mean, that is, that Alexander always and everywhere obeys Dionysius's law that "there is no strict likeness (ἀκριβὴς ἐμφέρεια) between the caused and the causes." There cannot be, not if "the causes in themselves remain separate and established above the effects *according to the principle of their own origin.*[26] Of course the trouble here is modal. If God in God's mode both causes and just *is* good, creatures in their mode only participate it. Such is the logic of participation, which regulates Alexander's thinking on transcendentals as divine attributes. Creatures share *per participationem* whatever God is *per naturam.*

Here Alexander's trinitarian line on beauty introduces a special puzzle. For Alexander the *ordo sacer divinarum personarum* identifies a structure or relation. Beauty is not, then, an attribute or perfection of an essence. Were beauty like that, creatures could share divine beauty as they do the divine one, true, or good—that is, *per participationem.* But can a "sacred order" be participated? Do perichoretic relations admit of degrees? What would it mean to say so?

Perhaps Alexander's gradations of *vestigia trinitatis* attempt to meet this challenge. That is the Augustinian strategy of *De trinitate*: limn the rational soul as asymptotically approximating but never quite attaining the trinity's *ordo.* Other, lesser creatures do not and cannot do this precisely because they lack remembering, understanding, and loving. It is just this lack, in fact, that makes them other and lesser in the first place. But if this is Alexander's answer, then why does he not apply it consistently? In *SH* I, Alexander insists that a creature's beauty is determined by mode-form-order.[27] But then the rational soul, most resplendent among creation's beauties,[28] is in *SH* I–II only *imago trinitatis* because of its triple powers of remembering, understanding, and willing. How do these triplets relate? And why does *SH* III not explain how the transition from *imago* to *similitudo*, involving grace's tripled triplet of activity, relates to either mode-form-order or remembering-understanding-loving?

Let us assume the process of justification (*processus iustificationis*) arranges steps toward deeper intimacy with the trinity. Each step would comprise a triplet that relates more integrally, more intimately, and more circumcessively than the last. This seems to capture Alexander's thinking. Why else would he work to show how grace's process mimics the trinitarian processions? Even so, the highest grade would not achieve "sacred order." It could not—not if perfect, circumcessive union is limited to God the trinity. If Alexander assumes it is, it is far from clear that we should too.[29] Still it follows necessarily for him that nothing but God is really and truly beautiful.

Alexander's assumption raises two more difficulties. The first is the strict limitation of perichoresis to the divine nature without remainder. Other Christian theologians—the Cappadocians, Maximus, John of Damascus—extended perichoretic logic to the incarnation. On this view perichoresis is not just *of* a nature *between* persons (God's) but also *of* a person *between* natures (God's and the human's).[30] By assertion rather than argument, Alexander forbids thought from moving in this direction. Because he does, he cannot allow created natures perfect perichoresis. This belongs to the *sancti trinity* only, and to us—somehow—by participation.

A second difficulty: Why should thought about beauty move along a trinitarian track at all? If at length the trinity's creatures mirror divine beauty by participation, then why ground beauty in trinitarian order at all? Why not—like Plotinus and Dionysius and Albert and Thomas—simply and cleanly class beauty as an attribute of the divine nature? If indeed beauty here below lies in the relative perichoresis of the powers of a *nature*, then Alexander's trinitarian preoccupation seems an ornamental rather than a lode-bearing feature of his thought. Might Brother Alexander end up refitting boilerplate Christian-Platonist aesthetics with trinitarian accents? If so, do these accents distort what Alexander means them to adorn?

These are large and difficult questions. They are also ones Alexander's texts do not answer, at least on my reading. So I sharpen rather than meet them, if only because their solutions appear to me now dim and blurred—a silhouette whose face I cannot yet make out. It is true that a recursive exegetical tangle does not by necessity rule out a systematic solution. In many cases it even births one. Still, I leave that task to theologians whose constructive lights outshine mine.

5. *You say you intend your historical interpretation for theological use. What difference does Brother Alexander's trinitarian teaching on beauty make theologically?*

I do not claim that excavating the *Summa*'s theology of beauty will (or should) reorient the field of theological aesthetics.[31] Still, Brother Alexander's peculiar line on beauty as trinitarian order may succor several workers in the (increasingly ecumenical) field. Let me note just two such labors.

One set of readers worries at a broadly scholastic theology of beauty undisciplined by Christian dogma. Robert Jenson claims that beauty is not the "dispositional property" of God but rather the "living exchange between

Father, Son, and Spirit...the sheer perichoresis...their communal music...God is a great *fugue*."[32] Stephen John Wright argues that theologies of beauty ought to be "more directed by doctrine than by antecedent metaphysical theories like the *analogia entis*."[33] And Katherine Sonderegger worries about reducing biblical names like beauty to "abstract honorifics."[34] Brother Alexander rather agrees. Indeed, the *Summa* yields not only a theology of *beauty* that is amenable to post-Barthian concerns about the *analogia entis*. As I argue in chapter 1, its very doctrine of being—God's and ours—is conditioned by trinitarian commitments. Readers who prefer Barth's *analogia fidei* to Przywara's (or Balthasar's) *analogia entis* will find that not *all* Western theologies of beauty remain innocent of Christian dogmatics.

Other readers worry that theologies of beauty have overlooked the Spirit. For example: against the Augustinian tradition of appropriating beauty to the Son, the Orthodox theologian Sergei Bulgakov follows Cyril of Alexandria in naming *the Spirit* as God's beauty.[35] Concern for the Spirit's eclipse is shared by Patrick Sherry and foregrounds pneumatic beauty in the work of Protestants like John Calvin and Jonathan Edwards.[36] From an ecumenical angle of vision, then, Balthasar's *ressourcement* may not resource enough. Doubtless the *SH* is deeply Augustinian. But its stress *ad intra* on the Spirit as *completio trinitatis* and *ad extra* on the Spirit's presence to us in grace making pleasing charts a path for thinking beauty beyond appropriation to the Son as image.

6. *Your argument deals in aesthetics. But it is flimsy exactly to the extent that you do not address a central feature of aesthetics: the experience of beauty.*

It is true that I have lavished asymmetrical attention on beauty's objective features. It is equally true that medievals were, by disposition or habit, fiercely interested in aesthetic experience. Brother Alexander is no exception. I have here read the *Summa* mostly aslant its teachings on aesthetic experience. But I have done so only to balance the scales, which at present skew heavily to one side. Most prominent and influential studies of beauty across the *Summa* regard aesthetic experience with disproportionate intensity.[37] And because attention is—here below anyway—zero-sum, attention to the subjective means inattention to the objective.

That my argument seeks equipoise need not excuse its near silence over aesthetic experience. Several lines of thought traced above open upon properly subjective questions. How, for example, does my final point on the trinitarian missions as shared delight (*fructus*) relate to Brother Alexander's teachings on pleasure? Do these apply to God, who seems also to delight? Are humans uniquely aesthetic animals? How might Alexander's thinking on the universal desire for trinitarian beauty illumine questions about the natural desire for God? And what might all this have to do with the highly affective inflection of Halensian theology? I have not answered or even entertained these questions here. For that I can only apologize and pledge further study as remit.

ACKNOWLEDGMENTS

If writing accrues debts, recording them is a joy. Sketches of the pages here gathered first appeared as a dissertation at Boston College. Among those who commented drafts or instructed errors or otherwise shaped the pages that follow are Boyd Taylor Coolman, Franklin T. Harkins, Philipp W. Rosemann, Stephen F. Brown, Jean-Luc Solère, Katherine Wrisley Shelby, Ty Paul Monroe, Fr. Liam Bergin, Lydia Schumacher, Aaron Gies, Vincent Strand, SJ, and Jordan Daniel Wood (*socius meus in scelere*). Fr. David Courtier at the Franciscan Institute gifted grants that took me to Rome and improved the work here. It was improved still more by Will Cerbonne and his team at Fordham University Press. I wear the debts owed my two readers—Mark D. Jordan and Mary Beth Ingham, CSJ, who lifted anonymity's veil—like honors, as both are heroes of mine. Whatever errors linger still in what follows, the above have spared me from committing innumerably more.

Others neither commented nor read the draft. Instead they have rendered a life beyond its pages possible. Among these are my parents, my in-laws, my sister and her husband and their children, my grandmother Kokkeler, my grandparents Coyle, the Woods, the Monroes, the Nelsons, the Coolmans, the Timpane-Rosses, the Marnuls, the Pappases, Austin Wilson and Jessina Leonard, and Fr. Richard Janowicz, my брати in formation for the St. Nicholas Eparchy. I owe my most recent debts to my colleagues, students, and monastics at Mount Angel Abbey and Seminary. Among them I single out Shawn Keough, Dcn. Owen Cummings, Liam de Los Reyes, and Abbot Jeremy Driscoll.

Still others have positively hindered writing. Even so, a single one of their many intrusions upon the writing of this book remains dearer to me than all of its pages. To these I owe the deepest debt: Finnegan Francis, Killian Townes, and Saoirse Reverie. And to my Megan—what can be said in public?

My final debt is due the LORD and his Church, who have no need of it and whose beauty it attempts and fails to speak.

Chapter 2 appeared in a different form as "Beauty among the Transcendentals in the *Summa Halensis*" in *Nova et Vetera* 18, no. 3 (2020): 875–907. A summary of portions of chapter 7 appeared as "Sin as Antitrinitarian Palimpsest in the *Summa Halensis*" in *Franciscan Connections: The Cord; A Spiritual Review* 68, no. 4 (2018): 22–27.

NOTES

FOREWORD

1. Friedrich Nietzsche, *The Gay Science*, ed. Bernard Williams, trans. Josefine Nauckhoff (Cambridge: Cambridge University Press, 2001), 119–20. Translation slightly revised.

2. As an example, I mention the pioneering study by Eugen Biser, *"Gott ist tot." Nietzsches Destruktion des christlichen Bewußtseins* (Munich: Kösel, 1962).

3. Friedrich Nietzsche, *Thus Spake Zarathustra*, trans. Thomas Common (New York: The Modern Library, 1917), 27 (Zarathustra's Prologue). Thomas Common's translation captures Nietzsche's Lutherizing German beautifully.

INTRODUCTION

1. For Alexander's biography, see Kenan B. Osborne, "Alexander of Hales: Precursor and Promoter of Franciscan Theology," *The History of Franciscan Theology*, ed. Kenan B. Osborne (St. Bonaventure: The Franciscan Institute, 1994), 1–38.

2. For a history of commenting on the Lombard across the thirteenth century, see especially the second chapter of Philipp W. Rosemann, *The Story of a Great Medieval Book: Peter Lombard's 'Sentences'* (Toronto: University of Toronto Press, 2007).

3. I comment more on the authorship question below. On the Franciscan context of the *Summa Halensis*, see the excellent summaries in Lydia Schumacher, *Early Franciscan Theology: Between Authority and Innovation* (Cambridge: Cambridge University Press, 2019), 1–54 and Ayelet Even-Ezra, "The *Summa halensis*: A Text in Context" in *The Summa Halensis: Sources and Context*, ed. Lydia Schumacher (Berlin: De Gruyter, 2020), 219–234.

4. Latin text of Alexander IV's *De fontibus paradisi* taken from the prolegomena to *Summa Halensis* I, ed. PP. Collegii S. Bonaventurae (Florence: Quaracchi, 1924–1948), vii–viii. English translation by Robert Prentice, "The 'De Fontibus Paradisi' of Alexander IV on the 'Summa Theologica' of Alexander of Hales'" in *Franciscan Studies* 5.4 (1945): 349–351.

5. SH I, n. 103 (1: 163): *"Ad secundum dicendum quod illud Augustini definit pulcritudinem visibilem sive corporalem; tamen dicitur de pulcritudine corporali sensibili, in quantum ducit ad intelligibilem sive spiritualem. Sicut enim "pulcritudo corporum est ex congruentia compositionis partium", ita pulcritudo animarum ex convenientia virium et ordinatione potentiarum, et pulcritudo in divinis ex ordine sacro divinarum personarum, qua una persona non ab alia, a qua alia per generationem, a quibus tertia per processionem."* All Latin from the *Summa Halensis* comes from the Quaracchi edition; all English translations are my own. This book went to press before it could make use of the felicitous, select translations in Oleg Bychkov's

and Lydia Schumacher's *A Reader in Early Franciscan Theology: The* Summa Halensis (New York: Fordham University Press, 2022).

6. Edgar de Bruyne, "Les premiers scolastiques" in *Études d'esthétique médiévale III: Le xiii siècle* (Bruges: De Tempel, 1946), 90–91.

7. I include all relevant studies on the *SH* in my bibliography. See, though, the wonderful spread of topics across the very recent *The Summa Halensis: Doctrines and Debates*, ed. Lydia Schumacher (Berlin: De Gruyter, 2020). Still, even here beauty is conspicuously absent.

8. This is especially true of Umberto Eco, "Transcendental Beauty" in *Art and Beauty in the Middle Ages* (New Haven: Yale University Press, 1986), 17–27 and "Beauty as a Transcendental" in *The Aesthetics of Thomas Aquinas*, trans. Hugh Bredin (Cambridge, MA: Harvard University Press, 1988), 20–48.

9. See Henri Pouillon, "La beauté, propriété transcendentale chez les scolastiques (1220–1270)," *Archives d'histoire doctrinale et littéraire du Moyen Age* (Paris: Librairie Philosophique J. Vrin, 1946), 263–314; de Bruyne, *Études d'esthétique*; and Władysław Tatarkiewicz, *History of Aesthetics: Volume 2: Medieval Aesthetics*, trans. R. M. Montgomery, ed. C. Barrett (Bristol: Thoemmes Press, 1970). It is no surprise that his narrow reading leads de Bruyne to concludes that "on espère peut-être qu'on se trouvera en présence d'un esthéticien mais on est vite détrompé" in his "Les premiers scolastiques," 88.

10. I think here of Hans Urs von Balthasar, *The Glory of the Lord IV: The Realm of Metaphysics in Antiquity* (San Francisco: Ignatius Press, 1989), 372–392; David Bentley Hart, *The Beauty of the Infinite: The Aesthetics of Christian Truth* (Grand Rapids: Wm. B. Eerdmans, 2004), 252; and Elisabeth Gössmann, *Metaphysik und Heilsgeschichte: Eine theologische Untersuchung der Summa Halensis* (Munich: Max Hueber Verlag, 1964), 193–196. Best, however, is the tireless work of Jan Aertsen. In chronological order, his texts that treat beauty in the *SH* are: "Beauty in the Middle Ages: A Forgotten Transcendental?" *Medieval Philosophy and Theology* 1 (1991): 68–97; "Die Frage nach der Tranzendentalität der Schönheit im Mittelalter" in vol. 1 of *Historia philosophiae medii aevi: Studien zur Geschichte der Philosophie des Mittelalters*, ed. Burkhard Mojsisch and Olaf Pluta (Amsterdam: B.R. Grüner, 1991), 1–22; "Schöne (das), II. Mittelalter" in *Historisches Wörterbuch der Philosophie*, ed. Joachim Ritter and Karlfried Gründer 8 (Basel: Schwabe and Co, 1992), 1351–1358; "The Concept of 'Transcendens' in the Middle Ages: What is Beyond and What is Common" in *Platonic Ideas and Concept Formation in Ancient and Medieval Thought*, ed. G. Van Riel and Caroline Macé (Leuven: Leuven University Press, 2004), 133–153; "Beauty: A forgotten transcendental?" in *Medieval Philosophy and the Transcendentals: The Case of Thomas Aquinas* (Boston/Leiden: Brill Publishers, 1996), 335–359; "The Triad 'True-Good-Beautiful:' The Place of Beauty in the Middle Ages" in *Intellect et imagination dans la philosophie médiévale*, ed. M. C. Pacheco (Turnhout: Brepols, 2006), 415–435; *Medieval Philosophy as Transcendental Thought: From Philip the Chancellor (ca. 1225) to Francisco Suárez* (Boston/Leiden: Brill Publishers, 2012).

11. Instructive here is Pouillon's judgment after reading the transcendental treatise that "Voilà tout ce que l'on trouve sur la beauté dans la première partie de la Summa fratris Alexandri" in "La beauté," 276.

12. Unparalleled is Oleg Bychkov, "A Propos of Medieval Aesthetics: A Historical Study of Terminology, Sources, and Textual Traditions of Commenting on Beauty in the Thirteenth Century" (PhD dissertation, University of Toronto, 1999). If it offers a meticulous analytic of various thirteenth-century masters on beauty, he does not speak the difference the trinity makes for the *SH*. Bychkov seems mostly to think of scholastic aesthetics as an ideal form with multiple instantiations, individuated one from another only *accidentaliter*. He highlights several differences, however, among scholastic theories of beauty in his "The Reflection of Some Traditional Stoic Ideas in the Thirteenth-Century Scholastic Theories of Beauty" in *Vivarium* 34.2 (1996): 141–160 and "Decor ex praesentia mali: Aesthetic Explanation of Evil in the Thirteenth-Century Franciscan Thought" in *Recherches de théologie et philosophie médiévales* 68, no. 2 (2001): 245–269. Curiously, neither of Bychkov's otherwise excellent articles on the trinity and aesthetics treat the *SH:* "What Does Beauty Have to Do with the Trinity? From Augustine to Duns Scotus" in *Franciscan Studies* 66 (2008): 197–212 and "The Beauty of the Trinity: Theological Aesthetics from Augustine to Duns Scotus," *The Opera Theologica of John Duns Scotus*, Archa Verbi Subsidia 4 (Münster: Aschendorff, 2012), 21–34. Also relevant is his "Bonaventure and the Late Medieval Tradition" in *Aesthetic Revelation: Reading Ancient and Medieval Texts after Hans Urs von Balthasar* (Washington DC: Catholic University of America, 2010), 268–322. His recent "Suspended Beauty? The Mystery of Aesthetic Experience in the *Summa Halensis*" in *The Legacy of Early Franciscan Thought*, ed. Lydia Schumacher (Berlin, Boston: De Gruyter, 2021), 111–128 mostly summarizes his dissertation. However different its reading, this book remains deeply indebted to Bychkov's scrupulous work.

13. Zachary Hayes, "Review of *Metaphysik und Heilsgeschichte: Eine theologische Untersuchung der Summa Halensis* by Elisabeth Gössmann" in *Speculum* 41, no. 1 (1966): 135.

14. With one or two exceptions, I largely share Schumacher's judgment that "although this Summa inevitably bears the marks of multiple authors . . . it nonetheless presents a coherent intellectual vision. . . . I myself have not been able to detect any substantial contradictions within its pages." Schumacher, *Early Franciscan Theology*, 8. See also Étienne Gilson, *History of Christian Philosophy in the Middle Ages* (New York: Random House, 1955), 327.

15. See my conclusion for textual references.

16. Andreas Speer, "Aesthetics" in *The Oxford Handbook of Medieval Philosophy* (New York: Oxford University Press, 2012), 669. Speer discusses Thomas Aquinas, but his claim is equally true of other scholastics.

17. Ludwig Wittgenstein, *Lectures on Aesthetics* 1.5–2 in *Lectures and Conversations on Aesthetics, Psychology, and Religious Belief*, ed. Cyril Barrett (Berkeley: University of California Press, 1967), 1.

18. Not that I here pretend to a sterile objectivity—quite the opposite. I confess at the outset that this book commits a double distortion. The first follows from the nearly 800 years that yawn between the *Summa*'s composition and my reading of it. If that past is lost, the reading of the *Summa* I offer is no doubt its partial rewriting. The second distortion follows from my narrow hermeneutical focus on beauty, which doubtless mutes other themes. Neither distortion bothers me much because neither can be helped. Not all distortion blinds, after all. A fisheye lens obscures the edges of a frame in order to draw attention to the center of the shot. And a city map straightens irregularities by restyling distances along grids that we might more easily find our way. Were it not for such distortions, our gaze would not focus where it ought. Or else we should not find our way around. An image or a map, if crude analogies be allowed, is very like what this book means to offer. I want here to draw attention to the patterns of theological beauty across the *Summa Halensis*—to map them, to understand, exposit, and wonder about their relation. And this means rewriting them.

19. *SH* I–II, n. 77 (2: 100): "Ipse ordo est pulcher."

20. For a thorough study on the authorship problem and its historiography, see Doucet's *Prolegomena* (1951), lix–lxxxi. These findings are summarized in Doucet's "The History of the Problem of the Authenticity of the Summa," *Franciscan Studies* 7 (1947): 26–41; 274–312. See also Schumacher, *Early Franciscan Theology*, 1–29.

21. Mathieu-Maxime Gorce, "La Somme théologique d'Alexandre de Halès est-elle authentique?" *The New Scholasticism* 5.1 (1931): 1–72, reprinted in his *L'essor de la pensée au moyen âge: Albert le Grand, Thomas d'Aquin* (Paris: Lib. Letouzey et Ané, 1933). Gorce attributes his findings to Pierre Mandonnet, such that Doucet often refers to both as "Gorce-Mandonnet."

22. Victorin Doucet, "The History of the Problem of the Authenticity of the Summa," *Franciscan Studies* 7 (1947): 310. For the story behind the *Summa*'s editing at Quaracchi, see Ignatius C. Brady's "The 'Summa theologica' of Alexander of Hales (1924–1948)," *Archivum franciscanum* 70.3–4 (1977): 437–447.

23. Doucet, *Prolegomena* (1951), ccclxix: "*Ipse Alexander quodammodo Summam fecit (critica externa), sed collaborantibus aliis (critica interna); item, ex propriis maxime scriptis, sed etiam ex alienis. Quare et authentica et halensiana quodammodo Summa dici potest, not autem simpliciter.*"

24. Schumacher is almost certainly right that the specter of authorial ambiguity and the difficulties of exorcising it have frightened readers away from the *Summa* (see her *Early Franciscan Theology*, 9). Indeed, Doucet may have even inadvertently contributed to this anxiety by claiming that the authorship puzzle formed the question "on which the whole doctrinal opinion of the thirteenth-century depends" in his "The History of the Problem," 38.

25. Both models are found across the two volumes edited by Lydia Schumacher.

26. J. S. Brewer, *Fr. Rogeri Bacon Opera hactenus inedita* I (London: Longman, Green, Longman, and Roberts, 1859), 326.

27. For an excellent theological defense of pseudepigrapha, plagiarism, and other standard practices of premodernity, see Paul J. Griffiths, "Kidnapping," in *Intellectual Appetite: A Theological Grammar* (Washington DC: The Catholic University of America Press, 2009), 163–186.

28. Lesley Smith, "Hugh of St. Cher and Medieval Collaboration," in *Transforming Relations: Essays on Jews and Christians throughout History in Honor of Michael A. Signer*, ed. Franklin T. Harkins (Notre Dame: University of Notre Dame Press, 2010), 255.

29. Smith, "Hugh of St. Cher," 258.

30. This is not to disparage readings of the *SH* with historical or paleographic interest. Theological readings like mine depend upon these others. I mean here only to affirm a dialectic between history and theology. These pressures, I take it, are productive for both disciplines. Still, I leave the historical tasks for those with training and interest of which I am not possessed.

31. *SH* I, n. 15 (1:25). As Bychkov notes in his "Suspended Beauty?," 124, the *SH* "often exhibits such ways of [aesthetic] reasoning as opposed to logical deduction. In fact, the Prologue . . . states clearly that theology is an emotional discipline that proceeds not by way of logical deduction but by way of 'taste'."

32. Simon Maria Kopf and Lydia Schumacher, "A Guide to Citing the *Summa Halensis*" in *The Summa Halensis: Sources and Context*, x.

1. TRANSCENDENTALS AND TRINITY

1. Khaled Anatolios, *Retrieving Nicaea: The Development and Meaning of Trinitarian Doctrine* (Grand Rapids: Baker Academic, 2011), 8.

2. Bruce Marshall, *Trinity and Truth* (New York: Cambridge University Press, 2004), 47.

3. Gössman, *MH* and Aertsen's *Medieval Philosophy*, 147.

4. Boyd Taylor Coolman, "'A Cord of Three Strands is Not Easily Broken: The Transcendental Brocade of Unity, Truth, and Goodness in the Early Franciscan Intellectual Tradition," *Nova et Vetera* 16.2 (2018): 564.

5. Aertsen, *Medieval Philosophy*, 135–176. Cf. Johann Fuchs, *Die proprietäten des seins bei Alexander von Hales* (Munich: Salensianischen Offizin, 1930).

6. As Aertsen discerns, Fuchs reads Scotus's transcendental thought into the *SH*. See his *Die Proprietäten des Seins*, 133–144. Cf. Allan B. Wolter's *The Transcendentals and Their Function in the Metaphysics of Duns Scotus* (Washington DC: The Catholic University of America Press, 1946). See also Gössmann, *MH*, 338.

7. *SH* I, n. 3 (1: 6).

8. *SH* I, n. 3 (1: 7): "*Ens secundum omnem sui differentiam . . . secundum differentes divisiones entis.*"

9. Aristotle, *Analytica Posteriora* 1.28.87b (LCL 391: 155). Or, as *SH* I, n. 1 (1: 4) renders *Analytica Posteriora* 1.10 (76b): "*Omnis scientia est alicuius generis subiecti, cuius partes et passiones per se considerat, sicut dicit Philosophus.*"

10. *De anima* 1.1.402b (LCL 288: 13).

11. *SH* I, nn. 11–12 (1: 20–22).

12. Gössmann, *MH*, 23.

13. *SH* I, n. 3 (1: 6).

14. *SH* I, n. 1 (1: 2).

15. There has been a recent spark of interest in the *SH* on the nature of theology. See Lydia Schumacher, "Theology as a Science in the *Summa minorum*," *Medioevo Romanzo* (2015): 367–384; Boyd Taylor Coolman, "On the Subject-Matter of Theology in the *Summa halensis* and St. Thomas Aquinas," *The Thomist* 79, no. 3 (2015): 439–466; Gregory F. LaNave, "'A Particularly Agitated Topic': Aquinas and the Franciscans on the Subject of Theology in the Mid-Thirteenth Century," *The Thomist* 79, no. 3 (2015): 467–491; Boyd Taylor Coolman, "Hugh of St. Victor's Influence on the Halensian Definition of Theology" in *Franciscan Studies* 70 (2012): 367–384; and Oleg Bychkov, "The Nature of Theology in Duns Scotus and his Franciscan Predecessors," *Franciscan Studies* 66 (2008): 5–62.

16. Gössmann, *MH*, 12; 25.

17. *SH* I, n. 72 (1: 112).

18. Aertsen, *Medieval Philosophy*, 147.

19. *SH* I–II, n. 8 (2: 17).

20. *SH* I, n. 21 (1: 31). The logic here is Aristotelian; see *Topica* 1.17.108a (LCL 391: 323). It is exactly this form of likeness—one that follows from generic identity—that the *Summa*'s denies between God and creatures. This is because being is not a genus, as Aristotle states in *Analytica Posteriora* (92b14) and *Metaphysica* B.3 (998b22).

21. *SH* I, n. 21 (1: 32).

22. See *Analytica Posteriora* 2.7 (92b) and *Metaphysica* 3.3 (998b).

23. Though Philip the Chancellor uses this language (*SDB* I, q. 3, ad 2), its source is likely Avicenna's *The Book of Healing* 1.5.21, translated in *The Metaphysics of the Healing: A Parallel English-Arabic Text =Al-Ilahīyāt Min Al-Shifā'* by Michael E. Marmura (Provo: Brigham Young University Press, 2005), 34–35.

24. Michael J. Rubin, "The Meaning of 'Beauty' and Its Transcendental Status in the Metaphysics of Thomas Aquinas" (PhD dissertation, The Catholic University of America, 2016), 5–6.

25. Philip the Chancellor, *SDB* q. 3, ad 2 (1: 19). All references to the *SDB* are drawn from *Cancellarii Summa de bono*, edited by Niklaus Wicki (Berne: Francke, 1985). See also Aertsen, *Medieval Philosophy*, 128.

26. Neither does the *SH* cite *convenientia* as the Arab philosophical tradition had used it, particularly Algazel's *Logica*. Cf. Aertsen, *Medieval Philosophy*, 98.

27. Aertsen, *Medieval Philosophy*, 138.

28. Note where the analogy breaks: accidents borrow being from substances as their principles, so too creatures from God. But accidents do not properly speaking "participate" substances like creatures do God. Accidents inhere in or subsist according to substances without themselves bearing the attributes of those substances.

29. Aertsen, *Medieval Philosophy*, 13; 29.

30. Aertsen, "Avicenna's Doctrine of the Primary Notions and its Impact on Medieval Philosophy" in *Islamic Thought in the Middle Ages* (Boston/Leiden: Brill Publishers, 2008), 21–42, and Michael E. Marmura's "Avicenna on Primary Concepts in the *Metaphysics* of his *al-Shifa*'" in *Probing Islamic Philosophy: Studies in the Philosophies of Ibn-Sīnā, al-Ghazālī, and Other Major Muslim Thinkers* (Binghamton: Global Academic Publishing, 2005), 149–168.

31. It seems the *SH* learns this strategy from Philip the Chancellor. Consider his *SDB* q. 9 (1: 30).

32. Aertsen, *Medieval Philosophy*, 140.

33. *Metaphysica* 7.12.1037b (LCL 271: 373).

34. *SH* I, n. 72 (1: 113).

35. *SH* I, n. 72 (1: 113).

36. For example: the *SH* says that according to the Philosopher, '*Unum' est ens indivisum in se, divisum autem ab aliis*. But this is not a proper definition. No, in fact both parts of it follow the prescriptions laid down here. The first part (*unum est ens indivisum*) is *una notio per abnegationem oppositae intentionis, quae est divisio vel multitudo*. And the second part only 'defines' one *per effectum consequentem, qui est distinguere ab aliis*. See *SH* I, n. 72 (1: 113).

37. *SH* I, n. 72 (1: 113): "[P]rimae ergo determinationes entis sunt primae impressiones apud intellectum: eae sunt unum, verum, bonum, sicut patebit."

38. *SH* I–II, n. 2 (2: 3): "*Ens est prima impressio intelligentiae.*"

39. The Quaracchi editors note Avicenna's *The Book of Healing* 1.5.

40. Avicenna, *Liber de philosophia prima sive scientia* 1.5. *Liber De philosophia prima: sive, Scientia divina* (Avicenna Latinus), ed. Simone Van Riet and G. Verbeke (Leuven: E. Peeters, 1977), 31–32. See also Aertsen, *Medieval Philosophy*, 80–86.

41. *Analytica Posteriora* 1.3.72b (LCL 391: 36–39).

42. Twice Aertsen notes that many scholastics prefer these to Avicenna's term *primae impressiones* exactly because of its implicit invocation of an external Agent Intellect. He argues that the *SH* evinces less handwringing over this term only to the extent that it connects this theory to one more licit, namely Augustine's (*Medieval Philosophy*, 84, 141).

43. Or, and in a less Kantian key, consider Henry of Ghent's gloss in his *Summa quaestionum ordinarum*, a. 24, q. 7, as in Aertsen, *Medieval Philosophy*, 84–85.

44. *SH* I–II, n. 2 (2: 3).

45. *Trin.* 8.3. See also Plato's *Meno* or Iamblichus's *De mysteriis* 1.3. or Plotinus's *Enn.* VI.5.

46. For more on the Franciscan inheritance of Augustine and Avicenna, see Lydia Schumacher's controversial but fascinating *Divine Illumination: The History and Future of Augustine's Theory of Knowledge* (Malden: Wiley-Blackwell, 2011).

47. *SH* I, n. 345 (1: 513).

48. Aertsen, *Medieval Philosophy*, 142.

49. *SH* I–II, n. 35 (2: 45). Aertsen misses this text, though it is found in Jacob Wood's "Kataphasis and Apophasis in Thirteenth-Century Theology: The Anthropological Context of the *Triplex Via* in the *Summa fratris Alexandri* and Albert the Great" in *The Heythrop Journal* 57, no. 2 (2016): 2.

50. As ever, the question is not whether the *SH* affirms the doctrine of analogy, but rather which one. Schumacher suggests that its analogy of proportionality hedges "much closer to the conception of univocity advocated by later Franciscans" (*Early Franciscan Theology*, 134–35). But this is itelf an argument that turns on proportion. Much closer, we might ask, than *whose*? Jacob Wood argues that there may well be more confluence between analogy taught by the early Franciscans and that of, say, Thomas Aquinas's *Scriptum*, than is typically imagined. See Jacob W. Wood, "Forging the Analogy of Being: John of La Rochelle's *De divinis nominibus* (Trier, Abtei St. Matthias, 162) and "The *Summa Halensis* on Knowing and Naming God" in *The Summa Halensis: Debates and Doctrines*, 32–57.

51. Aertsen, *Medieval Philosophy*, 159.

52. Aertsen, *Medieval Philosophy*, 100.

53. Aertsen, *Medieval Philosophy*, 128.

54. It is well known that later thinkers like Thomas Aquinas treat of other transcendental terms like *res* and *aliquid*. The simple explanation is that they inherited these "extra" transcendentals from Avicenna, who says much about them. But the story is more complicated. The twelfth-century *Ars Meliduna*, for instance, says: "*Nullum nomen conveniens cuilibet rei significat universale, ut 'res,' 'aliquid,' 'ens' et 'unum.'*" See Klaus Jacobi's "*Nomina transcendentia*: Untersuchungen von Logikern des 12. Jahrhunderts über transkategoriale Terme" in *Die Logik des Transzendentalen. Festschrift für Jan A. Aertsen*, ed. Martin Pickavé (New York: Miscellanea Mediaevalia 30, 2003), 23–36. If Jacobi's dating is correct, then the inclusion of *res* and *aliquid* among transcendental terms predated translations of Avicenna. Aertsen thinks this indicates a "native Latin tradition with respect to these terms," *Medieval Philosophy*, 43. It is interesting for my purposes that the *SH* might have rejected both the Avicennian and native Latin tradition of expanding the list of "firsts." It is true that there was already some precedent for doing so in Philip the Chancellor, who wrote his *Summa* well before the *SH*. Still, why does the *SH* reject what Thomas Aquinas (for instance) accepts? Why limit the transcendental terms to three? It is not entirely clear why Philip may have done so. But it seems suggestive that the *SH* transforms Philip's list of three into a site for trinitarian reflection.

55. Coolman, "The Transcendental Brocade," 583.

56. Jorge J. E. Garcia, "The Transcendentals in the Middle Ages: An Introduction" in *Topoi* 11, no. 2 (1992): 113–120. See also Jan Aertsen's "What Is First and Most Fundamental? The Beginnings of Transcendental Philosophy," *Qu'est-ce que la philosophie au Moyen Âge?* (New York, Berlin: Walter de Gruyter, 1998), 177–192 and Scott MacDonald's "The Relation between Being and Goodness,"

Being and Goodness. The Concept of the Good in Metaphysics and Philosophical Theology (Ithaca, NY: Cornell University Press, 1990), 31–55.

57. Dionysius, *DN* 12, no. 2 (PG 3: 978; PL 122: 1168).

58. Augustine, *vera rel.* 7. For Augustine's works I adopt all bibliographic conventions prescribed by the *Augustinus-Lexicon*.

59. Boethius, *De consolatione* 3.11.

60. *SH* I, n. 73 (1: 113–116).

61. *SH* I, n. 73 (1: 115). The *SH* goes on to quote *DN* 13.2.

62. The good is the *indivisio actus a potentia*, the true the *indivisio esse et quod est*, and the one *indivisio* itself, since *unum non ponit super ens nisi indivisionem*. See Philip's *SDB* q. 1 (1: 6); q. 2 (1: 10); and q. 7 (1: 27).

63. Aertsen, *Medieval Philosophy*, 120–21.

64. *SH* I, n. 88 (1: 140): "*Quamvis secundum rem coincidant in idem verum, unum, et bonum, tamen differunt intentiones eorum.*" Cf. Aertsen, *Medieval Philosophy*, 143.

65. Cf. Philip the Chancellor, *SDB* q. 7 (1: 27).

66. Cf. *SDB* q. 2 (1: 10).

67. *SH* I, n. 88 (1: 140). Cf. *SDB* q. 1 (1: 6).

68. Here seems an obvious difference from the transcendental doctrines of Thomas Aquinas and Denys the Carthusian, for whom the distinction between divine names and transcendental terms runs sharper. See Kent Emery Jr., "The matter and order of philosophy according to Denys the Carthusian" in *Was ist Philosophie im Mittelalter? =Qu'est-ce que la philosophie au Moyen Âge? =What Is Philosophy in the Middle Ages?* (New York, Berlin: Walter de Gruyter, 1998), 674–675.

69. Boethius, *De hebdomadibus* 6.

70. *SH* I, n. 72 (1: 113–115); n. 88 (1: 139–141); n. 102 (1: 160–161). Cf. Aertsen, *Medieval Philosophy*, 142. Note that Aertsen incorrectly identifies the second location of the systematic order as n. 83; the correct location is n. 88 (see note below).

71. *SH* I, n. 88 (1: 140): "*Quamvis secundum rem coincidant in idem verum, unum et bonum, tamen differunt intentiones eorum,* sicut supra dictum est in quaestione de unitate." (emphasis mine)

72. *SH* I, n. 73 (1: 114).

73. Aertsen, *Medieval Philosophy*, 144. Gössmann notes this too at *MH*, 338.

74. *SH* I, n. 73 (1: 114). This reappears in Bonaventure, *brev.* 1.6.2 and in Denys the Carthusian, *De ven. mundi*, a. 13, in *Doctoris Ecstatici D. Dionysii Cartusiani Opera Omnia, cura et labore monachorum ordinis Carthusiensis* (Montreuil-sur-Mer/Tournai/Parkminster 1896–1935), vol. 34, 238.

75. *SH* I, n. 73 (1: 115).

76. An axiomatic principle, likely mediated to the *SH* through *Liber de causis* 1.1.

77. See also the *SH*'s treatment of the name *ars Patris* for the Son. *SH* I, n. 453 (1: 649). The conversation is clearly indebted to the earlier one in Alexander's *Glossa* I, d. 31, 11 (12: 302).

78. *SH* I–II begins with an extended essay on "Whether the principles of efficient, exemplary, and final [causality] are from eternity?" The answer is negative. The question then proceeds to establish that these three causes *eaedem sint in essentia*. Then the question arises *De ordine istarum rationum inter se*, to which the solution is given: "*Nam quod sint plures, hoc est ex quodam respectu creatorum ad primum . . . non quod ipsum primum sit in se multiplex . . . Unde sicut dicitur de tribus personis.*" When the text turns to treat the causes *singulatim*, it continues to fill in this trinitarian frame for causality: exemplary causality is attributed to the Son (*SH* I–II, n. 10 [2: 18]), final causality to the *summum bonum* and so the Spirit (*SH* I–II, n. 16 [2: 25]), and efficient causality to the Father (*SH* I–II, n. 18 [2: 27]). More on this in a later chapter.

79. Aertsen, *Medieval Philosophy*, 147.

80. Gössmann hints at an answer at *MH*, 339.

81. *SH* I n. 73, (1: 115).

82. *trin.* 10.4.17–18 (CCSL 50: 320–321).

83. *SH* I–II, n. 338 (2: 410). Though Alexander admits that "*in aliis enim creaturis remanet ratio vestigii secundum unitatem, veritatem, et bonitatem,*" the human creature alone "*distinguitur in anima ratio memoriae, intelligentiae, et voluntatis.*" These remain distinct, however, from the *similitudo dei*.

84. *SH* I, n. 73 (1: 114–115).

85. *Glossa* I, d. 26, 6 (12: 256). Cf. Walter Principe's *Alexander of Hales' Theology of the Hypostatic Union* (Toronto: Pontifical Institute of Mediaeval Studies, 1967), 26.

86. For more on the typically Franciscan version of trinitarian speculation, see Russell L. Friedman's "The Trinity and the Aristotelian categories: different ways of explaining identity and distinction," in *Medieval Trinitarian Thought from Aquinas to Ockham* (Cambridge: Cambridge University Press, 2010), 5–49.

87. The same language is present later in a response to the question of "whether there is an order among the divine persons." See *SH* I, n. 320 (1: 471–472).

88. *SH* I–II, n. 482 (2: 684): "'*Ingenitus', sicut et ignorantia, dicitur dupliciter: negative et quasi contrarie. Primo modo convenit Patri, secundo modo convenit Spiritui Sancto.*" Innascibility applies here to the Holy Spirit because the Spirit is said to differ from the Father *a processione*, and not *a generatione*.

89. *Glossa* I, d. 28, 5d (12: 274). Cf. Principe, *Alexander of Hales' Theology of the Hypostatic Union*, 26.

90. Aertsen, *Medieval Philosophy*, 160.

91. Aertsen, *Medieval Philosophy*, 59.

2. TRANSCENDENTALS AS TRINITARIAN APPROPRIATION

1. Aertsen, *Transcendental Thought*, 147.

2. Elizabeth Gössmann, *MH*, 339 and Coolman, "The Transcendental Brocade."

3. *SH* I, n. 73 (1: 114).

4. Gilles Emery, *The Trinitarian Theology of St. Thomas Aquinas*, trans. Francesca Aran Murphy (New York: Oxford University Press, 2007), 312.

5. Why should Bonaventure provide the canon for the *SH* on appropriation? It is typically a delicate—even dangerous—thing to mix and match passages from various authors without registering difference. I risk it here because on this point Bonaventure compresses and summarizes, as I show below, exactly what the *SH* performs over much larger blocks of text. For the deep similarities between Halensian and Bonaventurean grammars of appropriation (in contrast to the Albertine-Thomist), see Emery's *Trinitarian Theology*, 317–320.

6. *brev.* 1.6.2. English emended from *Breviloquium*, trans. Dominic Monti (St. Bonaventure: The Franciscan Institute, 2005), 44–45. Latin taken from *Doctoris Seraphici S. Bonaventurae Opera Omnia* (Quaracchi: Ex Typographia Collegii S. Bonaventurae, 1882 [5: 214–215]).

7. Emery, *Trinitarian Theology*, 313.

8. For one example among many, take the discussion on "procession" at *SH* I, n. 305 (1: 441).

9. *SH* I, n. 447 (1: 640).

10. See this principle in action, for example, at *SH* I, n. 454 (650): "*Sumitur autem 'procedere' non quod attribuitur Filio, sed quod distinctivum est Spiritus Sancti ab aliis personis.*" Cf. Bonaventure, *brev.* 1.3.6–9 (5: 212) and *In I Sent.* 26.4 (1: 460–461). The personal properties were fixed by the second canon of the Fourth Lateran Council: "the Father begets, the Son is begotten, and the Holy Spirit proceeds."

11. *SH* I, n. 451 (1: 647): "*Nomina autem appropriabilia possunt supponere essentiam et personam.*"

12. Hilary of Poitiers, *De trinitate* 2.1 (SC 443: 276–277).

13. See Augustine's *trin.* 6.10.11 (CCSL 50: 241–242).

14. Lombard, *Sent.* I, d. 31, c. 2 (Brady 4: 225–229), trans. Silano, 166–169. Cf. Emery, *Trinitarian Theology*, 318. All Latin from *Magistri Petri Lombardi Parisiensis Episcopi Sententiae in IV Libris Distinctae*, ed. Ignatius Brady. Spicilegium Bonaventurianum 4–5 (Grottaferrata: Editiones Collegii S. Bonaventurae Ad Claras Aquas, 1971–1981). All English translations taken from Guilio Silano's *The Sentences*. Mediaeval Sources in Translation, 4 vols. (Toronto: Pontifical Institute of Mediaeval Studies, 2007).

15. *SH* I, n. 448 (1: 641–642): "*Processio Spiritus Sancti est sicut voluntatis a notitia et mente.*"

16. Bonaventure follows the *SH* closely at *brev.* 1.3.6–1.3.9 (5: 212) and *trip. via* 3.7.12 (8: 17).

17. *SH* I, n. 461 (1: 658). Lombard, *Sent.* I, d. 31, cc. 2–3 (Brady 4: 225–229), trans. Silano, 166–170, noted in Augustine, *doct. chr.* 1.5.5. For more on the history of this triad, see Jean Châtillon's classic "Unitas, aequalitas, concordia vel connexia. Recherches sur les origines de la théorie thomiste des appropriations," *Thomas Aquinas 1274–1974. Commemorative Studies* (1974), 337–380.

18. Augustine, *doct. chr.* 1.5.5.

19. Richard of St. Victor, *De tribus personis appropriatis in trinitate* 1 (Ribaillier 184).

20. Richard of St. Victor, *De tribus* 1 (Ribaillier 185).

21. Throughout I employ masculine pronouns for the trinitarian persons. I eschew all pronouns, however, for God or the divine essence.

22. Probably it is the *SH's* similar treatment of the first two triads that causes Bonaventure to claim in *brev.* 1.3 (5: 211–212) that the Augustinian *unitas-aequalitas-concordia* says much the same as Hilary's, if in different words (*per alia verba*).

23. Lombard, *Sent.* I, d. 36, cc. 3–5 (Brady 4: 261–262), trans. Silano, 200–202. For more on appropriation in "Les Maîtres Chartrains," see Châtillon, "Unitas, Aequalitas, Concordia," 354–358.

24. *SH* I, n. 461 (1: 658).

25. Cf. Emery, *Trinitarian Theology*, 315 and Dominique Poirel, "Scholastic Reasons, Monastic Mediations, and Victorine Conciliations: The Question of the Unity and Plurality of God in the Twelfth Century" in *The Oxford Handbook of the Trinity*, ed. Gilles Emery and Matthew Levering (Oxford: Oxford University Press, 2011), 170.

26. Dating difficulties render unclear whether Abelard or Hugh used the triad first. For more, see Boyd Taylor Coolman, "'In Whom I Am Well Pleased': Hugh of St. Victor's Trinitarian Aesthetics," *Pro Ecclesia* 23, no. 3 (2014), 338. Cf. Poirel, *Livre de la nature et débate trinitaire au XIIe siècle: Le De tribus diebus de Hughes de Saint-Victor*, Bibliotheca Victorina 14 (Turnhout: Brepols, 2002) and Constant Mews, "The World as Text" in *Scripture and Pluralism: Reading the Bible in the Religiously Plural Worlds of the Middle Ages and Renaissance*, ed. Thomas J. Heffernan and Thomas E. Burman (Boston/Leiden: Brill Publishers, 2005), 95–122.

27. Hugh of St. Victor denies the triad any relation to the personal properties *stricto sensu* and restricts it to the divinity properly. Cf. *DS* 1.3.26 (PL 176: 227). For more on Hugh of St. Victor's influence on the *SH*, see Boyd Taylor Coolman, "Hugh of St. Victor's Influence on the *Summa Halensis*" in *The Summa Halensis: Sources and Context*, 201–215.

28. While the newly implemented practice of commenting the Lombard's *Sentences* guaranteed wide exposure for these triads, Châtillon notes how the *SH* gathers the piecemeal treatment of appropriated triads of the *Sentences* into a single tractate: *De nominibus personalibus appropriatis*. Cf. Châtillon, "Unitas, Aequalitas, Concordia," 373–374.

29. *SH* I, n. 450 (1: 646).

30. *SH* I, n. 450 (1: 646).

31. Hugh of St. Victor, *DS* 1.3.26 (PL 176: 227). For a translation see Deferrari, *On the Sacraments*, 53.

32. *SH* I, nn. 405–432 (1: 596–625).

33. The language of *bonum* is Hugh's. There seems to be some fluidity in the early thirteenth century between terms standing in the third place: *voluntas* is

used most often, but *bonum, benignitas,* and *benevolentia* are sometimes substituted. Cf. *SH* I, n. 450 (1: 646); Bonaventure, *brev.* 1.6.5 (5: 215).

34. Hugh advances a more kataphatic account of this triad in *De tribus diebus.*

35. Emery, *Trinitarian Theology,* 317.

36. *DT* 6.15 (Ribaillier 247–248).

37. *SH* I, n. 450 (1: 646). Here the *SH* quotes in full the sense (if not quite the letter) of Richard's *De trinitate* 6.15 (Ribaillier 247–248).

38. Bonaventure, *In I Sent.* d. 34, a. un., q. 3 (1: 592) and *SH* I, n. 450 (1: 646). Cf. Emery, *Trinitarian Theology,* 320.

39. Emery, *Trinitarian Theology,* 320.

40. Thomas Aquinas's anxieties about the Richardian-Franciscan line are evident in *In I Sent.* d. 31, q. 1, a. 2. Thomas's concern here seems to follow from anxieties about natural knowledge of the trinity. If we tether the personal properties too closely to the essential attributes, we may end up granting pagans access to the *propria.* Thomas's anxieties are familiar. But from the Richardian-Franciscan perspective, the Dominican insistence (especially Albert's) upon a sharp distinction between essential attributes (*communia*) and personal properties (*propria*) courts another danger. It risks, that is, failing to account seriously for the peculiar *mode* of God being God. In other words, God is not *other* than trinity. Casting all the personal property business into the abyss of mystery surely protects against natural knowledge of the trinity. But the Richardian-Franciscan line seems to insist upon a contemplative turn back to this mystery after the light of faith is given—hence Richard's "necessary reasons." Though to different ends, Scotus critiques Thomas's trinitarian theology for rendering accidental "the *way* that [the Persons] originate." See Russell Friedman, "Medieval Trinitarian Theology from the Late Thirteenth to the Fifteenth Centuries" in *The Oxford Handbook of the Trinity,* ed. Gilles Emery and Matthew Levering (New York: Oxford University Press, 2011), 203.

41. Or perhaps Alexander's claim here runs stronger still. Perhaps it is not just that Christians *may* appropriate certain attributes to certain persons; perhaps they *must.* God's unique trinitarian mode (or *tropos,* as the Greeks like to say) of being requires that thinking and speaking about it register that mode. If God is and has his being as trinity, Alexander seems to mean, then we cannot speak God's attributes as other than trinity.

42. Emery, *Trinitarian Theology,* 320.

43. *SH* I, n. 73 (1: 114).

44. *SH* I, n. 88 (1: 140) and n. 73.

45. *SH* I, n. 89 (1: 143–144).

46. *SH* I, n. 89 (1: 142).

47. This point recurs throughout Richard of St. Victor's *DT,* but see especially 3.12.

48. *SH* I, n. 78 (1: 122).

49. *SH* I, n. 78 (1: 122).

50. Friedman, *Medieval Trinitarian Thought from Aquinas to Ockham* (Cambridge: Cambridge University Press, 2010), 17.

51. *SH* I, n. 78 (1: 123).

52. *SH* I, n. 89 (1: 142). See also n. 461 (1: 658), n. 484 (1: 686), n. 489 (1: 691). Bonaventure reinscribes this description in *brev.* 1.3 (5: 212).

53. Zachary Hayes, "Bonaventure's Trinitarian Theology in General" in *St. Bonaventure's Disputed Questions on the Mystery of the Trinity* (St. Bonaventure: The Franciscan Institute, 2000), 41.

54. This presages the later discussion *De innascibilitate*, *SH* I, nn. 480–484 (1: 681–687).

55. *SH* I, n. 89 (1: 142).

56. *SH* I, n. 89 (1: 144–145).

57. *SH* I, n. 89 (1: 145).

58. For more on the Son's singular personal property, see *SH* I, nn. 408–426 (1: 601–618).

59. *SH* I, n. 321 (1: 472) and n. 468 (1: 669–671).

60. A theme Bonaventure adopts and strengthens. On this point see Hayes's "Bonaventure's Trinitarian Theology," 53–54 and Hellmann, *Divine and Created Order in Bonaventure's Theology*, trans. J. M. Hammond (St. Bonaventure: The Franciscan Institute, 2001), 61–77.

61. *SH* I, n. 89 (1: 143–144).

62. *SH* I, n. 73 (1: 114).

63. *SH* I, n. 88 (140): "*Bonum* [appropriatur] *Spiritus Sanctus, cui appropriatur ratio finalis.*"

64. Interesting that Scotus retains the argument from two modes of production, though now scrubbed of the self-diffusive background at *Ordinatio* 1.9. un., n. 7 (Vatican, 4: 331). Cf. Richard Cross, *Duns Scotus*, (Oxford: Oxford University Press, 1999), 62.

65. *SH* I, n. 304 (1: 440).

66. *SH* I, n. 304 (1: 440).

67. A similar logic applies for the Spirit as final cause at *SH* I, n. 304 (1: 440).

68. *SH* I, n. 450 (1: 646).

69. *SH* I, n. 73 (1: 116).

70. John of Damascus, *De fide orthodoxa* (PG 94: 859).

71. See, for example, Philip the Chancellor, *SDB* I, tr. 3, q. 3 (250).

72. Coolman, "The Transcendental Brocade," 569.

73. *SH* I, n. 73 (1: 116).

74. Thomas Aquinas, *De veritate* q. 1, a. 3, s.c. 5.

3. BEAUTY AS TRANSCENDENTAL ORDER

1. Plato, *Hippias Major* 304e (LCL 167: 323).

2. The best recent study on the transcendental question in Thomas Aquinas is Michael J. Rubin's "The Meaning of 'Beauty' and Its Transcendental Status in

the Metaphysics of Thomas Aquinas" (PhD diss., The Catholic University of America, 2016).

3. In this I concur entirely with Bychkov's recent corrective to Balthasar's overwrought view. See his "Suspended Beauty?" especially 111–114.

4. *SH* I, n. 103 (1: 163).

5. To my mind, only Edgar de Bruyne registers this apparent aporia. See his "Les premiers scolastiques" in *Études d'esthétique médiévale* III, 89 and 97.

6. On one, *SH* I, nn. 72–86 (1: 112–136); on true, nn. 87–101 (1: 138–158); on good, nn. 102–130 (1: 160–199).

7. *SH* I, n. 103 (1: 162), or *An idem sit bonum et pulcrum.*

8. Together these comprise the question *Quid sit bonum secundum rationem suae intentionis* at *SH* I, nn. 102–104 (1: 160–163).

9. The primary proponents of the antitranscendental reading are Dieter Halcour, "Tractatus de transcendentalibus entis conditionibus" in *Franziskanische Studien* 41 (1959): 41–106 and Jan Aertsen, *Medieval Philosophy and the Transcendentals: The Case of Thomas Aquinas* (Boston/Leiden: Brill Publishers, 1996), hereafter "*Medieval Philosophy*." As I will show below, Aertsen's argument depends heavily upon Halcour's.

10. *SH* I–II, n. 75 (2: 99).

11. Among these readers are Henri Pouillon, "La beauté, propriété transcendantale chez les scolastiques (1220–1270)" in *Archives d'histoire doctrinale et littéraire du Moyen Age* (Paris: Vingt et unième année, 1946): 278–279 and Umberto Eco, *Art and Beauty in the Middle Ages* (New Haven, CT: Yale University Press, 1986).

12. De Bruyne, "Les premiers scolastiques," 90–91, 96.

13. Eco, *Art and Beauty*, 23.

14. Eco, *Art and Beauty*, 24; Cf. Eco, *The Aesthetics of Thomas Aquinas*, trans. Hugh Bredin (Cambridge, MA: Harvard University Press, 1988), 45.

15. Eco, *Art and Beauty*, 24; *The Aesthetics of Thomas Aquinas*, 45.

16. Eco, *Art and Beauty*, 24; *The Aesthetics of Thomas Aquinas*, 45. Eco attempts a palimpsest of his source, but he manages only a carbon copy; his source is Pouillon's "La beauté."

17. Aertsen makes similar arguments in his earlier "Beauty in the Middle Ages: A Forgotten Transcendental?" in *Medieval Philosophy and Theology* I (1991), 68–97 and "Die Frage nach der Transzendentalität der Schönheit im Mittelalter" in *Historia Philosophiae Medii Aevi, Festschrift für Kurt Flasch*, ed. Burkhard Mojsisch and Olaf Pluta (Amsterdam, Philadelphia: B. R. Grüner, 1991), 1–22.

18. Aertsen, *Transcendental Thought*, 172. Aertsen here invokes Thomas's treatment in *De veritate*, q. 1, a. 1.

19. Aertsen, *Transcendental Thought*, 172.

20. Cf. Halcour, "Tractatus de transcendentalibus," 49.

21. See Aertsen's "Das Schöne" in *Historisches Wörterbuch der Philosophie, Band 8: R–Sc*, ed. Joachim Ritter and Karlfried Gründer (Basel: Schwabe & Co Verlag, 1992), 1354. See also Aertsen, "The triad 'true-good-beautiful'," 429.

22. Eco, *The Aesthetics of Thomas Aquinas*, 45. Eco follows many in assuming John of La Rochelle penned *SH* I and *SH* III.

23. Eco, *The Aesthetics of Thomas Aquinas*, 46.

24. Aertsen, *Medieval Philosophy*, 337: "The question as to the transcendentality of the beautiful cannot be resolved until it has become clear what universal mode of *being* the beautiful expresses that is not yet expressed by the other transcendentals, and what its place is in the order of these properties." Cf. *Transcendental Thought*, 176.

25. Rubin, "The Meaning of Beauty," 91.

26. Rubin, "The Meaning of Beauty," 92.

27. Several scholars judge Aertsen's guideline as inadequate. See Michael Machias Waddel, "Truth Beloved: Thomas Aquinas and the Relational Transcendentals" (PhD dissertation, University of Notre Dame, 2000); Louis-Marie de Blignieres, *Le mystère de l'être: L'approche thomiste de Guérard des Lauriers*, preface by Serge-Thomas Bonino (Paris: J. Vrin, 2007); and D. C. Schindler, "The Transcendentals" in *Hans Urs von Balthasar and the Dramatic Structure of Truth: A Philosophical Investigation* (New York: Fordham University Press, 2004), 350–421. See also Rubin, "The Meaning of Beauty," 88–149.

28. Alain de Libera, *Albert le Grand et la philosophie: A la recherche de la vérité* (Paris: J. Vrin, 1990), 11.

29. Aertsen, *Transcendental Thought*, 135–176.

30. Aertsen, *Transcendental Thought*, 147 and 674.

31. This is especially curious given the fact that Aertsen himself, quoting Kretzmann, notices that Thomas "never presents the Trinitarian appropriation of the transcendentals unmistakably in his own voice." He continues: "This appropriation remains much more in the background of his work than it does in the writings of the representatives of the early Franciscan school at Paris, Alexander of Hales and Bonaventure." Aertsen, *Medieval Philosophy*, 412. Cf. Kretzmann, "Trinity and Transcendentals," 91.

32. Aertsen, *Transcendental Thought*, 169. Cf. Halcour, "Tractatus de transcendentalibus," 47.

33. Halcour assays the authorship question in his "Tractatus de transcendentalibus," 58–63. Emma Jane Marie Spargo demurs without having herself consulted the text and on the authority of Pouillon alone in *The Category of the Aesthetic in the Philosophy of Saint Bonaventure* (St. Bonaventure: The Franciscan Institute, 1953), 34.

34. *Tractatus de transcendentalibus*, q. 1 (Halcour 65).

35. Halcour, "Tractatus de transcendentalibus," 63.

36. Aertsen, *Transcendental Thought*, 170.

37. *Tractatus de transcendentalibus*, q. 1 (Halcour 67).

38. The former term belongs to Aertsen, *The Transcendentals*, 351; the latter to Coolman, in his "The Transcendental Brocade," 572. Both describe the same phenomenon, that each transcendental is synthetic to the extent that each

conceptually contains the transcendentals that precede it. Cf. Rubin, "The Meaning of Beauty," 93.

39. It is worth noting that Spargo's judgment that beauty be a transcendental for Bonaventure rests on this text alone, whose authorship she ascribes to Bonaventure: "From the point of view of causality, it can be said that the one refers to efficient causality, the true to formal causality, and the good to final causality. But the beautiful embraces all these causes," *The Category of the Aesthetic*, 36. Spargo's conclusion gets reinscribed in David E. Ost's "Bonaventure: The Aesthetic Synthesis" in *Franciscan Studies* 36 (1976): 243. For a more sophisticated treatment of Bonaventure on beauty's transcendentality, see Karl Peter's *Die Lehre der Schönheit nach Bonaventura* (Werl: Dietrich-Coelde-Verlag, 1964), especially 115–129.

40. Bychkov has recently defended Aertsen's position that the Assisi text innovates the *Summa*'s teaching on beauty as nontranscendental. But merely showing that the Assisi text interprets rather than merely repeats the *SH* does not yet show that it interprets the *SH inappropriately*. On my view the Assisi manuscript interprets the *SH*'s transcendental teaching on beauty *through* its claim that beauty in God is from the "sacred order" of the trinitarian persons. That Aertsen and Bychkov do not seriously treat the latter passage in the *SH* likely accounts for their dismissal of the Assisi text's interpretation. See Bychkov, "Suspended Beauty?"

41. Exceptions here are Pouillon's "La beauté," 276 and de Bruyne's "Les premiers scolastiques," 110.

42. Pouillon, "La beauté," 276.

43. *SH* I, n. 103 (1: 163).

44. Bonaventure, *itin.* 1.2–1.3; 4.2; 7.1 (5: 297; 306; 312).

45. *SH* I, n. 103 (1: 163): "*Ad secundum dicendum quod illud Augustini definit pulcritudinem visibilem sive corporalem; tamen dicitur de pulcritudine corporali sensibili, in quantum ducit ad intelligibilem sive spiritualem. Sicut enim "pulcritudo corporum est ex congruentia compositionis partium", ita pulcritudo animarum ex convenientia virium et ordinatione potentiarum, et pulcritudo in divinis ex ordine sacro divinarum personarum, qua una persona non ab alia, a qua alia per generationem, a quibus tertia per processionem.*"

46. Though Hagendahl does not cite any classical source for Augustine's definition of beauty at *civ.* 22.19 (CCSL 48: 838), he cites Cicero's *Tusc. disp.* 4.13.30–4.13.31 as the source for a near identical passage in Augustine's *ep.* 3.4. See Harald Hagendahl, *Augustine and the Latin Classics* (Stockholm: Almqvist & Wiksell, 1967), 319. Bychkov shows that Cicero's own definition owes to the Stoics, particularly Chrysippus. Galen reports 22. as holding that "beauty arises from the symmetry of parts." For more, see Bychkov's "The Reflection of Some Traditional Stoic Ideas in the Thirteenth-Century Scholastic Theories of Beauty" in *Vivarium* 34, no. 2 (1996): 141–160.

47. Remember Plotinus's arguments against Stoic grammars of beauty at *Enn.* I.6 (LCL 440: 235–263).

48. Halcour, "Tractatus de transcendentalibus," 49.

49. *Tractatus de transcendentalibus,* q. 1 (Halcour 67).

50. The other option is, of course, *circumincessio.* See John of Damascus, *De fide orthodoxa: Versions of Burgundio and Cerbanus,* ed. Eloi Marie Buytaert (St. Bonaventure: The Franciscan Institute, 1955): 45; 64. Cf. Emery, *Trinitarian Theology,* 301 and Peter Stemmer's "Perichorese: Zur Geschichte eines Begriffs" in *Archiv für Begriffsgeschichte* 27 (1983), 36. *Circuitio* is used again in Jacques Lefèvre d'Étaples's sixteenth-century *Traduction latine des livres de la foi orthodoxe de saint Jean de Damas.* Cf. August Deneffe's "Perichoresis, circumincessio, circuminsessio: Eine terminologische Untersuchung" in *Zeitschrift für katholische Theologie* 47, no. 4 (1923): 510.

51. *SH* I, n. 72 (1: 113).

52. Aertsen, *Medieval Philosophy,* 337; *Transcendental Thought,* 176.

53. *SH* I, n. 72 (1: 113–115), n. 88 (1: 139–141), and n. 102 (1: 160–161).

54. *SH* I, n. 89 (1: 143–144).

55. The text gets close in one place. *SH* I–II, n. 75 (2: 99) does ask *cum utrumque* [Dionysius] *addat super ens, quid addit pulcrum super ens quo differt a bono.* But the *respondeo* seems to ignore answering the question as posed. In fact, the text never again speaks of beauty "adding" anything to being, though the *respondeo* assumes that both good and true add to being.

56. Ordinarily—at least in other medieval texts—omission of a term need not necessarily disqualify the term's transcendentality. On this point in Thomas's texts, see Rubin, "The Meaning of Beauty," 21–87 (especially 56–57 on *res* and *aliquid* as precedent). Still, beauty's omission from lists of transcendentals in the *SH*, especially when taken together with the third criterion of appropriability, suggests that absence means more in the *SH* than it does in Thomas. And in any case, Alexander leaves it out at *Glossa* I, d. 3, n. 4 (12: 39).

57. *SH* I, n. 73 (1: 116).

58. Hans Urs von Balthasar *GOL* IV, 377. Balthasar's source is likely also Halcour, "Tractatus de transcendentalibus," especially 48.

59. Balthasar, *GOL* IV, 377: "Since the One, True, and Good of being referred back to the trinitarian causality of God as Father, Son, and Spirit, *there seemed to be no more room in God for another.*" (emphasis mine)

60. Halcour notes this difficulty at "Tractatus de transcendentalibus," 48. Aertsen repeats it in "Das Schöne," 1353.

61. Aertsen says very little about *SH* I–II, n. 75.

62. Étienne Gilson, *History of Christian Philosophy in the Middle Ages* (New York: Random House, 1955), 327.

63. *SH* I, n. 72 (1: 113).

64. *SH* I–II, n. 75 (2: 99).

65. See question 2 of the *SH* I–II *De creatura secundum quantitatem,* which comprises nn. 54–74 (2: 63–83).

66. Aertsen, *Transcendental Thought,* 140.

67. Aristotle, *Categoriae* 8b26–10a11.

68. Aristotle, *Categoriae* 8b26–27 (LCL 325: 62), my translation.

69. *ST* I–II, q. 49, a. 2, co.

70. These are, respectively, *SH* I–II, n. 78 (2: 101), n. 79 (2: 101), n. 80 (2: 102), n. 83 (2: 105).

71. In other words, the *SH* I seems more interested in the transcendental divine attributes—one, true, and good—as such; the *SH* I–II in their created traces (*vestigia*). The latter follows a long discussion *De vestigio* at *SH* I–II, nn. 34–40 (2: 44–49). For more on vestiges in the *SH*, see Elisabeth Gössmann's "Die Vestigium-Lehre" in her *MH*, 186–189.

72. Aside from our writing on two different figures, the deep difference between my suggestion here and Czapiewski's "ingenius solution" that attempts to make "beauty's absence from the list of transcendentals into evidence *did* consider it such a term*" is that he argues for beauty's transcendentality, and I against it. Rubin, "The Meaning of Beauty," 94–95. Cf. Aertsen, *The Transcendentals*, 353 and Czapiewski, *Das Schöne bei Thomas von Aquin* (Freiburg im Breisgau: Herder, 1964), 121–131.

73. Exceptions are Theodore de Régnon's *Études de Théologie sur la Sainte Trinité*, vol. 2 (Paris: Victor Retaux, 1892) [hereafter *EST*]; Albert Stohr, *Die Trinitätslehre des hl. Bonaventura: Eine systematische Darstellung und historische Würdigung. I Teil, Die wissenschaftliche Trinitätslehre* (Munster: Aschendorff-Verlag, 1923); and Kevin Patrick Keane's "The Logic of Self-Diffusive Goodness."

74. *SH* I, nn. 320–327 (1: 471–481).

75. *SH* I, nn. 6–26 (2: 14–37).

76. *SH* I, n. 103 (1: 162). Cf. Augustine, *div. qu.* 30 (PL 40: 19).

77. *SH* I–II, n. 76 (2: 100) will later draw an analogous distinction between *pulcrum* and *aptum*.

78. Note here the resonance with the famous dictum from Thomas's *ST* I, q. 39, a. 8. The *SH* likely adapts this definition from William of Auvergne's *De bono et malo*. *SH* I–II, n. 75 (2: 99) develops this point further.

79. *SH* I, n. 103 (1: 162).

80. *SH* I, n. 115 (1: 181).

81. *SH* I–II, n. 81 (2: 103). It seems curious at first blush that the *SH* should list *species* as the content of *species*. But this is explained at *SH* I, n. 115 (1: 181).

82. *SH* I, n. 113 (1: 117).

83. *SH* I–II, n. 37 (2: 46), n. 39 (2: 48), n. 485 (2: 673), n. 518 (2: 769). De Bruyne's rather neat citation "*pulchritudo creaturae est vestigium pulchritudinis increatae*" does not, so far as I can tell, actually occur in the text. De Bruyne, "Les premiers scolastiques," 110. Perhaps he misremembers *SH* I–II, n. 38 (2: 48): "*ut trinitas in creatura trinitati increatae respondeat.*"

84. *SH* I–II, n. 75 (2: 99).

85. *SH* I, n. 103 (1: 162).

86. *SH* I–II, n. 20 (2: 30–31).

87. *SH* I–II, n. 8 (2: 17).

88. *SH* I–II, n. 20 (2: 31). Alexander here glosses Augustine's *trin.* 6.10.12 (CCSL 50: 242–243).

89. *SH* I, n. 453 (1: 649).

90. *SH* I, n. 175 (1: 258). This matches almost exactly Alexander's *Glossa* I, d. 36, n. 5 (12: 357–360), though it differs from Alexander's *QDA* I, q. 46, n. 36 (Quaracchi: Ex Typographia Collegii S. Bonaventurae, 1960).

91. *SH* I, n. 103 (1: 162).

92. Aristotle, *De partibus animalium* 639b.12–13.

93. *SH* I, n. 107 (1: 168): "Causa enim finalis ratio est aliarum causarum." Cf. *SH* I–II, n. 115 (2: 181). Quoting Philip the Chancellor, Aquinas will repeat this in his *Commentaria in octo libros physicorum Aristotelis* 3.5.11 and, more pithily, at *De principiis naturae* 4.29: "*Unde dicitur quod finis est causa causarum, quia est causa causalitatis in omnibus causis.*" Latin from *De principiis naturae ad fratrem Sylvestrum* in *Opuscula philosophica*, ed. Raimundo Spiazzi (Turin/Rome: Marietti, 1954), 121–128.

94. *SH* I, n. 103 (1: 162). Cf. Dionysius, *DN* 4.7

95. *SH* I, n. 73 (1: 114).

96. This raises the objection Aertsen notes and Rubin repeats at "Transcendental Status," 78: "Distinction in meaning from the good does not necessarily entail conceptual distinction from all of the transcendentals." This seems true, so far as it goes—especially in view of the Thomistic texts that Aertsen and Rubin review. But this objection seems to presume that "conceptual distinction from all of the transcendentals" necessitates a transcendental in its own right. Or at least this is why Aertsen raises the objection: he attempts a refutation of beauty's transcendentality in Thomas. Why exactly this does not prove a final difficulty for the *SH* has everything to do with its peculiar criterion for transcendentality, namely that the transcendentals must function as trinitarian appropriations.

97. *SH* I, n. 73 (1: 114).

98. Alexander raises the question of *an abstractis hypostasibus sit intelligere ordinem naturae in trinitate et e converso* at *SH* I, n. 327 (1: 481). His answer, of course, is negative.

99. *SH* I–II, n. 8 (2: 16–17).

100. *SH* I, n. 73 (1: 116).

101. Pope Eugene IV, *Cantate Domino*, February 4, 1442.

102. For some, my interpretation here may recall Maritain's claim that for Thomas "beauty is the radiance of all the transcendentals united." Jacques Maritain, *Art and Scholasticism and The Frontiers of Poetry*, trans. Joseph Owens (New York: Charles Scribner's Sons, 1962), 173, note 66, though it has a longer history. Maritain seems to think that because beauty (in Thomas) relates to all the transcendentals, it must be some kind of "super-transcendental." He assumes that beauty

must itself be a kind of transcendental to relate to the others. It is this that distinguishes Maritain's reading of Thomas from the aesthetic logic of the *SH*. Maritain's line runs without the trinity—the *Summa*'s does not.

103. Alexander, you may recall, follows Richard of St. Victor in insisting that the order of God's essential attributes itself follows a trinitarian taxis. God, on this picture, is his attributes trinitarianly.

104. *SH* I–II, n. 135 (2: 207) claims that divine power, wisdom, and will "circumincedunt se."

105. *SH* I–II, n. 77 (2: 100).

106. Their inattention to the taxic and so trinitarian shape of beauty in *SH* I leads de Bruyne to conclude that "we hope perhaps to find ourselves in the presence of an aesthetician, but we are quickly undeceived." De Bruyne, "Les premiers scolastiques," 88.

107. Rubin, "The Meaning of Beauty," 6.

108. *SH* I–II, nn. 27–40 (2: 38–48), nn. 75–90 (2: 99–114).

109. *Tractatus de transcendentalibus*, q. 1 (Halcour 67).

4. THE BEAUTY THE TRINITY IS

1. *trin.* 6.10.12 (CCSL 50: 242), my translation.

2. Keane, "The Logic of Self-Diffusive Goodness," 46–47. For scope of importance, compare the role of order in Thomas Aquinas's corpus. It plays a minor role at *ST* I, q. 27, a. 4, ad 1, and then a larger role at *De potentia*, q. 10, aa. 2–3. But it pales when set against the *SH*'s question with eight *capitula* (nn. 320–327 [1: 471–482]).

3. For an excellent overview of the *SH*'s trinitarian theology, see Schumacher's double chapters in *Early Franciscan Theology*, 143–182.

4. *SH* I, nn. 296–494 (1: 414–696). Or, inclusive of the trinitarian missions, nn. 296–518 (1: 414–748).

5. Thanks to Boyd Taylor Coolman, whose lovely phrase (and life's work) this is.

6. Richard of St. Victor, *DT* 4.7 (Ribaillier 170). Cf. *SH* I, n. 404 (1: 592).

7. Augustine, *trin.* 5.9.10 (CCSL 50: 216–217). Cf. *SH* I, n. 396 (1: 584).

8. Theo Kobusch, "The Summa Halensis: Towards a New Concept of 'Person'" in *The Summa Halensis: Debates and Doctrines*, 153–170; he points up "a new emphasis on the idea of moral being" (162).

9. *SH* I, n. 387 (1: 570): "Persona est, secundum Boethium, 'substantia rationalis naturae individua'."

10. *SH* I, n. 387 (1: 570): "*Nam Richardus ponit duas; prima est haec: 'persona est intellectualis naturae incommunicabilis existentia', secunda est haec: 'persona est existens per se solum iuxta quemdam rationalis existentiae modum'.*" The quotations derive from *DT* 4.22 and 4.24, respectively.

11. *SH* I, n. 387 (1: 570): "*Magistri vero ponunt tertiam talem: persona est hypostasis, distincta proprietate ad dignitatem pertinente.*" The Quaracchi editors

suggest it comes from Alan of Lille's *Regulae theologicae*, c. 32 (PL 210: 637), but the formulation is not quite there. Most probably Weber is right to suggest that it comes from Alexander himself at *Glossa* I, d. 23, 9b (12: 501). Cf. Hubert Philipp Weber, *Sünde und Gnade bei Alexander von Hales: Ein Beitrag zur Entwicklung der theologischen Anthropologie im Mittelalter* (Innsbruck: Tyrolia-Verlag, 2003), 119–141. In his "Alexander of Hales's Theology in His Authentic Texts (Commentary on the *Sentences* of Peter Lombard, Various Disputed Questions)," *The English Province of the Franciscans (1224–c.1350)*, ed. Michael J.P. Robson (Boston, Leiden: Brill Publishers, 2017), Weber translates the definition as "a hypostasis with distinct *properties* which belong to dignity." He then goes on to associate this definition with Porphyry's "bundle of properties," which Brother Alexander references as *aggregatio proprietatum* at *SH* I, n. 377 (1: 501). But of course the trouble here, as that last text points up, is that *proprietate* is singular. And so it must be in a trinitarian context. A divine person is not an aggregation of properties but rather an *individuum, quia est substantia habens* proprietatem *quam non est in alio reperire* (*SH* I, n. 377).

12. Kobusch, "Towards a New Concept of 'Person,'" 162.

13. *SH* I, n. 387 (1: 570–571), esp. ad 9 (1: 571).

14. De Régnon, *EST*, vol. 2, 344–345.

15. Emery, *Trinitarian Theology*, 104.

16. "Numbering" the trinity is a dicey business. Gregory Nazianzen already noted its difficulty in *Or.* 31.18 (SC 250: 310). Brother Alexander knows these challenges. He treats the issue at *SH* I, nn. 313–319 (1: 458–470).

17. *SH* I, n. 467 (1: 668).

18. *SH* I, n. 467 (1: 668). Cf. Richard of St. Victor, *DT* 4.17.

19. Here personal properties differ in kind from *relationes* and *notiones*, which number four and five respectively. Brother Alexander offers an extended answer to why "*quinque sunt notiones, quatuor relationes, tres personales proprietates*" at *SH* I, n. 465–468 (1: 666–671).

20. *SH* I, n. 467 (1: 668).

21. See *SH* I, n. 341 (1: 505): "*In divino esse necessario ponitur natura et ordo naturae secundum rationem originis.*" See also n. 22 (1: 52), n. 307 (1: 445), n. 312 (1: 456), n. 316, ad 3 (1: 464), 321 (1: 472), n. 327 (1: 481), n. 467 (1: 668). Cf. Albert Stohr, *Die Trinitätslehre*, 105.

22. Richard of St. Victor, *DT* 4.15 (Ribaillier 177).

23. Here I recall that Friedman's heuristic between emanation and relation accounts for distinguishing the persons. He presents a subtler account than I have in his "Divergent Traditions in Later-Medieval Trinitarian Theology"; his *Medieval Trinitarian Thought*; and much more extensively in his *Intellectual Traditions at the Medieval University*.

24. Friedman, *Medieval Trinitarian Thought*, 17.

25. Here is where things get tricky. If Brother Alexander commends the emanation account, he grounds trinitarian difference in hypostatic origin. But if personal

properties derive from origin, and if the Father be *principium sine principio*, then the question invariably follows: Whence his *innascibilitas*? Thomas will pose the same question, remember, to Bonaventure. For the definitive defense of Bonaventure against rather slipshod accusations—John Baptist Ku's *God the Father in the Theology of St. Thomas Aquinas* (New York: Peter Lang, 2013), 86, associates Bonaventure with Eunomius of Cyzicus—see Jordan Daniel Wood's forthcoming "No Proto-Father: A Neoplatonic Defense of Bonaventure against Thomas Aquinas."

26. Friedman, *Medieval Trinitarian Thought*, 17.

27. Relation, it seems obvious to say, exercises far less dominion here than it will in Albert or Thomas.

28. *SH* I, n. 405, ad 2–3 (1: 597).

29. *SH* I, n. 406 (1: 598). Alexander later allows that "deus" may also refer to one or more of the divine persons, but not the divine essence as such. See *SH* I, n. 359 (1: 537) and n. 488 (690). Cf. Keane, "The Logic of Self-Diffusive Goodness," 79.

30. *SH* I, n. 405, ad 2–3 (1: 597).

31. *SH* I, n. 379 (1: 559).

32. Though this is complicated, not least because Brother Alexander uses both *innascibilitas* and *paternitas* to name the Father's personal property. In any case both are notions proper to the Father, even if both also vie for his personal property. See *SH* I, n. 467 (1: 667–668), nn. 480–484 (1: 681–687). Cf. Gössmann, *MH*, 387.

33. *SH* I, n. 482 (1: 685).

34. *SH* I, n. 484, ad 1 (1: 686). Cf. Stohr, *Die Trinitätslehre*, 125–128.

35. Many of these are already indexed in William of Auxerre's *Summa Aurea* I, tr. 8, c. 5 (1: 134–140). But William learns many of them from Peter Lombard (*I Sent.*, d. 28, c. 3 [Brady 4: 211]) and Peter of Poitiers (*I Sent.*, c. 29 [PL 211: 900d–901a].

36. *SH* I, n. 482 (1: 684–685). Here Bonaventure will disagree with Brother Alexander, or rather side with one strand of Alexander's thought over the other. At *In I Sent.* d. 29, dub. (1: 517) and d. 28, q. 3 (1: 501), Bonaventure writes that "*proprietas personalis Patris est paternitas, non innascibilitas.*" Still sometimes Brother Alexander appears ambivalent. He draws a sharp distinction between properties and notions at *SH* I, n. 465–468 (1: 666–671), but calls both *paternitas* and *innascibilitas notiones* and *proprietates* at n. 484, ad 1 and 4 (1: 686).

37. *SH* I, n. 483 (1: 685–686). Cf. Alexander of Hales, *Glossa* I, d. 1, n. 14i (12: 14).

38. *SH* I, n. 482 (1: 684).

39. *SH* I, n. 483 (1: 685).

40. Alexander distinguishes *paternitas in actu* from *paternitas in potentia* at *SH* I, n. 484 (1: 687). The distinction means to answer the question of *utrum remota paternitate intelligi possit persona innascibilis*. By identifying *innascibilitas* with *paternitas in potentia*, Alexander allows that *innascibilitas* remains in the Father even without the generation of the Son. This point bears directly

upon Bonaventure's later claim that many knew *innascibilitas* through reason's deliverances but *paternitas* only through revelation's.

41. *SH* I, n. 297, ad 23 (1: 428): *"Licet igitur non sit diffusivum sui ut in se consideratur, nihilominus est diffusivum prout est in persona non-ente ab alio."* Cf. Gössmann, *MH*, 364.

42. Wilhelm E. Gössmann, "Die Methode der Trinitätslehre in der Summa Halensis," *Münchener Theologische Zeitschrift* 6 (1955), 258. Cf. Gilles Emery, *La trinité créatrice: trinité et création dans les commentaires aux* Sentences *de Thomas d'Aquin et de ses précurseurs Albert le Grand et Bonaventure* (Paris: J. Vrin, 1995), 22.

43. This recalls the Neoplatonic axiom *ab unio simplici non est nisi unum.* This axiom grounds and necessitates the Neoplatonic account of emanation: it explains (or rather shows) how the many derive from One. The medievals knew about the axiom through al-Farabi or Avicenna or *Liber de causis* 22, though Albert the Great thinks the axiom is shared among *omnes ante nos philosophi* (*De causis* I, tr. 1, c. 10, p. 22, 3 and tr. 4, c. 8, p. 55, 76–79).

44. *SH* I, n. 301, ad 3 (1: 435). Emery notes a similar response in Bonaventure (*In I Sent.*, d. 9, a. un., q. 1 and d. 5, a. 2, q. 2 [1: 180–181; 118]), one that "diffère de celle des dominicains." Emery, *La trinité créatrice*, 362.

45. Or so Keane argues in "The Logic of Self-Diffusive Goodness," 96. The second argument from the internal gift of love comes from William of Auxerre's *SA* I.2.2. The third (from most excellent charity), fourth (from true love's generosity), and fifth (from *condilectum*) derive from Richard (*DT* 3.14–15).

46. Keane correctly identifies the Aristotelian vintage of this distinction; see *Ethica Nicomachea* 3.1.1110a–1111b, *Metaphysica* 7.7.1032, and *Magna Moralia* 1.10.1187a–12.1187b. I will add that the same distinction does important work throughout the work of Avicenna, (see his *The Book of Healing* 9.4 [327]).

47. *SH* I, n. 304 (1: 438). See also n. 319 (1: 469).

48. *SH* I, n. 312 (1: 454).

49. *SH* I, n. 296 (1: 419). Cf. Keane, "The Logic of Self-Diffusive Goodness," 138–140 and De Régnon, *EST*, vol. 2, 380–390.

50. *SH* I, n. 303 (1: 437). Cf. Keane, "The Logic of Self-Diffusive Goodness," 106. Brother Alexander sometimes collects images for trinitarian procession: see *SH* I, n. 310 (1: 447–448).

51. *SH* I, n. 416–417 (1: 607–608), n. 419 (1: 610–611). Cf. Keane, "The Logic of Self-Diffusive Goodness," 138.

52. The Son persists, in fact, as *semper nascitur*—per Alexander at *SH* I, n. 302 (1: 436). Keane misconstrues "the predilection of the early Franciscans for describing the Son's generation as a dynamic, ongoing process to one perduring in its completed perfection." The latter, Keane says, typifies the "static" depiction of the trinity in Thomas Aquinas. But Keane is only partly right. It is true that Brother Alexander thinks the *semper nascitur* option can be defended against the Augustinian option for *semper natum*. But Alexander (like the Lombard) allows

both: "*ex hoc igitur est quod inspiciendo ad praesentialitatem aeternitatis, dicitur de Filio 'semper nascitur'; inspiciendo vero ad perfectionem vel completionem, dicitur 'semper natus.'*" For Augustine, see *div. qu.* 37; for Peter Lombard, see *Sent.* I, d. 9, c. 4 (Brady 4: 106–109), trans. Silano 54–57. Cf. Keane, "The Logic of Self-Diffusive Goodness," 115–117 and De Régnon, *EST*, vol. 2, 501–503.

53. *SH* I, n. 418 (1: 609): "*Cum Filius rationem medii habeat . . .*"

54. *SH* I, n. 319 (1: 468), n. 320 (1: 471–472), n. 324 (1: 475–477), n. 418 (1: 609–610), n. 421 (612–613), n. 425 (1: 618), and so on. Cf. Keane, "The Logic of Self-Diffusive Goodness," 136.

55. Though not between *God* and world, since the Son too is creator. See *SH* I, n. 425 (1: 618). Cf. Alexander of Hales, *QDA* q. 9, d. 2, m. 2, sol (ed. Quaracchi, tome 1, n. 53, 97).

56. *SH* I, n. 330, ad 4 (1: 486).

57. *SH* I, n. 467 (1: 668).

58. *SH* I, n. 432 (1: 625), n. 465 (1: 666), and n. 467 (1: 668).

59. *SH* I, n. 467 (668). Alexander is clear at *SH* I, n. 305, ad 2 (1: 441) that he speaks *processio* of both Son and Spirit only analogously (*per prius et posterius*)—it belongs properly to the Spirit and only analogously to the Son.

60. *SH* I, n. 305 (1: 441). Cf. Keane, "The Logic of Self-Diffusive Goodness," 119.

61. *SH* I, n. 490–494 (1: 692–699).

62. *SH* I, n. 304 (1: 440), among very many other places.

63. *SH* I, n. 304 (1: 440).

64. *SH* I, n. 325 (1: 478).

65. Creation does, however, when it becomes the object of the doting Spirit's creating and redeeming gifts. See *SH* I, n. 310, ad 13 (1: 451).

66. Alexander often describes *diffusio voluntatis* with affective language (*amor, affectio, dilectio*). For instance: "*perfectissima diffusio voluntatis est illa quae est per amorem sive per dilectionem*" (*SH* I, n. 304 [1: 438]) or "*communicat ergo se bonitas vel per modum naturae vel per modum voluntatis sive affectionis*" (*SH* I, n. 317 [1: 465]).

67. *SH* I, n. 307, resp. and ad 5 (1: 444).

68. *SH* I, n. 307 (1: 445). Of course Alexander borrows this pattern of thought from Richard's *DT* 5.17.

69. *SH* 1, n. 308 (1: 446).

70. *SH* I, n. 327 (1: 481): "*Non ab alio a quo alius, ab alio a quo alius, ab alio a quo non alius.*"

71. Sergius Bulgakov, *The Comforter*, trans. Boris Jakim (Grand Rapids: Wm. B. Eerdmans, 2004), 68.

72. Gregory Nazianzen, *Or.* 42.15 (SC 384: 80–82); Basil, *Against Eunomius* 3.1–2 (SC 305: 145–153); and Athanasius, *Letter to Serapion* 1.28 (PG 26: 596).

73. Gregory of Nyssa, *Against Eunomius* 1.16 (PG 45: 311B).

74. See *SH* I, nn. 328–332 (1: 482–491).

75. Brother Alexander distinguishes this double purpose by separating a

cluster of questions on order (*SH* I, nn. 320–327 [1: 471–481]) from another on equality (nn. 328–332 [1: 482–487]).

76. *SH* I, n. 320 (1: 471): "dispositio partium in toto."

77. Bonaventure says much the same. Cf. Hayes, "Bonaventure's Trinitarian Theology," 213.

78. As ad 2 will note, "*notio aliquando significatur distincte, ut cum dico 'paternitas', aliquando indistincte, sed per additionem determinatur.*" The relation between notions and personal properties is intimate but not identical, since a common notion—active spiration, say—cannot constitute a personal property. For more on the exact difference between notions and properties, see *SH* I, nn. 465–479 (1: 666–680). The *SH* notes that the "*communis opinio de numero notionum, proprietatum, et relationum*" holds five, four, and four, respectively (*SH* I, n. 465 [1: 666]). Alexander will later argue for three personal properties, excluding *innascibilitas* (*SH* I, n. 482 [1: 685]) like Bonaventure will later at *brev.* 1.3 (5: 212). Bonaventure earlier catalogued four personal properties at *In I Sent.* d. 26, a.u., q. 1, resp. (1: 452) and q. 4, f. 2 and resp. (1: 460). Cf. Zachary Hayes, "Introduction," *Saint Bonaventure's Disputed Questions on the Mystery of the Trinity* (St. Bonaventure: The Franciscan Institute, 2000), 39–40.

79. *civ.* 19.13 (CCSL 48: 679): "*parium dispariumque sua cuique loca tribuens dispositio.*" English translation from *City of God XI–XXII*, trans. William Babcock, *WSA* I/7 (Hyde Park: New City Press, 2013), 368.

80. Cf. Alexander of Hales, *QDA* I, q. 5, m. 2 (Quarrachi 1: 48).

81. *SH* I, n. 321 (1: 472).

82. Cf. Alexander of Hales, *Glossa* I, d. 11, n. 5 (12: 137); d. 20, n. 8a–8h (12: 214), d. 27, n. 10c (12: 269).

83. *SH* I, n. 321 (1: 472). Bonaventure asks the same at *In I Sent.*, d. 20, a. 2, q. 2 (1: 373).

84. There is a bit of lexical slippage here. At *SH* I, n. 320 (1: 471) first calls its preferred order for the trinity the *ordo secundum originem naturae, qui est principii ad illud quod est de principio*. The conclusion of the *solutio*, however, posits an *ordo naturae vel originis* in the trinity. And the next question (*SH* I, n. 321 [1: 472]) uses both *ordo naturae vel originis* and simply *ordo naturae*. However ambiguous the language, it is clear from context that these terms bear identical content.

85. *SH* I, n. 325 (1: 474).

86. *SH* I, n. 321, ad 2 (1: 473). Thomas's answer to this question at *ST* I, q. 42, a. 3 compresses Alexander's.

87. *SH* I, n. 322 (1: 473–474).

88. *SH* I, n. 323 (1: 474).

89. *SH* I, n. 89 (1: 142): "*principium sine principio.*" See also n. 461 (1: 658), n. 484 (1: 686), n. 489 (1: 691). The latter phrase likely originates with Marius Victorinus: it appears in *Cand. ep.* 1.3 (CSEL 83: 1.4), *Ad Cand.* 16.10 (CSEL 83: 1.33–34), and *Adv. Ar.* 1.3 (CSEL 83: 1.58). Augustine repeats it in *ord.* 2.5.16, *f. et symb.* 9.18–19, and *Gn. litt. imp.* 3. All this recalls *Enn.* VI.8.11 (LCL 468: 260).

90. *SH* I, n. 297 (1:425).

91. *SH* I, n. 322, ad 2 (1: 474).

92. *SH* I, n. 323, ad 1 (1: 475) repeats Alexander's worry *"quod destrueretur summus ordo et connexio in divinis personis"* and *"confunderetur summa germanitas."*

93. Alexander of Hales's undisputed *QDA* I, q. 8 (67–78) also treats the so-called *controversia Graecorum et Latinorum circa processionem ab utroque.*

94. *SH* I, n. 324 (1: 475).

95. *SH* I, n. 324 (1: 477). I note Alexander's leniency toward the Greeks here (and also at *Glossa* I, d. 11 (12: 212). It will vanish in Bonaventure, who argues that the error of the Greeks follows *ex ignorantia, ex superbia, et [ex] pertinacia.* See his *In I Sent.* d. 11, a. un., q. 1, co (1: 212). Albert too speaks of "haeresis" at *In I Sent.* d. 11, a. 6 (25: 348). Cf. Emery, *Trinitarian Theology,* 296.

96. *SH* I, n. 323 (1: 475).

97. *SH* I, n. 324, ad 3, ob 3 (1: 476; 477).

98. This answers the fourth objection (n. 324, ad 4 [1: 477]), too, which asked whether procession from two is not superfluous. Should not everything about God be necessary and nothing superfluous? Alexander redeploys the distinction between *per modum naturae* and *per modum voluntatis.* As in ad 3, the objection applies only to production *per modum naturae* and so to the generation of the Son. But it cannot apply to the production *per modum voluntatis,* "whose perfection is the height of love."

99. One such asks whether indexing the procession of the Spirit to the divine will mean that the Son proceeds involuntarily. And does this in turn mean that the Spirit proceeds unnaturally? Not necessarily, since "natural" and "voluntary" modes of diffusion function principally as tools for speaking the processions (not like understanding and loving for Thomas Aquinas). Keane's resolution of this issue, however, betrays his penchant for process metaphysics. See his "The Logic of Self-Diffusive Goodness," 97–98, n. 58.

100. *SH* I, n. 115 (1: 181). Cf. n. 110 (1: 171).

101. *SH* I, n. 318, ad 1 (1: 467).

102. *SH* I, n. 318 (1: 467).

103. Aristotle remembers the Pythagorean preference for three in *De caelo* 1.1.268a.11–16 (LCL 338: 4–5).

104. See Augustine's *mus.* 1.12.22–26 and 6.4.7.

105. *SH* I, n. 318, ad 2 (1: 467).

106. *SH* I, n. 319, ob 1, op 1 (1: 468–469). Cf. Richard of St. Victor's *DT* 5.14.

107. *SH* I, n. 319, ob 2, op 2, ad 2 (1: 468–470). Cf. *DT* 5.11–5.12.

108. *SH* I, n. 319, ob 5 (1: 469). Cf. *DT* 3.14–3.15. W.E. Gössmann's "Die Methode der Trinitätslehre in der Summa Halensis," 260; E. Gössmann, *MH,* 366–368; De Régnon, *EST,* vol. 2, 405.

109. *SH* I, n. 319, ob 3, op 3, ad 3 (1: 468–470).

110. *SH* I, n. 319 (1: 468).

111. *SH* I, n. 319, ad 4 (1: 470).

112. The logic here owes to Richard of St. Victor's *DT* 5.12 (Ribaillier 210).

113. *SH* I, n. 327 (1: 481–482).

114. *SH* I, 327 (1: 481).

115. This is not to say, of course, that this God could not therefore *cause* beautiful things. Plotinus offers something very like this when he identifies beauty with *Nous* and not the One. The One need not (and cannot) be Beauty itself—neither can the One be intelligible. But it does not follow that beautiful or intelligible things do not proceed from the One.

116. Thomas attributes names like "supersubstantial beauty," "beauty in itself," "the font of all beauty" to the divine essence in his commentary *De divinis nominibus* 4.7–8, ed. Ceslai Pera (Turin/Rome: Marietti, 1950), 111–120. He links divine beauty with simplicity at §336. And at §337 (Pera: 113), Thomas writes that "*pulchritudo autem* participatio *primae causae quae omnia pulchra facit: pulchritudo enim creaturae nihil est aliud quam similitudo divinae pulchritudinis in rebus participata.*" Brother Alexander never uses "participate" with beauty, and for obvious reasons.

117. Even when it does—even when Thomas associated beauty with the Son—it does in the mode of trinitarian appropriation. Still then beauty names a divine attribute, even if it is one appropriable to a particular person.

118. *SH* I, n. 103 (1: 163).

119. *SH* I–II, n. 77 (2: 100).

120. *SH* I, n. 320, ad 2 (1: 472): "*Notionem indistincte sive confuse.*" Also at *SH* I, n. 314 (1: 460) Alexander writes that "in the divinity there is not number simply, but a number *of persons.*"

121. *SH* I, n. 319 (1: 468). Alexander here glosses Richard of St. Victor's *DT* 5.14.

122. *SH* I, n. 319 (1: 468).

123. *SH* I, n. 327 (1: 481).

124. Bychkov, "What Does Beauty Have to Do with the Trinity? From Augustine to Duns Scotus," *Franciscan Studies* 66 (2008): 197–212, and Emery, *Trinitarian Theology*, 209–214.

125. See Augustine's *trin.* 6.10.11 (CCSL 50: 241), which interprets Hilary's *De trinitate* 2.1 (CCSL 62: 38).

126. *Sent.* I, d. 27, c. 3–4 and d. 31, c. 2, nn. 1–9 (Brady 4: 205–207; 225–229); trans. Silano 149; 166–169.

127. For William of Auxerre, see *SA* I, tr. 8, c. 8, q. 4 (Ribaillier 16: 175). I make reference to the relevant texts of the other scholastics below. For more on William, see Boyd Taylor Coolman, *Knowing God by Experience: The Spiritual Senses in the Theology of William of Auxerre* (Washington, DC: CUA Press, 2004), especially 161–183.

128. Scotus, *Reportatio* I-A, d. 34, q. 3, n. 16. Allan Wolter and Oleg Bychkov, *John Duns Scotus: The Examined Report of the Paris Lecture (Reportatio I-A). Latin Text and English Translation*, 2 vols. (St. Bonaventure: The Franciscan Institute, 2004, 2008).

129. Alexander of Hales, *Glossa* I, d. 31, nn. 17–18 (12: 306).

130. Obviously it is possible—indeed likely—that someone else (convention suggests John of La Rochelle) penned the passages under view in *SH* I. It is also entirely possible that Alexander himself did, and that he is simply changed his mind on the matter. But these questions are not mine to answer, nor do they interest me much. For my own conviction about the authorship question, I refer the reader back to my introduction.

131. *Super Dionysium de divinis nominibus*, Opera omnia v. 37.1, ed. by P. Simon (Münster: Aschendorff, 1972), 183. Cf. Bychkov, *Aesthetic Revelation*, 300.

132. *In I Sent.*, d. 31, a. 6 (Borgnet 26: 106–109). Cf. Bychkov, *Aesthetic Revelation*, 300.

133. See Ulrich of Strasburg, *DSB* II, tr. 3, c. 4. *Corpus Philosophorum Teutonicorum Medii Aevi* 1.2, ed. Alain de Libera (Hamburg: Felix Meiner, 1987), 54–63. Cf. Bychkov, *Aesthetic Revelation*, 300.

134. *ST* I, q. 39, a. 8: "*Species autem, sive pulchritudo, habet similitudinem cum propriis filii. Nam ad pulchritudinem tria requiruntur. Primo quidem, integritas sive perfectio . . . Et debita proportio sive consonantia. Et iterum claritas. . . .*" See also *In I Sent.*, d. 31, q. 2, a. 1, *Opera omnia* v. 6 (Parma: P. Fiaccadori, 1856), 251.

135. Bychkov, *Aesthetic Revelation*, 301. Balthasar says much the same in *GOL* 4.

136. For instance, *In I Sent.*, d. 27, p. 2, a. un., q. 3 and d. 31, p. 1, a. un., q. 3. For more on Bonaventure on "Christ beauty," see, in reverse chronological order: Bychkov, *Aesthetic Revelation*, 298–321; Balthasar, "Bonaventure," *GOL* 2, trans. Andrew Louth, Francis McDonagh, and Brian McNeil (San Francisco: Ignatius Press, 1984), 260–362; Karl Peter, *Die Lehre von der Schönheit nach Bonaventura* (PhD diss. at University of Basel, 1964); and Emma Jane Marie Spargo, *The Category of the Aesthetic in the Philosophy of Saint Bonaventure* (St. Bonaventure: The Franciscan Institute, 1953). For a critical evaluation of Balthasar's reading of Bonaventure, see Bychkov's *Aesthetic Revelation*, 78–100, 268–321.

137. Scotus, *Rep.* I-A, d. 3, q. 3 and d. 34, q. 3. Cf. Bychkov, *Aesthetic Revelation*, 303.

138. See, for instance, *SH* I, n. 448 (1: 641) and *SH* II–II, n. 36 (3: 53). Bychkov claims that Alexander "refers, on several occasions, to the *identity* between *species* and beauty in the context of the appropriation of this quality to the Son," Bychkov, *Aesthetic Revelation*, 302, my emphasis. But the texts do not bear out his claim. In the first (*SH* I, n. 448), Alexander asks after the appropriations *aeternitas, species,* and *usus.* Then he merely reproduces the famous text from Augustine's *trin.* 6.10.11, which associates *pulchritudo* with *species* and *imago.* But after that quotation Alexander leaves *pulchritudo* aside entirely. And in the second text (*SH* II–II, n. 36), Alexander raises an objection that suggests an appropriative relation—not an identity—between *pulchritudo* and *species*: "*Modus enim* appropriatur *potentiae sive virtuti,* species vero pulchritudini, *ordo vero bonitati.*"

139. *SH* I, n. 448 (1: 641–642) and nn. 413–418 (1: 603–610).

140. *SH* I, n. 448 (1: 641).

141. *SH* I, n. 414, ad 1 (1: 605) and n. 416 (1: 607).

142. *SH* I, n. 415 (1: 606). Alexander dedicates an article to John of Damascus's claim that Spirit too is image. See *SH* I, n. 418 (1: 608–609).

143. *SH* I, n. 419 (1: 609–610).

144. *SH* I, n. 413 (1: 604).

145. *SH* I, n. 413 (1: 605).

146. *SH* I, n. 417 (1: 608).

147. Bychkov, *Aesthetic Revelation*, 320.

148. See Boethius's defense of analogy or proportion as a species of equivocation in his *In Categorias Aristotelis* I, (PL 64: 166B).

149. *SH* I, n. 319 (1: 468). Alexander here glosses Richard of St. Victor's *DT* 5.14.

150. *SH* I, 304 (1: 440).

151. *SH* I, n. 297 (1: 425).

152. *SH* I, n. 295, ad 6 (1: 418).

PART III: THE TRINITY'S BEAUTY *AD EXTRA*

1. *SH* I, 304 (1: 440).

2. *SH* I, n. 297 (1: 425).

5. THE BEAUTY CREATION IS

1. Francis, *Laudato Si': On care for our common home* (2015), n. 239.

2. Francis here quotes Bonaventure's *qu. disp. de myst. trinitatis*, 1, 2 concl.

3. *In I Sent.*, d. 14, q. 1, a. 1. Cf. Emery, *Trinitarian Theology*, 343.

4. At *SH* I, n. 297, ad 12 (1: 427), Alexander does predicate creation of the divine essence. But here he does so only to deny that generation can be predicated of it (à la Joachim of Fiore), since while generation introduces a distinction among the persons, creation does not.

5. *SH* I, n. 488 (1: 690).

6. *SH* I, n. 488 (1: 690). Cf. Gössmann, *MH*, 183–184.

7. *SH* I, n. 488 (1: 690). Cf. Keane, "The Logic of Self-Diffusive Goodness," 153.

8. *SH* III, n. 12, ad 1–2 (4: 31). Cf. Emery, *La trinité créatrice*, 288.

9. *SH* I, n. 405, ad 2–3 (1: 597).

10. *SH* I, n. 379 (1: 559).

11. *SH* I, n. 418 (1: 609): "*Cum Filius rationem medii habeat . . .*"

12. *SH* I, n. 319 (1: 468), n. 320 (1: 471–472), n. 324 (1: 475–477), n. 418 (1: 609–610), n. 421 (612–613), n. 425 (1: 618), and so on. Cf. Keane, "The Logic of Self-Diffusive Goodness," 136.

13. Emery, *La trinité créatrice*, 199. Cf. Alexander's *QDA* 1, d. 2, m. 2, sol, n. 53 (1: 97).

14. *SH* I, n. 425 (1: 618). Cf. Alexander of Hales, *QDA* q. 9, d. 2, m. 2, sol. n. 53 (1, n. 53, 97).

15. See Basil's *De fide* n. 2 (PG 31: 467–468). Basil's quip reappears in Bonaventure, *In I Sent.*, d. 29, a. 1, q. 2, arg. 1 and ad 1 and in Thomas Aquinas, *In I Sent.*, d. 29, q. un., a. 2, q. 1, arg. 1. Cf. Emery, "Trinity and Creation: The Trinitarian

Principle of the Creation in the Commentaries of Albert the Great, Bonaventure, and Thomas Aquinas on the *Sentences,*" *Trinity in Aquinas* (Ypsilanti: Sapientia Press, 2003), 42.

16. *SH* I, n. 422 (1: 614).

17. *SH* I, n. 422 (1: 614): "*Non enim dicitur Verbum 'creaturae Verbum,' sed Verbum dicitur quo fit creatura.*" Alexander seems here to have the error of Almaric in view. See n. 45 below.

18. *SH* I, n. 64 (1: 96).

19. *SH* I, n. 304 (1: 440).

20. *SH* I, n. 325 (1: 478).

21. *SH* I, n. 403 (1: 440): "*Spiritus Sanctus non diffundit se alii personae, sed creaturis.*"

22. *SH* I, n. 430–432 (1: 622–625).

23. *SH* I, n. 431 (1: 624).

24. *SH* I, n. 73 (1: 114). Cf. *SH* I, n. 88 (1: 140).

25. The example is mine, though I adapt it from Alexander's at *SH* I, n. 104 (1: 163).

26. *SH* I–II, n. 8, b (2: 17).

27. *SH* I–II, n. 8, obj. 2 and ad 2 (2: 16–17). The order Alexander attributes to Aristotle—"*primo ponit formalem exemplarem, secundo efficientem, tertio finalem, quia efficiens agit secundum exemplar aliquid propter finem qui consequi- tur ex eo quod fit*"—derives from *Physica* 2.3 and *Metaphysica* 4.2.

28. *SH* I–II, n. 8 (2: 17).

29. *civ.* 11.21 (CCSL 48: 339–341).

30. John Scottus Eriugena, *Periphyseon (De divisione naturae),* bk. 2, ed. I. P. Sheldon-Williams and Ludwig Bieler (Dublin: Dublin Institute for Advanced Studies, 1972), (555C–556A), 68–70.

31. *SH* I–II, n. 18 (2: 28).

32. *SH* I–II, n. 18, ad 1 (2: 28).

33. Brother Alexander's quotation at obj. 2 derives from Augustine's *Gn. litt.* 4.15.27 (PL 34: 307). But there is strong reason to suspect that the "heretic" Alexander names has something to do with Avicenna. Alexander's depiction here of a heretic who demands that the self-diffusion axiom apply to efficient causal- ity and so crude natural necessity reads very like Aquinas's (mis)representation of Avicenna at *De potentia* 3. Whatever the case, these caricatures bear almost no resemblance to Avicenna's subtler, superior, and actual doctrine on divine will and necessity in creation.

34. This trick enables scholastics to retain the Neoplatonic axiom largely divested of its meaning. God is now "free" not to create, since God always already accomplishes the perfection of his self-diffusive goodness in, well, his own goodness. So Alexander can deny both creation's efficient necessity and its guaranteed perseverance through time [*SH* I–II, n. 18, ad 2 (2: 28)]. On this point in Aquinas, see John F. Wippel's "Norman Kretzmann on Aquinas's attribution of will and of freedom to create to God," *Religious Studies* 39, no. 3 (2003): 287–298. Of

course this lands wide of the Neoplatonic concern—and Avicenna's, too, for that matter. On their view drawing so sharp a distinction between efficient and final causality cannot but court voluntarism. Not that they endorse a crude necessitarianism. Both Plotinus and Avicenna, for example, advocate the importance of the divine will in the act of creation; they both simply deny God a gnomic "choice" in the matter. See Plotinus, *Enn.* VI.8 and Avicenna, *Metaphysica* 8.7. Cf. Julie Swanstrom, "The Metaphysics of Causation" and Rahim Acar, *Talking about God*.

35. *SH* I–II, n. 18, ad 3 (2: 28–29). Cf. Anselm, *Cur deus homo* 1.11 (PL 158: 376) and *De vertitate* 12 (PL 158: 480).

36. Thus Alexander presumes some positive response to his question at *SH* I–II, n. 18, c (2: 28).

37. *SH* I–II, n. 18, ad 5 (2: 29).

38. *SH* I, n. 175 (1: 259).

39. *SH* I, n. 176 (1: 260).

40. *SH* I, n. 48 (1: 75). See also *SH* I, n. 46, 3 (1: 73).

41. At *Epis.* 58.21–22, Seneca distinguishes between "idea" and "eidos." See *Seneca the Younger, vol. IV: Epistles 1–65*, trans. Richard M. Gummere (Cambridge, MA: Harvard University Press, 1917), LCL 75, 398–400.

42. *SH* I–II, n. 10 (2: 18): "*Distinguens inter ideam et eidon, ut idea sit species divina, eidos vero forma in materia.*"

43. *SH* I–II, n. 10 (2: 18–19). Cf. *SH* I, n. 175 (1: 258). This almost exactly matches Alexander's *Glossa* I, d. 36, n. 5 (12: 357–360), though it differs from Alexander's *QDA*, q. 46, n. 36.

44. *SH* I, n. 46, III ad 1 (1: 73).

45. Thomas Aquinas flags and associates this error with the Amalricians at *ST* I, q. 3, a. 8. The Quaracchi editors point to several texts in the *SH* as leveling indirect critiques of Amalric and his followers (see *SH* I–II, prolegomena §78 [2: lvi]). Brother Alexander gets most explicit at *SH* I, n. 175 (1: 259), where he rejects an argument on the basis *quod propinquissimum est illi haeresi quae dicit omnia esse Deum.* Alexander names Amalricianism *illi haeresi* because of its formal condemnation at the Fourth Lateran Council.

46. Doolan, *Aquinas on the Divine Ideas as Exemplar Causes* (Washington DC: CUA Press, 2008), 42.

47. *SH* I, n. 168 (1: 250). Cf. *Enn.* V.1.6 (LCL 444: 33).

48. Emery, "Trinity and Creation," 43.

49. However celebrated, the move poses serious philosophic difficulties for Christians. How to explain multiplicity, especially now that we have claimed essential identity between *Nous* as principle of multiplicity and the sublimely simple God? Archetypical among Christian responses are both the perspectival (the divine ideas only appear multiple from our vantage as creatures) or the voluntarist (God simply "wills" the many from One). The *SH*—like many more—moves along both of these tracks. Still, neither resolves the properly metaphysical question of how God can know (and therefore somehow be)

plurality before God creates it. The perspectival solution simply denies that there is any properly metaphysical problem; the voluntarist one points to something like the wave of a divine wand.

50. *SH* I, n. 296 (1: 419): "*Ubi ponitur generatio, ponitur multiplicatio et differentia generantis et geniti; sed dicendo Deum intelligere se, non dico differentiam nec multiplicationem aliquam, quia nihil aliud est Deum intelligere se quam quasi conversio eius supra se; ergo non est idem generare et intelligere.*" That is not, notice, (1) to deny that he deploys it at all or (2) to indulge a warmed-over dichotomy between Richardian and Augustinian models of trinitarian theology.

51. This is especially true where Alexander defends filioquist arguments. See, for example, *SH* I, n. 324 d and ad 2 (1: 476–477).

52. Notice how trinitarian appropriation structures the first half of *SH* I: *De unitate divinae naturae* (nn. 72–86 [112–137]), *de veritate divinae naturae* (nn. 87–101 [138–159]), *de bonitate divinae naturae* (nn. 102–130 [160–200]); then *De potentia divina* (nn. 131–162 [201–245]), *de scientia divina* (nn. 163–265 [246–359]), *de voluntate divina* (nn. 266–294 [360–413]).

53. *SH* I, n. 415 (1: 606).

54. *SH* I–II, n. 12 (2: 20). Cf. Bonaventure, *In I Sent.*, d. 6, a. un., q. 3, ad 3 and 4 (1: 129–130).

55. *SH* I–II, n. 10 (2: 18). This seems an odd assertion, at least by Neoplatonic lights.

56. Aristotle, *De partibus animalium*, 639b.12–13.

57. *SH* I, n. 107 (1: 168): "*Causa enim finalis ratio est aliarum causarum.*"

58. *SH* I, n. 104 (1: 163).

59. *SH* I–II, n. 17, ad 1–2 (2: 26).

60. Cf. Avicenna, *The Book of Healing* 6.5, trans. Marmura 220 and Robert Wisnovksy's "Final and Efficient Causality in Avicenna's Cosmology and Theology," *Quaestio: The Yearbook of the History of Metaphysics* 2 (2002): 97–123.

61. *SH* I, n. 449 (1: 643–644). Brother Alexander reproduces Richard of St. Victor, *De tribus appropriatis personis in trinitate.* See Jean Ribaillier's edition in *Opuscules théologiques: texte critique avec introduction, notes et tables* (Paris: J.Vrin, 1967), 184.

62. For this turn of phrase and several of the insights that follow it, I owe a debt of gratitude to Boyd Taylor Coolman's "The Pneumatic Finality of Goodness—Metaphysics: Transcendental Pneumatology in the *Summa halensis*," an unpublished paper offered at St. Bonaventure's University on 12 July 2017.

63. See *SH* I, n. 450, ad 1–2 (1: 646) for an example, though others abound.

64. *SH* I, n. 304 (1: 440), n. 309 (447), n. 311 (451), n. 317 (465), n. 319 (468), and so on.

65. *SH* I, n. 110 (1: 172).

66. *Liber de causis*, prop. 1. Cf. Propositions 56 and 70 in Proclus's *Elements of Theology*.

67. *SH* I, n. 295 (1: 418). I say "triple" and not yet "trinitarian" for reasons that become clear below.

68. *brev.* 2.12.1 (5: 230).

69. The term "likeness" (*similitudo*) functions doubly. In a loose sense it refers to all manner of likeness—trace, image, and likeness. In its narrower acceptation, however, it refers specifically to the deiform rational soul. Brother Alexander's *Summa* likely knows this double use of *similitudo* from John of La Rochelle's *Summa de anima* c. 32, ed. Jacques Guy Bougerol (Paris: J. Vrin, 1995), 102–103.

70. Bonaventure calls these the *triplex gradus expressionis* at *brev.* 2.12.1 (5: 230).

71. *SH* I–II, n. 34 (2: 45).

72. *SH* I–II, nn. 34–40 (2: 44–49).

73. *SH* I–II, n. 37 (2: 46).

74. *SH* I–II, n. 33 (2: 43).

75. This triplet holds pride of place in other scholastics like William of Auxerre, though it plays only a secondary role in the *SH*. For more on the triplet in William, see Coolman's *Knowing* God, 161–183.

76. Augustine, *Gn. litt.* 4.3.7 (PL 34: 299).

77. License to transpose this triplet into a spiritual key seems to be granted by Claudianus Mamertus's *De statu animae* 2.5–2.6 (PL 53: 743–745).

78. *SH* I–II, n. 34 (2: 44).

79. *SH* I–II, n. 28, ad 5 (2: 41).

80. Gössmann, *MH*, 186.

81. This line, borrowed from Augustine's *c. Prisc.*, q. 39 (PL 40: 746), recurs across Alexander's treatment of this particular triplet.

82. *SH* I–II, n. 30, ad 1 (2: 42).

83. *SH* I–II, n. 30, ad 1 (2: 42).

84. *div. qu.* 18 (PL 40: 15).

85. *SH* I–II, n. 34 (2: 44). This triplet gets more play in the treatise on the angels, particularly at n. 116 (2: 158–159). Cf. Dionysius, *De cael. hierarch.* 11.2 (PG 122: 1059).

86. In two articles Boyd Taylor Coolman notes how this "Halensian *cum* Nyssan-Dionysian" triplet features in Brother Alexander's opening question on the nature of theology (*SH* I, n. 3 [1: 6]). Cf. Coolman's "Hugh of St. Victor's Influence on the Halensian Definition of Theology," *Franciscan Studies* 70 (2012): 367–384 and, more recently, "On the Subject Matter of Theology in the Summa halensis and St. Thomas Aquinas," *The Thomist* 79, no. 3 (2015): 439–466. Note the presence of this triplet, too, in *De doctrina theologiae* 3.8 (Vat. lat. 782), ed. Francisco de Asís Chavero Blanco in his "La quaestio *De doctrina theologiae* del manuscrito Vat. Lat. 782: introdducción y edición," *Carthaginensia* 15, no. 27[1999]: 31–72).

87. *SH* I–II, n. 75 (2: 99). Cf. n. 33 (43).

88. *SH* I–II, n. 33 (2: 44).

89. *SH* I–II, n. 30 (2: 42). Cf. *SH* I, n. 111 (1: 174).

90. *SH* I, n. 113 (1: 175).

91. *SH* I, n. 113 (1: 175–176).

92. *SH* I, n. 113 (1: 178).

93. *SH* I, n. 113 (1: 178): *"Dicimus quod etsi cognoscantur res sine illis [modus, species et ordo], non cognoscuntur cognitione theologica: ad illam enim necessaria sunt haec."*

94. *SH* I, n. 114 (1: 180).

95. *SH* I, n. 114 (1: 180). Cf. *SH* I–II, n. 37 (2: 47).

96. The image is Alexander's. See *SH* I–II, n. 37 (2: 47).

97. *SH* II–II, n. 35, ad 1–2 (3: 52).

98. *SH* I–II, n. 39 (2: 48). Alexander makes an exception in the case of nonrational creatures, whose death or destruction signals the erasure of the created trace. Yet the vestige remains to the extent that as an idea in the mind of God no creature *omnino cedit in non-ens*. Cf. Augustine, *civ.* 19.12 (CCSL 48: 675–678).

99. Proclus, *Theology of Plato* 3.9.

100. *CD* I/I, trans. Geoffrey William Bromiley (Edinburgh: T&T Clark, 1975), 334, emphasis mine.

101. Already in Brother Alexander's first question, he is keen to distinguish theology from philosophical sciences on the grounds that *non agunt de deo secundum mysterium trinitatis vel secundum sacramentum humanae reparationis. SH* I, n. 2, ad 1–4 (1: 5). Cf. Albert the Great's *SDN,* c. 2, n. 56, ad 2 (Cologne edition, vol. 37.1: 81).

102. *SH* I, n. 10 (1: 19). A reply to the second objection that the author of the Hermetic corpus knew the trinity because he writes *Monas monadem genuit* states that the author knew this *non per naturalem rationem, sed per doctrinam vel inspirationem.* Cf. William of Auxerre, *SA* III, tr. 4, q. 1 (f. 151a). Cf. Gössmann, *MH,* 184–185.

103. *SH* I, n. 10 (1: 19). For more on the philosophers' need of grace, see *SH* III, n. 606 (4: 944–950). Here the *SH* is faithful to Alexander's position at *Glossa* I, d. 2, n. 6 (12: 29).

104. This will be Bonaventure's position, which seems very close to Brother Alexander's. See Bonaventure, *In I Sent.*, d. 3, a. un., q. 4 (1: 76b).

105. This distinction holds even when it seems like Brother Alexander forgets it. At *SH* I, n. (1: 19), for instance, when Alexander reproduces the position of the *Glossa*: *"[philosophi] cognitionem ipsius trinitatis per propria ipsarum personarum non habuerunt nec habere potuerunt, nisi per doctrinam aut inspirationem; sed notitiam trinitatis per appropriata ipsis personis, scilicet potentiam, sapientiam et benignitatem,* habuerunt et habere potuerunt." Alexander responds that even when non-Christians seem to know an appropriated attribute like goodness, they do not know it as truly appropriated because they do not know the trinitarian *propria.*

106. Emery, *Trinitarian Theology,* 326. Brother Alexander offers a similar example at *SH* I, n. 405, ad 4 (1: 597), where he says that philosophers might know God as "principle" of the world, but not "principle" as Father of Son and Spirit and world.

107. *SH* I–II, n. 35 (2: 45).

108. *SH* I–II, n. 81 (2: 103).

109. Søren Kierkegaard, "The Seducer's Diary," *Either/Or: Part I. Kierkegaard's Writings*, vol. 3, trans. Howard V. and Edna. H. Hong, (Princeton: Princeton University Press, 1987), 301–445.

110. *SH* I–II, n. 40 (2: 49), reproducing Augustine's *De vera rel.* 22.43 (PL 34: 140).

111. Cf. Aristotle, *De partibus animalium* 1.5.645a (LCL 323: 98–99).

112. *SH* I–II, n. 40 (2: 49).

113. Bychkov, "A Propos of Medieval Metaphysics," 23.

114. For a long list of related uses of order and hierarchy, see Marie-Dominique Chenu's classic *Nature, Man, and Society in the Twelfth Century: Essays on New Theological Perspectives in the Latin West*, trans. and ed. Jerome Taylor and Lester K. Little (Toronto: University of Toronto Press, 1997), 81–82, n. 60.

115. *SH* I–II, n. 77 (2: 101)

116. This use features prominently across *SH* I–II, nn. 86–98 (2: 109–120).

117. *civ.* 19.13 (CCSL 48: 679): "*Ordo est parium dispariumque sua cuique tribuens loca dispositio.*" For this definition at work in the first sense, see *SH* I, n. 320 (1: 471); in the third, see *SH* I–II, n. 86 (2: 109).

118. *SH* I, n. 324 (1: 476): "*Ergo ordo in divinis personis sit exemplar huiusmodi ordinis.*"

119. Gössmann and Bychkov privilege the providential.

120. *SH* I–II, n. 75 (2: 99). I excerpt this passage from a larger objection that asks after the difference between truth and beauty. If both truth and beauty have something to do with *species* or *forma*, then how do they differ? Brother Alexander's answer is known to some commentators, but highly enigmatic: *veritas est dispositio ex parte formae relata ad interius, pulcritudo vero est dispositio ex parte formae relata ad exterius.* He borrows this quip from William of Auxerre, though it is not immediately clear how it coheres with Alexander's own aesthetic. He was just busied writing on the triplet that indwells creatures—what has this to do with *forma relata ad exterius*? Whatever else this means, it cannot refer simply or exclusively to bodies. It is possible that the *ad exterius* connects the beauty that indwells each creature to the creature's own natural desire for beauty, which it finds in other creatures. But getting clear on this puzzle would require a complete study on aesthetic experience or the subjective aspects of beauty that I cannot here perform.

121. The Isidore passage quoted at *SH* I–II, n. 76 is found also in Albert's *STh* II, tr. 11, q. 62, m. 1 (Borgnet 32: 596) and Ulrich of Strasburg's *DSB* II, tr. 3, c. 4, n. 9 (De Libera 3: 59). Cf. Bychkov, "A Propos," 211.

122. *SH* I–II, n. 76 (2: 100). Cf. Isidore of Seville, *Sentences* 1.8.18 (PL 83: 551–552).

123. *SH* I–II, n. 76 (2: 100).

124. *SH* I–II, n. 77 (2: 100–101). Alexander and others adopt this distinction from Augustine's *lib. arb.* 1.1 (PL 32: 1221–1222). Cf. Thomas Aquinas's *ST* I, q. 48, a. 5 or *De malo* q. 1, a. 4.

125. *SH* I–II, n. 77 (2: 101).

126. *SH* I–II, n. 78 (2: 101).

127. *SH* I–II, n. 78 (2: 101).

128. Bychkov discusses Alexander's arguments in his "A Propos of Medieval Aesthetics," 47.

129. *SH* I–II, n. 79 (2: 102).

130. This is the stipulative definition given at *SH* I–II, n. 79 (2: 101).

131. *SH* I–II, n. 79 (2: 102).

132. *SH* I–II, n. 79 (2: 102). Here Alexander reproduces Augustine's *civ.* 16.8.2 (CCSL 48: 509–510).

133. *SH* I–II, n. 79 (2: 102).

134. *SH* I–II, n. 80 (2: 102–103).

135. Only the middle example is Alexander's, or rather Augustine's reported by Alexander. See *SH* I–II, n. 80, obj. 2.

136. *SH* I–II, n. 80, obj. 3.

137. *SH* I–II, n. 80, ad 2 (2: 102).

138. Cf. Augustine's *nat. b.* 8 (CSEL 25.6.2: 858). See also *Gn. litt.* 1.8 (CSEL 28/3/2: 11) and 1.17 (CSEL 28/3/225); *div. qu.* 83.44 (CCSL 44A: 65.3–4); *vera rel.* 21.41 (CCSL 32: 213). Cf. Bychkov, "*Decor ex praesentalia mali*," 248.

139. Cf. Augustine's *lib. arb.* 3.9.27 (CCSL 29: 290–291). Cf. Bychkov, "*Decor ex praesentalia mali*," 249.

140. *SH* I–II, n. 80, ad 2 (2: 102).

141. *SH* I–II, n. 81 (2: 103).

142. Peter Lombard, *Sent.*, I, d. 46, c. 3 (SB 4: 314). The Lombard's editors associate the first position with Hugh of St. Victor's *DS* 1.4. There, Hugh argues that "*bonum fuit esse et bona et mala. Et voluit utrumque esse deus, quia utrumque bonum esse fuit . . . Et id circo non voluit deus malum, cum voluit ut esset et malum*" (1.4.5 [PL 176: 236A]). Later at *DS* 1.4.13, Hugh argues that "*quoniam malum esse vult et malum non vult . . . Et tamen vult esse malum, et in eo non nisi bonum vult, quia bonum est malum esse; et non vult ipsum malum, quia bonum non est ipsum malum*" (PL 176: 239C–D). The author of the *Summa sententiarum,* perhaps a *reportatio* of Hugh's lectures and well known to thirteenth-century scholastics, argues the same at tr. 1, c. 13 (PL 176: 65C–66C). Cf. Bychkov, "Decor ex praesentia mali," 259.

143. Bychkov, "*Decor ex praesentia mali*," 260–264.

144. *Glossa* I, d. 46 (12: 458–475) and II, dd. 34 and 36 (13: 325–334, 351–359).

145. For Albert, see *In I Sent.*, d. 46, a. 2 (Borgnet 26: 425–428), *STh* I, tr. 6, q. 27, c. 5 (Borgnet 31: 283–287) and II, tr. 11, q. 62, m. 2 (Borgnet 32: 598–604). For Thomas, see *Sent.* I, d. 46, q. 1, a. 3 and *ST* I, q. 19, a. 9. For Ulrich, see *DSB* II, tr. 3, c. 4, n. 7 (De Libera 3: 57–58). Cf. Bychkov, "*Decor ex praesentia mali*," 252.

146. That Alexander's texts (both his 'authentic' writings and the *SH*) stoke the thirteenth-century controversy is Bychkov's argument across his excellent "*Decor ex praesentia mali:* Aesthetic Explanation of Evil in Thirteenth-Century

Franciscan Thought," *Recherches de théologie et philosophie médiévales* 68, no. 2 (2001): 245–269. See also Mark Edwards, "Evil in Dionysius the Areopagite, Alexander of Hales, and Thomas Aquinas" in *The Summa Halensis: Sources and Context*, 55–70.

147. *SH* I–II, n. 82 (2: 104).

148. Or so Alexander (*SH* I–II, n. 82, obj. 2 [2: 104]) reads Dionysius at *DN* 4.19: "*Inconveniens autem est quod malum conferat ad completionem omnis et toti non imperfectum esse per se ipsum largiatur.*"

149. *SH* I–II, n. 82 (2: 105).

150. At *SH* I–II, n. 82 (2: 104–105), Alexander quotes Augustine's *civ.* 11.23 (CCSL 48: 341–343) and Isidore's *Sententiae* I.9.5 (PL 83: 552) in support of a chiaroscuro theodicy.

151. Alexander defines mutable things at *SH* I–II, n. 83 (2: 105): "*Et dico mutabilia ea quae mutantur in esse.*"

152. This, anyway, forms the common denominator among obj. 1–3.

153. *SH* I–II, n. 83 (2: 105).

154. *SH* I–II, n. 83 (2: 106).

155. *SH* I–II, n. 83, obj. 1 (2: 106)

156. *SH* I–II, n. 83 (2: 106).

157. *SH* I–II, n. 83 (2: 106).

158. Albert the Great seems to borrow these topics and their structure. See his *STh* II, tr. 11, q. 62, m. 2 (Borgnet 33: 599–604). Cf. Bychkov, "A Propos of Medieval Aesthetics," 52–53.

159. *SH* I–II, n. 84, contra 1 (2: 106).

160. *SH* I–II, n. 84, contra 2 (2: 106).

161. For more, see *div. qu.* 66.3; *ex. prop. Rom.* 36–64; and *Simp.* 1.1. Cf. William S. Babcock, "Augustine's Interpretation of Romans (A.D. 394–396)," *Augustinian Studies* 10 (1979): 55–74.

162. *SH* I–II, n. 84 (2: 107).

163. *SH* I–II, n. 84, ad 1 (2: 107).

164. Thus for Alexander miracles become necessary only after creation's damage. This does not explain, however, why Alexander disallows wonders *ante lapsum*—unlike miracles, wonders do not seem necessarily to presuppose damage.

165. Alexander's title proves a bit misleading, as he does not much consider sacraments in the arguments that follow.

166. *SH* I–II, n. 85, ob 1 and 3 (2: 107). Bychkov seems to report ob 1 as Alexander's own view when he writes "if beauty is a kind of arrangement, a mean term is always necessary between its elements, which also applies to the relationship between God and man: in this case, the mean term that restores harmony is Christ." But this particular argument does not feature in ad 3, where Alexander enumerates six different *congruentia* for the incarnation's beauty. See Bychkov, "A Propos of Medieval Aesthetics," 52.

167. Gössmann, *MH,* 191.

168. This recalls Brother Alexander's division of salvation history into *opera conditionis* and *opera reparationis* at *SH* I, n. 3 (1: 5–6).

169. He confirms this at *SH* I–II, n. 85, ad 3 (2: 108): "*Dicendum quod, licet pulchritudo universi quantum ad secundum statum,* potuerit esse sine incarnatione, *non tamen potuit esse ut multiplex congruentia servaretur.*" For more on this question, see *SH* III, n. 4 (4: 14–17).

170. *SH* I–II, n. 85, ad 3 (2: 108).

171. I hasten to note how this remains a distinct question from the now infamous "had Adam not sinned" question that Brother Alexander considers at *SH* III, n. 23 (4: 41–42). Though the question under consideration considers modal alternatives, it is decidedly posed under the condition of sin. So even some of the arguments tendered in favor of the incarnation's peculiar fittingness assume the fall. Of them, only the argument from the pseudo-Augustinian *DSA* 9 (PL 35: 1591) recurs in *SH* III, n. 23 (4: 41–42). I direct the interested reader to Justus Hunter's *If Adam Had Not Sinned: The Motive for the Incarnation from Anselm to Scotus* (Washington DC: CUA Press, 2019). See also Hunter's more recent "The Contribution of the *Summa Halensis* to the Reason for the Incarnation" in *The Summa Halensis: Debates and Doctrines,* 141–152, which elaborates on these points.

172. *SH* I, n. 324 (1: 476).

6. THE BEAUTY THE SOUL IS

1. *SH* I, n. 103 (1: 162).

2. For the analytical account of this question, see Pius Künzle, *Das Verhältnis der Seele zu ihren Potenzen. Problemgeschichtliche Untersuchungen von Augustin bis und mit Thomas von Aquin* (Freiburg: Universitätsverlag, 1956); and Magdalena Bieniak's excellent *The Soul-Body Problem at Paris, ca. 1200–1250: Hugh of St-Cher and His Contemporaries* (Leuven: Leuven University Press, 2010), 91–118 and "The Soul-Body Union in the *Summa halensis*" in *The Legacy of Early Franciscan Thought,* 37–49. More recently still, see Lydia Schumacher, "The *De anima* Tradition in Early Franciscan Thought: A Case Study in Avicenna's Reception" in *The Summa Halensis: Sources and Context,* 155–170.

3. The following studies offer a larger scope on psychological debates in the early thirteenth-century: Richard C. Dales's *The Problem of the Rational Soul in the Thirteenth Century* (Boston/Leiden: Brill Publishers, 1995), Dag Nikolaus Hasse's *Avicenna's* De Anima *in the Latin West: The Formation of a Peripatetic Philosophy of the Soul 1160–1300* (London: The Warburg Institute, 2000), and Bieniak's *The Soul-Body Problem at Paris.*

4. Alain de Libera, *Archéologie du sujet,* 2 vols. (Paris: J. Vrin, 2007–2008). He summarizes his argument in "When Did the Modern Subject Emerge?," *American Catholic Philosophical Quarterly* 82, no. 2 (2008): 181–220.

5. De Libera, "When Did the Modern Subject Emerge?," 204.

6. *trin.* 3.4.10 (CCSL 50: 137). Cf. De Libera, "When Did the Modern Subject Emerge?," 204.

7. Robinson thinks de Libera's work might address Charles Taylor's "neglect of the contribution the Middle Ages makes to the concept of 'self'" in his magisterial *Sources of the Self.* See Robinson's "Sources of the Self and Early 13th Century Augustinian Responses to Aristotle's Noetic" in his "The Early 13th Century Latin-Augustinian Reception of the Peripatetic Agent Intellect," 192–227.

8. De Libera notes and exposits "L'interprétation scolastique du modèle périchorétique de l'âme," especially Aquinas's and Bonaventure's, in his first volume. See *Archéologie du sujet: naissance du sujet,* 297–342.

9. I borrow this term and very much else from Bieniak's unparalleled *The Soul-Body Problem at Paris.*

10. McGinn, "Introduction," 69. See also Künzle, *Das Verhältnis,* 28.

11. *trin.* 10.11.18 (CCSL 50: 330).

12. See Bieniak, *The Soul-Body Problem,* 99; and Künzle, *Das Verhältnis der Seele,* 34–38.

13. For more on the authorship question, see Bernard McGinn's helpful introduction to *Three Treatises on Man: A Cistercian Anthropology* (Kalamazoo: Cistercian Publications, 1977), 1–100.

14. Lombard, *Sentences* 1, d. 3, c. 2, n. 8 (Brady 4:74), trans. Silano 24–25: "This is so because they exist substantially *in* the soul or mind itself . . . these exist *in* the spirit substantially . . . yet they exist severally *in* their own substance." And later, in n. 9: "As Augustine says . . . these three have been divinely and naturally established *in* the mind, and also how great a thing it is *in* the mind whereby even the eternal and unchangeable nature can be recalled, gazed, upon, and desired." Later, in c. 3, n. 3: "The mind is here understood not as the soul, but as that which is most excellent *in* the soul." Again, in c. 3, n. 4: "These three things, even though they are mutually distinct, yet are said to be one because they exist substantially *in* the spirit."

15. Lombard, *Sentences* 1, d. 3, c. 2, n. 8 (Brady 4:74): *"Ecce ex quo sensu illa tria dicantur esse unum vel una substantia."*

16. McGinn, "Introduction," 74: "It is obvious that the stress is on inclusiveness rather than consistency or system."

17. See, for example, *DSA* 4, 7, 9, 13, 34, 35, and 37. Cf. McGinn, "Introduction," 69. All English quotations are taken from Erasmo Leiva's and Sr. Benedicta Ward, SLG's translation of "Treatise on the Spirit and the Soul" in *Three Treatises on Man.*

18. *DSA* 13 (PL 40: 789), trans. "Treatise on the Spirit," 200.

19. Other defenses of the identity thesis can be found in Hugh of St. Cher, the anonymous *Quaestio si anima est sua potentia,* and William of Auvergne. For more on these, see Bieniak, *The Soul-Body Problem,* 102–107.

20. Two sites are to be found in Philip's *SDB.* But he raises the question again in his *Quaestio disputata De imagine et similitudine nostra,* ed. Niklaus Wicki in

his *Die Philosophie Philipps des Kanzlers. Ein philosophierender Theologe des frühen 13. Jahrhunderts* (Fribourg: Academic Press Fribourg, 2005), 171–181. Most interesting is the second place Philip faces the question in *SDB*, though detailing that would take me too far afield. It is enough to say here that though Philip shifts his argumentative strategy in the latter part of the text, his commitment to the identity thesis has not flagged. Different here is the inclusion of a fresh metaphysical division, one that (scholars agree) he learned from Alexander of Hales midway through the composition of his *SDB*. On this point, see Künzle, *Das Verhältnis der Seele*, 109–110, and Bieniak, *The Soul-Body Problem*, 107–112. That Alexander's distinction meant to combat the identity thesis does not stop Philip from adopting it without endorsing a divergent conclusion. I flag this only (1) to note the closeness of the theological community in Paris during the early decades of the 13th century and (2) to weigh the gravitas of Alexander's influence upon his peers.

21. *SDB* I.3.4 (Wicki 1: 250).

22. *SDB* I I.3.4 (Wicki 1: 250): "*Preterea, circumincedentes sunt illi actus. Quod enim volo intelligo et memini, et quod memini intelligo et volo, et quod intelligo memini et volo, sicut Augustinus dicit in libro* De trinitate. *Hoc autem inducitur ut ponatur similitudo ad divinas personas sese circumincedentes, sicut dicit Iohannes Damascenus.*" Neither Künzle nor Bieniak note this passage or the explicit logic of perichoresis throughout Philip's psychology.

23. Surely De Libera has it right that historically "Augustin est toujours cité par les médiévaux . . . comme garant de la thèse de l'identité essentielle entre l'âme et ses facultés." He seems not to recognize that some other of Augustine's texts point in the opposite direction. Cf. De Libera, *Archéologie du sujet*, 302.

24. *trin.* 15.27.48, trans. Hill 422 (CCSL 50a: 529–530): "Nor do these three differ in them, as in us memory is one thing, understanding another and love or charity yet another"; and *ep.* 169.2.6 (Teske 109): "But these three should not for this reason be thought to be comparable to the Trinity so as to match it in every respect . . . This likeness, then, is first found to be unlike the Trinity insofar as these three, memory, understanding, and will, *are in the soul but are not the soul.* That Trinity, however, is not in God but is God" (Teske 110).

25. Here I follow Mark D. Jordan's view that for scholastics an *auctoritas* typically references "a textual precedent deserving attention" rather than a mere historical figure. Jordan, *Rewritten Theology: Aquinas after His Readers* (Malden/Oxford: Blackwell Publishing, 2006), 64.

26. Hasse, *Avicenna's* De anima *in the Latin West*, 21. Such is true in the *SH* anyway, where Alexander variously calls both Avicenna and Aristotle *philosophus*. Avicenna is the *philosophus* in question at least 18 times. Cf. Hasse, *Avicenna's* De anima *in the Latin West*, 53.

27. *De anima* 1.5, from Avicenna Latinus, *Liber de anima seu sextus de naturalibus I–III*, ed. S. Van Riet (Leuven/Leiden: E. Peeters/Brill, 1972), 81. Cf. Künzle, *Das Verhältnis*, 100.

28. Avicenna Latinus, *Liber de philosophia prima sive Scientia divina* 8.5 (405). I report here the traditional view, though scholarship debates whether Avicenna imagined God to have an essence at all.

29. Boethius, *De trinitate* 2 (PL 64: 1250).

30. William of Auxerre, *SA* II, tr. 9, c. 1, q. 6 (Ribaillier 17: 243).

31. *SA* II, tr. 9, c. 1, q. 6 (Ribaillier 17: 243).

32. *SA* II, tr. 9, c. 1, q. 6 (Ribaillier 17: 243–244).

33. Actually, "quality" is not an accurate translation in Latin or English. *Isagoge* 3.21–22 (Busse 8) reads: "One item is said to differ most properly from a diverse item when it is distinguished by a specific difference—as man differs from a horse by a *specific difference* (εἰδοποιῷ διαφορᾷ), that of rational." Not only does Porphyry distinguish "difference" and "quality" lexically; he also distinguishes them conceptually, since his third and fourth chapters treat each respectively. Translation taken from Jonathan Barnes's *Porphyry: Introduction* (Oxford: Oxford University Press, 2003), 9. Greek from *Porphyrii Isagoge et in Aristotelis Categorias Commentarium*, ed. Adolfus Busse (Berlin: Reimer, 1887), 8.

34. On exactly this question Thomas Aquinas will differentiate between (1) an accident "which is the opposite of 'substance' and includes under itself nine categories of things" and (2) an accident "as being one of the four predicates put down by Aristotle in the *Topics* and as being one of the five universals put down by Porphyry." The first is an accident properly speaking, the second something midway between substance and accident—what Thomas calls a "natural property." He concludes: "the powers of the soul are intermediate between the essence of the soul and an accident, as natural or essential properties, that is, as properties that are a natural consequence of the essence of the soul." See *De spiritualibus creaturis*, q. 11, co.

35. *SA* II, tr. 9, c. 1, q. 6 (Ribaillier 17: 244).

36. *SA* II, tr. 9, c. 1, q. 6 (Ribaillier 17: 243).

37. I borrow from Boyd Taylor Coolman the concept of a "Halensian school," which stands in for what Roest calls the "old Franciscan school." And this in apparent contrast to "the middle Franciscan school" and later forms of Scotism and Ockhamism. Still it seems to me that the present dearth of research on the so-called "middle Franciscan school" (the mature Bonaventure, John Peckham, John of Wales, Matthew of Aquasparta, Peter John Olivi, and Vital du Four) renders difficult any sharp distinctions among it and the earlier or latter ones. Cf. Bert Roest, *Franciscan Learning, Preaching, and Mission c. 1220–1650* (Boston/Leiden: Brill Publishers, 2015), 121.

38. For a highly compressed biography, see Bougerol's introduction to his edition of Jean de La Rochelle, *Summa de anima*, ed. J.-G. Bougerol (Paris: Vrin, 1995), 9–13.

39. Neither Alexander's *QDA* nor what is edited of the scattered *QDP* treat of the soul-powers question as posed.

40. Étienne Gilson, *History of Christian Philosophy in the Middle Ages* (New York: Random House, 1955), 329.

41. Many associate another disputed question over the issue with Alexander, edited by Odon Lottin in his *Psychologie et morale aux XIIe et XIIIe siècles*, vol. 1 (Louvain: Abbaye du Mont César, 1942), 490–492. But I rather doubt it bears Alexander's hand for reasons Walter H. Principe describes in *The Theology of the Hypostatic Union in the Early Thirteenth Century, vol. 2: Alexander of Hales' Theology of the Hypostatic Union* (Toronto: Pontifical Institute of Mediaeval Studies, 1967), 51. Cf. Künzle, *Das Verhältnis der Seele*, 120–121.

42. Alexander of Hales, *Glossa* I, d. 3, nn. 1, 5, 11, 16, 22.

43. *Glossa* I, d. 3, n. 29 (12: 50–52).

44. *Glossa* 1, d. 3, n. 34d. Cf. *Glossa* 1, d. 3, n. 30 (12: 52).

45. *Glossa* 1, d. 3, 46a (12: 64). Cf. *DSA* 13 (PL 40: 789).

46. *Glossa* 1, d. 3, 46b (12: 64): "*In omni eo quod est citra Primum, differt quod est et esse; ergo quo potest et quod potest: ergo anima et sua potentia.*" Cf. Boethius, *De trinitate* 2 (PL 64: 1250).

47. *Glossa* I, d. 3, n. 46c (12: 65).

48. Bieniak suggests that there is conceptual precedent for the distinction in Gilbert of Poitiers, though there is also ample precedent in the Neoplatonic tradition. Cf. Bieniak, *The Soul-Body Problem*, 109–110.

49. *Glossa* I, d. 3, 46c (12: 65): "*Essentia est illud quo res est id quod est, ut homo humanitate. Substantia vero quo res est substans sive subsistit inseparabiliter. Subiectum est cui adveniunt aliqua et sine quorum aliquo vel quolibet res potest esse.*"

50. *Glossa* I, d. 3, 46c (12: 65).

51. *Glossa* I, d. 3, 46c (12: 65).

52. *Glossa* I, d. 3, 12 (12: 32).

53. *Glossa* I, d. 3, 46c (12: 65). This also explains why Alexander sometimes says at *Glossa* I, d. 26 (12: 254) that "*in creatura autem differt 'quod est' et 'quo est'. 'Quo est' est essentia, 'quod est' est substantia, ut: non est homo sua humanitas.*" *Quod est* here stands in for an actualized *essentia*, or an abstract essence that's been gifted existence. On this reading, then, Alexander is not identifying *substantia* itself with 'quod est,, but rather as the direct result of an *essentia* in act.

54. Principe notices that the distinction between the essence of a substance and its non-accidental properties marks a lynchpin for his doctrine of transubstantiation at *Glossa* IV, d. 10, 4g (4: 156). Principe, *Alexander of Hales' Theology of the Hypostatic Union*, 51.

55. *Glossa* I, d. 3, n. 46c (65): "*Subiectum dicitur anima respectu accidentium.*" Alexander speaks of the subject as bearer of accidents elsewhere too. See, for example, *Glossa* I, d. 26, n. 6 (12: 256), II, d. 26, n. 10 (13: 245); II, d. 35, n. 9c (13: 341); *QDA* 51, nn. 118–127 (938–941). Cf. Principe, *Alexander of Hales' Theology of the Hypostatic Union*, 52.

56. *Glossa* I, d. 3, 47 (12: 66): "'*Et haec eadem trinitas permanebit' et secundum illam est imago. Non ergo peribit esse imaginis, nec est accidentale hoc modo.*"

57. Hasse shows, for instance, that John's "first-hand knowledge" of Avicenna's *De anima* exceeded that of his peers; he cited passages unknown to them. Hasse, *Avicenna's* De Anima *in the Latin West*, 49–50.

58. Robinson offers a summary of views on the dating of these two works in his "The Agent Intellect in Two Early-Thirteenth Century Franciscan Texts: John of Rochelle's *Summa de Anima* and Book 2 of the *Summa fratris Alexandri*" in "The Early Thirteenth Century Latin-Augustinian Reception of the Peripatetic Agent Intellect," 96. Cf. Jean Rohmer, "La théorie de l'abstraction dans l'école franciscaine de Alexandre de Halès à John Peckham," *Archives d'histoire doctrinale et littéraire du moyen-âge* 3 (1928): 105–184 and Hasse, *Avicenna's* De Anima *in the Latin West*, 51–54.

59. Hasse, *Avicenna's* De Anima *in the Latin West*, 51, n. 227. Cf. Ryan, "Jean de La Rochelle on the Soul and its Powers," 53.

60. Ryan summarizes Bougerol's index of textual similarities between the *SH* and John's *SDA* at "Jean de La Rochelle on the Soul and its Powers," 55.

61. John of La Rochelle, *SDA* c. 60, ed. J.-G. Bougerol (Paris: J. Vrin, 1995), 181–184 and *SH* I–II, n. 349, (2: 424–425). That is not, of course, to say they bear no difference on the soul whatever. Robinson shows, for instance, that the *SH* refines John's position on the agent intellect. John imagined three agent intellects—one in God, another in the soul, and still another in the angel. The *SH* denies the last. The *SH* also embeds John's position on the individual agent intellect within "the Augustinian claim that the soul is an *imago dei*, which gives the basis for its self-perfecting capacity . . . [Brother Alexander] fuses [the individual agent intellect] with the *imago Dei* doctrine more completely than John does." Robinson, "The Early Thirteenth Century Latin-Augustinian Reception of the Peripatetic Agent Intellect," 119–122.

62. *SDA* c. 60, 1–30 (182–183); *SH* I–II, n. 349, obj. 1–3 (2: 494).

63. *SDA* c. 60, 1–9 (182).

64. *SDA* c. 60, 10–17 (182).

65. *SDA* c. 60, 18–30 (182–183).

66. *SDA* c. 60, 49–53 (183).

67. *SDA* c. 60, 54–66 (183). The position depicted here undoubtedly belongs to Philip the Chancellor, whose texts John of La Rochelle knew well. Cf. Ryan, "Jean de La Rochelle on the Soul and its Powers," 24. See also J.-M. Vernier's introduction to his translation of Jean's text in *Somme de l'âme* (Paris: J. Vrin, 2001), 8.

68. *SDA* c. 60 (184).

69. *SH* I–II, n. 349 (2: 424–425).

70. Künzle argues for a close relation between John and the *SH* at *Das Verhältnis der Seele*, 124. Both Bieniak and Denise Ryan challenge the close association Künzle sees, though only Bieniak registers her interpretation as a disagreement. She reads John to affirm the identity thesis at c. 35 (Bougerol 113), but acknowledges that it is fairly ambiguous. Notice, though, that he here

affirms identity *at the level of substance*. Cf. Bieniak, *The Soul-Body Problem*, 117 and Ryan, "Jean de La Rochelle on the Soul and its Powers," 115–120.

71. A note at *SDA* c. 60 (184) reports that a fifteenth-century manuscript (National Central Library of Fiorenza ms. 970) appends the following: "*Haec tria, scilicet memoriam, intelligentiam et voluntatem, dicit Augustinus idem esse quod animam quia complent et efficiunt idem esse anima, sicut dicit Magister in Sententiis. Et ideo dicit Augustinus quod haec tria, mens, notitia et amor non sunt in anima ut in subjecto, ut color in corpora, quia non sunt adventitia ipsi anima, sed complentia esse ipsius quod est adventitium, ut color corpori non complet esse eius; nec valet obiectio de prima materia: non videtur idem esse quod et posse suscipere formam quamlibet talis potentia, non est aliqua potentia sed inferioritas. Potentiae precedunt omnem materiam et omnem formam. Unde non dicitur proprie materia habere aliquam potentiam vel aliquid posse.*" Bieniak knows, too—or so a footnote suggests—this tacks William of Auxerre's response to the prime matter argument at the very end of John's question, exactly where the response shows up in the *SH*. Künzle admits that one of John's statements earlier in the *Summa de anima* leaves a "zwiespältigen Eindruck." But why, Künzle asks, would John first register Alexander's solution and then append to it the strongest of objections against Philip's identity thesis if he himself held it?

72. *SH* I–II, n. 349, ad 3 (3: 425).

73. Gilson, *Christian Philosophy in the Middle Ages*, 329.

74. For more on the image in Alexander's "authentic" texts, see Italo Fornaro's *La teologia dell'immagine nella Glossa di Alessandro d'Hales* (Vicenza: Edizioni L.I.E.F., 1985).

75. *SH* I–II, n. 336 (2: 408–409).

76. Alexander treats the same question in more detail at *SH* I–II, n. 338 (2: 410–411), where he asks: *Qua ratione dicatur 'ad imaginem Dei'* and *Utrum homo possit dici ad imaginem Filii quaeritur.*

77. *SH* I–II, n. 336, obj. 1 (2: 408). Cf. Hilary of Poitiers, *De synodis* 13 (PL 10: 490).

78. *SH* I–II, n. 336, obj. 3 and 4 (2: 408).

79. *SH* I–II, n. 336 (2: 409).

80. *SH* I–II, n. 336, ad 3 (2: 409). Cf. ad 4.

81. *SH* I–II, n. 336, ad 4 (2: 409).

82. *SH* I–II, n. 337 (2: 409).

83. *SH* I–II, n. 337, ad 1 (2: 410).

84. It seems odd that here Brother Alexander refers to the transcendental triplet instead of *modus-species-ordo*, which he typically features more prominently in his treatments of the trace.

85. *SH* I–II, n. 337, ad 1 (2: 410).

86. *SH* I–II, n. 337, ad 1 (2: 410).

87. *SH* I–II, n. 337, obj. 2 and 3 (2: 409).

88. *SH* I–II, n. 337, ad 2 (2: 410).

89. *SH* I–II, n. 104 (2: 131–133) and n. 183 (2: 238–239). Curiously enough, Alexander's account of angelic incorporeality does not commit him to Thomas Aquinas's view that each individual angel constitutes its own species. On this point, see *SH* I–II, n. 115 (2: 156).

90. *SH* I–II, n. 337, ad 2 (2: 410).

91. Cf. *SH* I–II, n. 338, II (2: 411).

92. *SH* I–II, n. 337, ad 2 (2: 410).

93. *SH* I–II, n. 340, I (2: 412).

94. *SH* I–II, n. 340, II (2: 413).

95. *SH* I–II, n. 340, III (2: 413–414).

96. *SH* I–II, n. 339, I, sol (2: 411).

97. *SH* I–II, n. 339, I ad 1 (2: 411).

98. *SH* I–II, n. 339, II (2: 411): "*Imago in cognitione, similitudo in dilectione.*" The distinction here comes from the *De spiritu et anima* 10 and 39 (PL 40: 789; 809).

99. *SH* I–II, n. 339, II, sol (2: 411–412).

100. *SH* I–II, n. 341, I (2: 414).

101. *SH* I–II, n. 341, II (2: 414).

102. *SH* I–II, n. 341, I (2: 414).

103. *SH* I–II, n. 341, II, obj. 2 (2: 414). This argument has both Aristotelian and Neoplatonic precedent—call these horizontal and vertical versions of act. On the horizontal level (Aristotle's), nothing can be reduced to act by anything not already in act (*Metaphysica* 9.8.1049b24–28). Neoplatonists erect this axiom vertically. Consider, for example, *Liber de causis*, prop. 17.

104. *SH* I–II, n. 341, II, ad 2 (2: 414).

105. Friedman, *Medieval Trinitarian Thought*, 17.

106. The first derives from the *Glossa Ordinaria*, which reads Sirach 17:1 to say that memory and will proceed from understanding. This either abrogates trinitarian *ordo* or confuses the received assignment of appropriation—the Father as understanding, Son as will, and so on. This problem, Alexander assures, is only aspectual. Acquired memory in becoming may and does hang upon some prior understanding and its willed recall. But it is not so in the order of being. The logic here implicitly turns on an Aristotelian insight, that priority may be given priority in time, though not by reason. See *Metaphysica* 9.8.1049b14–16 (LCL 271: 455): "To every potentiality of this kind actuality is prior, both in formula and in substance; in time it is sometimes prior and sometimes not."

107. *SH* I–II, n. 342, II (2: 415). Cf. *SDA* c. 35, 31–39 (112).

108. Brother Alexander's phrase is *necessario concomitantur*. Cf. *SDA* c. 35, 45–48 (112).

109. *SH* I–II, n. 342, II, obj. 1 (2: 415).

110. *SH* I–II, n. 342, II (2: 415).

111. *SH* I–II, n. 452 (2: 576): "*Penes quae principaliter consistit pulchritudo universi sunt creaturae rationales.*"

7. THE BEAUTY GRACE GIVES

1. Alister E. McGrath, *Iustitia Dei: A History of the Christian Doctrine of Justification*, third. ed. (New York/Cambridge: Cambridge University Press, 2005), 68. For Brother Alexander on the matter, see *SH* III, n. 608 (4: 956–957). Gérard Philips shows that many canonists of Alexander's time denied that grace posits anything in the soul in his *L'union personnelle avec le Dieu vivant. Essai sur l'origine et le sens de la grâce créée* (Leuven: Leuven University Press, 1989), 81.

2. A very helpful contextual treatment of the *SH*'s doctrine of grace can be found in Vincent Strand, SJ, "The Ontology of Grace in Alexander of Hales and John of La Rochelle," *The Summa Halensis: Debates and Doctrines*, 171–191. Cf. Richard Cross, *Duns Scotus* (New York/Oxford: Oxford University Press, 1999), 108.

3. John of La Rochelle, *Quaestiones disputatae de gratia* q. 7, edited by Ludwig Hödl in *Die neuen Quästionen der Gnadentheologie des Johannes von Rupella OM (+1245) in Cod. lat. Paris 14726* (Munich: Max Hueber Verlag, 1964), 63.

4. McGrath, *Iustitia Dei*, 177.

5. McGrath, *Iustitia Dei*, 71. Cf. Cross, *Duns Scotus*, 109.

6. Scotus admits, for instance, that a habit of grace is not necessary for justification, at least not absolutely considered at *ord.* 1.17.1.1–2, n. 160, ed. Carolus Balić (Vatican: Typis Polyglottis Vaticanis, 1951 [5: 215]).

7. See Gregory of Rimini, *In I Sent.*, d. 17, q. 1, a. 2. Here again they worry about obligation's constraint upon God. For Scotus, Ockham, and Gregory, God in his infinite and absolute freedom must not be obliged to accept a person as *gratus* just because she bears the habit of grace. (For Scotus anyway, she bears that habit only because she has *already* been predestined as *grata* by God. Cf. Cross, *Duns Scotus*, 108.) All admit, however, that God does not in fact accept as *gratus* those without the habit in the order he has established; they want only to protect God's absolute freedom to do otherwise, had God so wished. Cf. McGrath, *Iustitia Dei*, 154.

8. Cross, *Duns Scotus*, 109.

9. McGrath, *Iustitia Dei*, 177.

10. *SH* III, n. 633 (4: 1001).

11. *SH* III, n. 608 (4: 957).

12. *SH* I, n. 512, ad 3 (1: 732): "*Missiones Filii et Spiritus Sancti . . . in hoc quod est inhabitare animam vel esse in anima secundum rationem fructus.*" Cf. n. 511, II (1: 729), n. 514 (1: 737).

13. *SH* II-II, nn. 63–67 (3: 80–82).

14. *SH* II-II, n. 63 (3: 80): "*Ad primum dicendum est quod hae quatuor definitiones assignantur in comparatione ad quatuor causas.*"

15. *SH* II-II, n. 63 (3: 80). Cf. *civ.* 12.9.1 (CCSL 48: 363–364).

16. *SH* II-II, n. 63 (3: 80). Cf. n. 64 (3: 80–81).

17. *SH* II-II, n. 65 (3: 81). Cf. Anselm, *De conc. virg. et orig. pecc.* 3.27 (PL 158: 436).

18. *SH* II-II, n. 63 (3: 80).

19. *SH* II-II, n. 66 (3: 81).

20. *SH* II–II, n. 63 (3: 80).

21. *SH* II–II, n. 67 (3: 82).

22. *SH* I, n. 73 (1: 114).

23. Brother Alexander's focus here falls on rational creatures, so it seems curious that he asks after mode–form–order rather than the memory–understanding–will. How to explain this? Two options, each compatible with the other. First, the switch might have to do with Alexander's source, William of Auxerre, who prefers the former triplet to the latter on this point. See *SA* II, 11.2.2.1 (2: 326–327). Cf. Coolman, *Knowing God by Experience*, 180. Second, Alexander places heavy emphasis on sin's corrosive effects on the *will* in particular (and so *loving*, in Augustine's triplet, rather than remembering or understanding). Alexander calculates sin's damage using *modus–species–ordo*, then, because it offers him a triplet for evaluating the will in relative isolation from the memory or understanding.

24. *SH* I, n. 33, ad 2 (1: 50).

25. *SH* II–II, n. 33 (3: 51).

26. *SH* II–II, n. 35, ad 1–2, a–b (3: 52).

27. *SH* II–II, n. 35, ad 1 (3: 53).

28. *SH* II–II, n. 35, ad 1 (3: 53). Later in ad 2 Brother Alexander indexes these to the immaterial causes.

29. Here I depict a combination of obj. 1 and 2 of *SH* II–II, n. 36 (3: 53). I should note, however, that objection 1 contains something curious. There an objector seems to introduce an entirely new triad. He indexes *modus* to *potentia* or *virtus*, *species* to *pulchritudo*, and *ordo* to *bonitas*. We saw *verum–pulchrum–bonum* at *SH* I–II, n. 75 (2: 99) and *potentia–sapientia–bonitas/voluntas* nearly everywhere across *SH* I. This triplet of *potentia/virtus–pulchritudo–bonitas* appears to perform a remix of some kind. It is also absent (to my mind) from the remainder of the *SH*.

30. *SH* II–II, n. 36, ad 2 (3: 54).

31. *SH* II–II, n. 28, ad 3 (3: 28).

32. *SH* II–II, n. 28, ad 1 and 2 (3: 28).

33. *SH* II–II, n. 340 (3: 346).

34. *SH* II–II, n. 523 (3: 517).

35. These are at *SH* III, nn. 65–86 (4: 96–129) and nn. 87–95 (4: 130–137) respectively.

36. *SH* III, n. 98 (4: 142).

37. *SH* III, n. 53, ad 4 (4: 79): "*Humana vero natura est ei [Filio Dei] unita ut adiacens, quia homo, prius non existens, unitur Filio Dei ab aeterno existenti, et ita quoad hoc tenet modum accidentis, quamvis non sit accidens.*"

38. *SH* III, n. 101 (4: 147).

39. *Gratia unionis* was a common enough theme in the early thirteenth-century. The *Summa sententiarum* used the concept to mediate a debate between Abelard and Gilbert of Poitiers on exactly how Christ as man was Son of God.

Even so, Principe claims that it was the Lombard who first used the construction "gratia unionis." The concept is developed further by William of Auxerre.

40. *SH* I, n. 245, ad 3 (1: 337).

41. McGrath, *Iustitia Dei*, 103. McGrath is correct, I think, only if we qualify that the *gratia* under consideration here is *gratia unionis*, not *gratia* in general. For a representative case of the Dominican line, see Thomas Aquinas at *ST* I–II, q. 13, a. 10, co. For the standard Franciscan line, see Bonaventure at *In II Sent.*, d. 29, a. 2, q. 2c (2: 702–704). Matthew of Aquasparta reports and rejects something very like Thomas's argument at *Quaestiones disputatae de gratia* q. 4 (ed. Doucet 94–96).

42. *SH* III, n. 96 (4: 139).

43. *SH* III, n. 99 (4: 144–145).

44. There is a disproportionately large literature on Alexander's role in burnishing the created-uncreated grace distinction. Best, however, is Vincent Strand, SJ, "The Ontology of Grace in Alexander of Hales and John of La Rochelle." Other treatments can be found in my bibliography.

45. *SH* III, n. 99 (4: 144): "*Intelligendum est primo, ad solutionem huius quaestionis, quod gratia unionis duplex est. Est enim unionis disponens et est gratia unionis complens. Disponens est gratia creata, complens vero et perficiens est gratia increata; et haec est ipse Spiritus Sanctus.*"

46. *SH* III, n. 99 (4: 144).

47. *SH* III, n. 99 (4: 144).

48. *SH* I, n. 307, resp. and ad 5 (1: 444).

49. *SH* III, n. 99 (4: 144).

50. Hugh of St. Cher, for example, rejects the grace of union as a medium and implies that whatever else it is, it is not a disposition in the human nature. See also Walter H. Principe, *Hugh of St-Cher's Theology of the Hypostatic Union* (Toronto: Pontifical Institute of Mediaeval Studies, 1970), 109. Thomas Aquinas later rejects Alexander's tight connection between the grace of nature and created disposition in human nature. For Thomas, the grace of union simply is the "*esse personale quod gratis divinitus datur humanae naturae in persona verbi*" (*ST* III, q. 6, a. 6, co). The medium or principle of union, then, simply "*est persona filii assumens humanam naturam*" (*ST* III, q. 7, a. 13, co). So for Thomas, the disposition of grace in Christ's human nature follows from (but is not itself) the grace of union (*ST* III, q. 7, a. 13, ad 2). See also his *Quodlibet* 9, q. 2, a. 1, ad 3 and *De veritate* q. 29, a. 2.

51. *SH* III, n. 99 (4: 144–145).

52. *SH* III, n. 99 (4: 145).

53. *SH* III, n. 99 (4: 145).

54. *SH* III, n. 99 (4: 145): "*Item, Spiritus Sanctus est nexus et vinculum et communio Patris et Filii, ut dicit Augustinus, et hoc eo quod est amor. Sicut ergo Spiritui Sancto convenit esse unionem divinarum personarum in divina natura, et est ostensivum unitatis earum, ita conveniet ei ut sit unio naturarum in una persona Filii.*"

55. *SH* III, n. 100 (4: 146–147).

56. *SH* III, n. 100 (4: 147).

57. *SH* III, n. 100 (4: 147).

58. *SH* III, n. 101 (4: 148): "*Est ergo prior secundum rationem intelligentiae gratia unionis quam gratia secundum quam est caput, licet eadem sit secundum substantiam, quia aliiter non esset caput nostrum nisi crederemus gratiam unionis.*"

59. In his unpublished "'The Spirit Comes to Christians through Christ': Capital Grace in the *Summa halensis*," Boyd Taylor Coolman writes that Alexander "thus grounds the entire economy of grace in this 'grace of union,' namely, that by which human nature was united to the divine nature in the Incarnation."

60. Of course scholastics knew the Pauline trope and Augustine's *totus Christus*. It is present too already in twelfth-century discussions—see Peter of Poitiers, *IV Sent.*, c. 20 (PL 211: 1215–1219). But the Lombard seems to set the course for discussion at III *Sent.*, d. 13, c. 1, n. 2. From there, all scholastics who comment the *Sentences* develop the doctrine. See, for example, William of Auxerre, *SA* III, nn. 102–114 (4: 148–160); Albert, *In III Sent.*, d. 13, aa. 2–3 (15.2: 134); Bonaventure, *In III Sent.*, d. 13, a. 2 (2: 283–291); and Thomas Aquinas, *In III Sent.*, d. 13, q. 2, a. 1, *ST* III, q. 8, or *In Eph.* c. 1, l. 8, nn. 47–57.

61. Weber, *Sünde und Gnade*, 307.

62. *SH* III, n. 102 (4:148).

63. Avicenna, *De anima* 5.8.19, trans. and ed. F. Rahman, *Avicenna's de anima, being the psychological part of Kitāb al-Shifā'* (London/New York: Oxford University Press, 1959), 266. For more on early scholastic reception of Avicenna's neurology, see Hasse, *Avicenna's De Anima in the Latin West*, 100–106.

64. *SH* III, n. 103 (4: 150).

65. *SH* III, n. 104 (4: 151).

66. Alexander treats supposition at *SH* I, nn. 358–359 (1: 535–537).

67. *SH* III, n. 104 (4: 151).

68. *SH* III, nn. 105–108 (4: 151–154).

69. *SH* III, n. 110 (4: 155).

70. Plato, *Phaedrus*, 246a–254e.

71. Hugh of St. Victor, *DS* 2.1.12 (PL 176: 412).

72. Brother Alexander assigns value to each: the first is, he says, *perfectissima*. Interesting that in the *itin.*, Bonaventure will reverse the value of the first two. He moves from considering the trinitarian union at 6.1–6.3 to contemplating the hypostatic union at 6.4–6.7. See especially *itin.* 6.5 (5: 311).

73. *SH* III, n. 111 (4: 156–157).

74. Boyd Taylor Coolman tantalizes with the suggestion that Thomas Gallus, last of the Victorines, may account for the presence of Dionysian themes like *influentia* in the early Franciscans. See his *Knowledge, Love, and Ecstasy in the Theology of Thomas Gallus*, 34–37.

75. *SH* III, n. 112 (4: 157–158).

76. *SH* III, n. 112 (4: 158).

77. *SH* III, n. 112 (4: 158). The quotation here derives from Hugh of St. Victor's *DS* 2.2.1 (PL 176: 415).

78. Leo XIII, *Divinum Illud Munus* (1897), §6. Leo here paraphrases Augustine's *s.* 187.

79. *SH* III, n. 99 (4: 144) and n. 110 (4: 155).

80. *SH* III, n. 110 (4: 155), n. 112 (4: 158), n. 636 (4: 1007). See also *SH* I, n. 308 (1: 446), n. 318 (1: 467–469), and n. 430 (1: 623).

81. *SH* I, n. 308 (1: 446).

82. I do not here consider the tangled complex of grace's other kinds, like *gratia gratis data* (*SH* III, nn. 646–672 [4: 1023–1060]). Neither do I sort sanctifying grace into its various modes, as Alexander does at *SH* III, n. 614 (4: 969): "*praeveniens, subsequens, operans, cooperans, et sic de aliis differentiis gratiae.*" Rather I consider sanctifying grace in general and as it relates to the trinity.

83. *SH* III, n. 608 (4: 956–957).

84. *SH* III, n. 608 (4: 957).

85. Lombard, *Sent.* I, d. 17, cc. 1–6 (Brady 4: 141–152), trans. Silano 88–97.

86. Philipp W. Rosemann's "Fraterna dilectio est Deus: Peter Lombard's Thesis on Charity as the Holy Spirit" in *Amor amicitiae: On the Love that is Friendship: Essays in Medieval Thought and Beyond in Honor of the Rev. Professor James McEvoy*, ed. Thomas A.F. Kelly and Philipp W. Rosemann (Leuven: Peeters, 2004), 409–36 offers the soberest Catholic account of the Lombard's controversial thesis. Others, like Aage Rydstrøm-Poulsen's otherwise magisterial *The Gracious God: Gratia in Augustine and the Twelfth Century* (Copenhagen: Akademisk Forlag, 2002), fall to Thomism's perennial temptation to make of the twelfth-century the final stretch on the long march to Thomas Aquinas.

87. Praepositinus, a supporter of the Lombard's thesis, already diagnosed the conflation of efficient and formal causality as chief among his opponents' concerns. Simon of Tournai proposed a solution: "Man is righteous by the virtue of righteousness as the formal cause, Simon of Tournai teaches, but he is made righteous by God as the efficient cause. In the same way, when a believer loves, his concrete love as a formal cause is different from the source of this love, namely the efficient cause." Cf. Rydstrøm-Poulsen, *The Gracious God*, 422, 435. As Praepositinus already divined, this will be the character of many responses to the Lombard's charity thesis.

88. See Bonaventure, *In II Sent.*, d. 44, dub. 3 (2: 1058).

89. Philips, *L'union personnelle avec le Dieu vivant*, 81–82. Cf. Strand, "The Ontology of Grace," and Monsour, "The Relation between Uncreated and Created Grace in the Halensian *Summa*," 86–90. As Strand notes, *gratia creata* is found in both Alexander's *Glossa* and in his early *QDA*. It is also found (though not explained) in Philip the Chancellor's *SDB*. Cf. *SDB* I (364).

90. See Alexander of Hales, "Quaestiones disputatae de gratia," in *Alexander de Hales Quaestiones Disputatae de Gratia Editio Critica: Un Contributo Alla*

Teologia Della Grazia Nella Prima Metà del Sec. XIII, ed. Jacek Mateusz Wierzbicki (Roma: Antonianum, 2008). Alexander's *Quaestiones disputatae de gratia* belongs to the *QDP*, not all of which have yet been critically edited.

91. Strand casts doubt over McGrath's judgment at *Iustitia Dei*, 161, that "it is possible to argue that the main features of the early Franciscan school's teaching on justification are essentially identical with the early teaching of Alexander of Hales." Strand argues that because McGrath tendered this judgment before the critical edition of Alexander's *Quaestiones disputatae de gratia*, McGrath fails to see how John "considerably developed the work of his master concerning the ontology of grace" ("The Ontology of Grace," 176. John writes on the ontology of grace in three places: in his *Tractatus de gratia*, *Quaestiones disputatae de gratia*, and likely the *SH*. We have no critical edition of the former two, though Ludwig Hödl's *Die neuen Quästionen der Gnadentheologie des Johannes von Rupella* offers select questions and a complete table of contents.

92. Strand argues that Alexander of Hales's account improves upon Philip the Chancellor's; John of La Rochelle's upon Alexander of Hales's; and the *SH*'s upon John of La Rochelle's.

93. *SH* III, n. 609 (4: 959). Cf. n. 99 (4: 144).

94. *SH* III, n. 609 (4: 959).

95. Cf. John of La Rochelle's *Quaestiones disputatae de gratia*, 69. McGrath, who claims that all early Franciscans deny the soul as *capax Dei*, seems not to notice John's departure on this point.

96. Cf. *SH* III, n. 609 (4: 959).

97. Cf. *SH* III, n. 609, ad 4 (4: 960).

98. Aristotle, *Categoriae* 5.2a.34–36.

99. *SH* III, n. 610 (4: 962).

100. *SH* III, n. 611 (4: 964).

101. *SH* III, n. 611, ad 3 (4: 964).

102. *SH* III, n. 612 (4: 967). Alexander indexes a number of definitions of grace here, some of which will interest those studying scholastic grace debates. Some among them are found already in Alexander, *Glossa* II, d. 26, n. 6c (13: 243). Detailing them here would take me too far afield. But interested readers will find this question treated ably in Monsour's "The Relation between Uncreated and Created Grace in the Halensian *Summa*," 90–91. Cf. Weber, *Sünde und Gnade*, 309–312.

103. *SH* III, n. 613 (4: 967): "*Gratia est habitus mentis universaliter vitae totius ordinativus.*" The Quaracchi editors, Monsour, and Strand locate a similar definition in Philip the Chancellor's *SDB* I (Wicki, 357). The exact provenance of this definition seems unclear. Wicki refers readers to a text of Bernard's that does not quite offer a suitable source. And Albert the Great associates the definition with Augustine at *In III Sent.*, d. 26, a. 4, obj. 3 (Borgnet 27: 449) and *Summa theologica* II, tr. 16, q. 98, m. 3 (Borgnet 33: 228). For an overview of this question, see Monsour's "The Relation between Uncreated and Created Grace in the Halensian *Summa*," 91–94, particularly n. 17.

104. *SH* III, n. 613 (4: 967).

105. Dionysius, *Celestial Hierarchy* 3.2.

106. *SH* III, n. 631 (4: 997).

107. *SH* III, n. 631 (4: 997).

108. *SH* III, n. 632 (4: 1000).

109. *SH* III, n. 632 (4: 1000).

110. The Quaracchi editors note that the quotations Alexander (loosely) reproduces come not from Richard, but rather from Hugh's *Soliloquium de arrha animae* (PL 176: 951C–967C). Either the editors or Brother Alexander misidentify the text as *De arrha sponsi ad sponsam*, an erroneous conglomeration of Hugh's *De arrha animae* and *De amore sponsi ad sponsam*.

111. Here again, Hugh of St. Victor, *De arrha* (PL 176: 951): "*Dic mihi, quaeso, anima mea, quid est quod super omnia diligis? Ego scio, quod vita tua dilectio est et scio quod sine dilectione esse non potes.*"

112. *SH* III, n. 633 (4: 1002).

113. *SH* III, n. 633 (4: 1002).

114. In fact, Brother Alexander parses merit's work according to the *rationes* of the immaterial causes at *SH* III, n. 633, ad a-1 (4: 1002).

115. *SH* III, n. 633 (4: 1001).

116. *SH* I–II, n. 342, II (2: 415): "*Item, dubitabit aliquis de hoc quod dicit Augustinus, in libro De trinitate, quod actus isti sese sunt circumincedentes, meminisse, intelligere, velle, ut sit similitudo potentiarum ad personas divinas, sicut dicit Damascenus: verbi gratia quod memini, intelligo, volo, et quod intelligo, memini et volo, et quod volo, memini et intelligo.*"

117. *SH* III, n. 609 (4: 959): "*Quia ergo Spiritus Sanctus amor est, immo et virtus prima amoris, inde est, cum datur nobis, transformat nos in divinam speciem, ut sit ipsa anima assimilata deo.*" Cf. Philips, "La théologie de la grâce," 115, who may overread *speciem* here as "beauty." Why Brother Alexander here uses *species* rather than *pulcher* or *pulchritudo* is far from clear. As I argued in chapter 5, *species* in the *SH* almost always names the Son's likeness to the Father. A connection between his point here and the Spirit's role in the incarnation is possible but tenuous.

118. Bonaventure will, particular at *brev.* 5. For a detailed and highly subtle account of Bonaventure on this point (and in comparison to the *SH*), see Katherine Wrisley Shelby's "The *Influentia* of Grace in *The Commentary on the Sentences* and the *Breviloquium*," in her "St. Bonaventure's Theology of Grace," 157–213. Cf. her "Part V: On the Grace of the Holy Spirit," in *Bonaventure Revisited: Companion to the* Breviloquium, 215–244.

119. *SH* I, n. 103 (1: 162).

120. Doucet warns that part of this treatise (nn. 514–518) may be a later addition, "perhaps taken from Odo Rigaldus." See Doucet, "The History of the Problem of the Authenticity of the Summa (cont.)," 310.

121. *SH* I, nn. 495–518 (1: 697–748).

122. *SH* I, n. 512, II (1: 733).

123. *SH* I, n. 512 (1: 732).

124. *SH* I, n. 503 (1: 714): "*Unde concedo quod haec definitio "mitti est cognosci"* etc. *datur per effectum; unde cum efficitur aliquid in mente in quo habet cognosci processio Filii vel Spiritus Sancti, tunc dicitur mitti Filius vel Spiritus Sanctus, et intelligo non de quocumque effectu, sed de effectu pertinente ad gratiam gratum facientem.*" Still, Alexander clarifies that this "knowing" *in mente* is not a mere cognitive act like others. *SH* I, n. 505, ad 1 (1: 719). Cf. Augustine, *trin.* 4.5.29 (Hill 174).

125. *SH* I, n. 511, I (1: 729).

126. *SH* III, n. 99 (4: 144–145).

127. Alexander affirms the trinity's general presence to all rational creatures (*SH* I, n. 508, ad 3 [1: 723]), but restricts the trinitarian missions to those who possess *gratia gratum faciens* (*SH* I, n. 512 [1: 731]). Difficulties of sequence loom here. What exactly is the order of things? Does the inhabitation cause the enjoyment or vice versa? And when exactly does *gratia gratum faciens* figure? These are the challenges Cunningham's *The Indwelling of the Trinity* considers. I avoid these here, directing the interested reader to Cunningham's criticisms and Monsour's response at "The Relation between Uncreated and Created Grace in the Halensian *Summa*," 232–253.

128. See, for instance, *SH* I, n. 511, resp and ad 3c (1: 727–730), n. 512, I–II, ad 1, and ad 3 (1: 730–733), and n. 515, ad 6 (1: 738).

129. Cunningham notices William of Auxerre and Odo Rigaldus both depict the presence of the trinitarian missions as *fructus* at *The Indwelling of the Trinity*, 107–108.

130. Philips, "La théologie de la grâce," 109.

131. *doctr. chr.* 1.4.4 (PL 34: 20): "*Frui enim est amore alicui rei inhaerere propter seipsam.*"

132. *civ.* 14.7 (CCSL 48: 422): "*Amor ergo inhians habere quod amatur, cupiditas est, id autem habens eoque fruens laetitia.*"

133. Monsour, "The Relation between Uncreated and Created Grace in the Halensian *Summa*," 219.

134. *SH* III, n. 608 (4: 957). To be sure and despite the differences I highlight above, Scotus too conceives justice as a form of beauty and likeness. See *Reportatio* 1-A, d. 17, p. 1, q. 2, n. 67 (WB 479–80).

135. *SH* III, n. 647, II (3: 1025): "*Gratia gratum faciens est ipsa salus.*"

136. The trope is hardly exclusive to Christianity. Plato already recommends "likeness to God" as the height of the good life in *Theaetetus* 176a–b. Plotinus continues this at *Enn.* I.6.6 and I.6.9. See also Proclus, *In Tim.* III, 296.7–297.1. Neoplatonists also knew a need for divine aid in the form of grace. See, for instance, Iamblichus, *De myst.* 1.12 and 5.10.

137. Monsour, "The Relation between Uncreated and Created Grace in the Halensian *Summa*," 208.

138. *SH* I–II, n. 40 (2: 49).

139. *SH* III, n. 608 (4: 957).

140. Hart, *The Beauty of the Infinite*, 252.

CONCLUSION

1. Aidan Nichols, *Discovering Aquinas: An Introduction to His Life, Work, and Influence* (Grand Rapids/Cambridge: Wm. B. Eerdmans Publishing Co, 2003), 142. Cf. Mark D. Jordan, *Rewritten Theology: Aquinas After His Readers* (Malden/Oxford: Blackwell Publishing, 2006), 187.

2. As I note, de Bruyne mourns that "we hope, perhaps, to find ourselves in the presence of an aesthetician, but we are quickly undeceived," "Les premiers scolastiques," 88. And, after reading the question on beauty's relation to the good—the very passage where Brother Alexander links beauty to trinity— Pouillon pronounces that "this is all we find about beauty in the first part of the *Summa halensis*," "La beauté," 276.

3. *SH* I, n. 103 (1: 163).

4. *SH* I, n. 319 (1: 468).

5. *SH* I, n. 297 (1: 425).

6. *SH* III, n. 633 (4: 1001).

7. "Pulcritudo" features more heavily across the *SH*, however, than the Quaracchi editors notice. By my count, the word alone crops up at 97 *different* passages, recurring more often within each. *Decor* appears frequently too (mostly in citations), though not nearly as frequently as *species* does.

8. Balthasar, *The Glory of the Lord IV,* 372–392.

9. *SH* I, n. 103 (1: 163).

10. *SH* I, n. 103 (1: 163).

11. *Metaphysica* 7.12. 1037b (LCL 373: 372–373): "For there is nothing else in the definition (τῷ ὁρισμῶν) but the primary genus (τό πρῶτον λεγόμενον γένος) and the differentiae (αἱ διαφοραί)."

12. He supports this claim at *SH* I–II, n. 75 (2: 99).

13. *SH* I, n. 72 (1: 113): "*Si ergo notificetur, hoc non poterit esse nisi per posteriora, hoc est per abnegationem oppositae intentionis et per positionem effectus consequentis.*"

14. *SH* I, n. 72 (1: 113).

15. For a similar problem in Thomas Aquinas, see Rubin, "The Meaning of 'Beauty'," 6–10 and Aertsen, *The Transcendentals*, 30.

16. Albert the Great, *SDN* (Simon 37.1: 183–184). *DN* 4.7. Cf. *STh.* I, tr. 6, q. 26, c. 1, a. 2, p. 3.

17. The Quaracchi editors of the *SH* claim a "great affinity" between the *SH* and Albert's *STh*. Albert, they say, had the *SH constanter prae minibus habuerit*. See Doucet's *Prolegomena*, ccxxxv–ccxxxvi. For a complete, persuasive, and text-by-text account of Albert's dependence on Alexander's aesthetics, see Bychkov's "A Propos," 27–30. In fact, the textual intimacy between the *SH* and

Albert's *STh* caused some scholars to doubt Albertian authorship. For more on this question, see Matthieu-Maxime Gorce, "Le problème des trois Sommes: Alexandre de Halès, Thomas d'Aquin, Albert le Grand," *Revue Thomiste* 36 (1931): 293–301 and Albert Fries, "Zur Problematik der *Summa theologiae* unter dem Namen des Albertus Magnus," *Franziskanische Studien* 70 (1988): 68–91.

18. Determining exactly how Thomas sourced Alexander's aesthetics requires further study. At the very least we can note Alexander's ubiquitous presence across Albert and then Albert's undisputed influence on Thomas. Bychkov also argues that Brother Alexander influenced not just thought on beauty, but the use of certain sources. It is, Bychkov shows, only after Alexander sets Dionysius's *DN* 4.19 against Augustine's *Enchiridion* 10.1 that Albert (*SDN* 4.19 [Simon 37.1: 249ff]) and then Aquinas (*In I Sent.*, d. 46, q. 1, a. 3; *ST* I, q. 19, a. 9) comment these texts. But again, this hardly means the Dominicans agree with Alexander's interpretations of these texts. Bychkov, "A Propos," 193–194. As to Ulrich: for more on the similarities between the *SH* and Ulrich's *DSB* (which sometimes reproduces whole passages from the former), see Bychkov, "A Propos," 34.

19. I can report only preliminary soundings here. Bonaventure too associates beauty with order (*In II Sent.*, d. 9, a. un., q. 6, ad 3 [2: 252]), foregrounds the trinity as its exemplar (*In II Sent.*, d. 9, praenotata [2: 238] and q. 8, ad 4 [2: 256]), maps creation with triplets, construes sin as antitrinitarian disorder (*In II Sent.*, d. 32, a. 3, q. 1 [2: 770]), and limns grace trinitarianly. Still, he does not always pick up Brother Alexander's lines. Bonaventure's theological aesthetics bears a more christological shape. He is quicker to call Christ "totius pulchritudinis fonti et origini" (*De perfectione evangelica* 3.3 [5: 176]), for instance, or argue *"quod in Filio recte reperitur ratio omnis pulcritudinis"* (*In I Sent.*, d. 31, p. 2, a. 1, q. 3, ad 1 [1: 544]). Bonaventure does not, it seems, retain Brother Alexander's strict conceptual distinction between *species* as an appropriation for the Son and *pulcritudo* as description of trinitarian taxis.

20. The following post-Bonaventure Franciscan texts on beauty await study and comparison: Roger Marston, *Quaestiones disputatae de emanatione aeterna*, q. 4 (Quaracchi: Collegii S. Bonaventurae, 1932), 69–89; *Quaestiones disputatae de fide*, qq. 2 and 6 (Quaracchi: Collegii S. Bonaventurae, 1957), 65, 141–164; *Quaestiones disputatae de anima beata*, qq. 3–4 (Quaracchi: Collegii S. Bonaventurae, 1959), 226–262; and *Quodlibeta quatuor ad fidem codicum nunc primum edita*, II, q. 5, ed. Girard Etzkorn and Ignatius Brady (Grottaferrata: Collegio S. Bonaventura, 1994), 153–159; John Peckham, *Quodlibet* I, q. 4 and III, qq. 5 and 10, ed. Girard Etzkorn and Ferdinand Delorme (Grottaferrata: Collegio S. Bonaventura, 1989), 12, 141–142, and 153, and *Quaestiones disputatae*, qq. 6–7, ed. Girard J. Etzkorn, Hieronymus Spettmann, and Livarius (Grottaferrata: Collegii S. Bonaventurae, 2002), 525.

21. Trent Pomplun, "Notes on Scotist Aesthetics in Light of Gilbert Narcisse's *Les raisons de Dieu*," *Franciscan Studies* 66 (2008): 252. Pomplun here reports the collective judgments of Edgar de Bruyne, Francis Kovach, and Gérard Sondag.

Cf. de Bruyne, *Études d'esthétique médiévale*, 3 vols. (Bruges: Rijkuniversiteit te Gent, 1946); Kovach, "Divine and Human Beauty in Duns Scotus," *Deus et Homo ad mentem I. Duns Scoti* (Rome: Societas Internationalis Scotistica, 1972), 445–459; and Sondag, "The Conditional Definition of Beauty by Scotus," *Medioevo* 30 (2005): 191–206.

Particularly striking parallels between Alexander and Scotus crop up where Scotus discusses the relational-Stoic account of beauty (*ord.* II, d. 3, p. 1, q. 7, n. 251 [Vatican 7: 513–514]), on the trinitarian shape of beauty (*ord.* I, d. 3, p. 2, q. un, n. 298 [Vatican 3: 181–182]), on the appropriated *vestigia trinitatis* as created beauty (*rep.* I-A, d. 3, q. 3, n. 80 [WB: 206]), on the beauty of bodies as relational (*ord.* I, d. 17, p. 1, qq. 1–2, n. 62 [Vatican 5: 163–164]) beauty of the universe in general (on created grace as *quaedam pulchritudo et similitudo deiformis* (*rep.* 1-A, d. 17, p. 1, q. 2, n. 67 [WB: 479–480]).

22. Denys's *De venustate mundi et pulchritudine Dei* sources the *SH* rather heavily, particularly for a self-professed student of Thomas Aquinas. See his text in *Doctoris Ecstatici D. Dionysii Cartusiani Opera Omnia, cura et labore monachorum ordinis Carthusiensis* (Montreuil-sur-Mer/Tournai/Parkminster 1896–1935), vol. 34. There is also relevant material on beauty in Denys's *Elementatio philosophica*, prop. 92 (Op. om. 33: 97B–97C). Kent Emery Jr. claims that "consideration of divine Beauty presses toward contemplation of the trinity . . . Denys repeats an old-fashioned theological motif (developed, e.g., by Alexander of Hales and Bonaventure)." Emery, "The Matter and Order of Philosophy according to Denys the Carthusian," *Was ist Philosophie im Mittelalter? Qu'est-ce que la philosophie au Moyen Âge? What is Philosophy in the Middle Ages?* (New York, Berlin: Walter de Gruyter, 1988), 667–679. Cf. Emery, "Fondements théoriques de la reception de la beauté dans les écrits de Denys le Chartreux," *Les Chartreux et l'art: XIVe–XVIIIe siècles: actes du Xe Colloque international d'histoire et de spiritualité cartusiennes*, ed. Daniel Le Blévec and Alain Girard (Villeneuve-lès-Avignon: Editions du Cerf, 1989), 307–324.

23. *SH* III, n. 99 (4: 144–145).

24. *SH* I–II, n. 8 (2: 17).

25. *SH* I, n. 21 (1: 32).

26. *DN* 2.8. Greek from *Corpus Dionysiacum I: De divinis nominibus*, ed. Beate Regina Suchla (New York, Berlin: Walter de Gruyter, 1990), 132. Witness also Plotinus's *Enn.* I.2.2 (LCL 440: 131).

27. *SH* I–II, n. 81 (2: 103).

28. *SH* I–II, n. 452 (2: 576): "*Penes quae principaliter consistit pulchritudo universi sunt creaturae rationales.*"

29. At *SH* III, n. 111 (4: 156–157), Alexander suggests that the "one" in Christ's prayer at John 12:11 admits only three options: *in natura una* (as in the trinity), *in persona una* (as in Christ's person), or *in voluntate una* (as in the saints).

30. Maximus, *Amb.* 5.14 (PG 91: 1053B). Also unlike Alexander, Maximus then extends this to deification at *Amb.* 41.5 (PG 91: 1308B).

31. Brother Alexander's teaching on beauty is very much the sort of *theologia gloria*, for instance, that is challenged by Natalie Carnes's fascinating *Beauty: A Theological Engagement with Gregory of Nyssa* (Eugene: Cascade Books, 2014).

32. Robert Jenson, *Systematic Theology*, vol. 1 (Oxford: Oxford University Press, 1997), 234–236.

33. Stephen John Wright, *Dogmatic Aesthetics: A Theology of Beauty in Dialogue with Robert W. Jenson* (Minneapolis: Fortress Press, 2014), 50.

34. Katherine Sonderegger, *Systematic Theology*, vol 1: The Doctrine of God (Minneapolis: Fortress Press, 267).

35. Beauty as Spirit features across his works. The best conspectus of his position here, however, is in his *Sophia, the Wisdom of God: An Outline of Sophiology* (Lindisfarne Books, 1993), 98.

36. Patrick Sherry, *Spirit and Beauty: An Introduction to Theological Aesthetics* (Oxford: Clarendon Press, 1992).

37. This is primarily true of Pouillon's "La beauté, propriété transcendentale chez les scolastiques (1220–1270)" and de Bruyne, "Les premiers scolastiques," though less so of Bychkov's "A Propos of Medieval Aesthetics."

BIBLIOGRAPHY

1. PRIMARY SOURCES

Albert the Great. *Commentarii in libros Sententiarum.* 6 vols. Borgnet Edition
25–30. Paris: 1893–1894.

———. *Super Dionysium De divinis nominibus.* Edited by Paul Simon. Cologne
Edition. Vol. 37, bk. 1. Münster: Aschendorff, 1972.

Alexander of Hales. *Glossa in quatuor libros Sententiarum Petri Lombardi.*
Bibliotheca Franciscana Scholastica Medii Aevi 12–15. 4 vols. Quaracchi: Ex
Typographia Collegii S. Bonaventurae, 1951–1957.

———. *Summa theologica Doctoris Irrefragabilis Alexandri de Hales Ordinis
Minorum (Summa halensis).* 4 vols. Quaracchi: Ex Typographia Collegii S.
Bonaventurae, 1924–1948.

———. *Quaestiones Disputatae "antequam esset Frater."* Bibliotheca Franciscana
Scholastica Medii Aevi 19–21. Quaracchi: Ex Typographia Collegii S. Bonaventurae, 1960.

———. *Quaestionis disputate de gratia: editio critica.* Edited by Jacek Mateusz
Wierzbicki in *Studia Antoniana* 50. Rome: Antonianum, 2008.

Anonymous. *Liber de causis.* Translated by Dennis J. Brand. Milwaukee:
Marquette University Press, 1981.

Anselm. *Cur deus homo.* Patrologia Latina 158. Turnhout: Brepols, n.d.

———. *De conceptu virginali et de originali peccato.* Patrologia Latina 158.
Turnhout: Brepols, n.d.

———. *De veritate.* Patrologia Latina 158. Turnhout: Brepols, n.d.

Aristotle. *Analytica Posteriora.* Translated by Hugh Tredennick and E. S. Forster
in *Aristotle: Posterior Analytics. Topica.* Loeb Classical Library 391. Cambridge, MA: Harvard University Press, 1960.

———. *Categoriae.* Translated by Harold P. Cooke in *Aristotle: The Organon, Vol. 1:
The Categories. On Interpretation. Prior Analytics.* Loeb Classical Library 325.
Cambridge. MA: Harvard University Press, 1938.

———. *De anima.* Translated by Walter Stanley Hett in *Aristotle: On the Soul.
Parva Naturalia. On Breath.* Loeb Classical Library 288. Cambridge, MA:
Harvard University Press, 1957.

———. *De caelo.* Translated by William Keith Chambers Guthrie in *Aristotle: On
the Heavens.* Loeb Classical Library 338. Cambridge, MA: Harvard University
Press, 1939.

———. *De partibus animalium.* Translated by A. L. Peck in *Aristotle: Parts of
Animals. Movement of Animals. Progression of Animals.* Loeb Classical
Library 323. Cambridge. MA: Harvard University Press, 1937.

———. *Ethica Nicomachea*. Translated by H. Rackham in *Aristotle: Nicomachean Ethics*. Loeb Classical Library 73. Cambridge. MA: Harvard University Press, 1934.

———. *Magna Moralia*. Translated by G. Cyril Armstrong in *Aristotle: Metaphysics, Vol 2: Books 10–14. Oeconomica. Magna Moralia*. Loeb Classical Library 287. Cambridge, MA: Harvard University Press, 1935.

———. *Metaphysica*. Translated by Hugh Tredennick in *Aristotle: Metaphysics, Vol. I: Books 1–9*. Loeb Classical Library 271. Cambridge, MA: Harvard University Press, 1933.

———. *Topica*. Translated by Walter Stanley Hett in *Aristotle: On the Soul. Parva Naturalia. On Breath*. Loeb Classical Library 288. Cambridge. MA: Harvard University Press, 1957.

Athanasius. *Letter to Serapion*. Patrologia Latina 26. Turnhout: Brepols, n.d.

Augustine. *De civitate dei*. Corpus Christianorum Series Latina 47–48. Turnhout: Brepols, 1995.

———. *De trinitate libri XV*. Corpus Christianorum Series Latina 50–50a. Turnhout: Brepols, 1967.

Augustine*, *De spiritu et anima*. Patrologia Latina 40. Turnhout: Brepols, n.d. Translated into English by Erasmo Leiva and Sr. Benedicta Ward. In *Three Treatises on Man: A Cistercian Anthropology*. Kalamazoo: Cistercian Publications, 1977.

Avicenna. *Liber De Philosophia Prima: Sive, Scientia Divina* (Avicenna Latinus). Edited by Simone Van Riet and G. Verbeke. Louvain: E. Peeters, 1977.

———. *Liber de anima seu sextus de naturalibus I–III* (Avicenna Latinus). Edited by Simone Van Riet. Louvain, Leiden: Éditions Orientalistes; E.J. Brill, 1968.

———. *Metaphysica*. Translated in *The Metaphysica of Avicenna: A critical Translation-Commentary and Analysis of the Fundamental Arguments in Avicenna's Metaphysica in the Danes Nama-i 'ala'i*. Translated by Peter Morewedge. New York: Colombia, 1973.

———. *The Metaphysics of the Healing: A Parallel English-Arabic Text (Al-Ilahīyāt Min Al-Shifā')*. Islamic Translation Series. Translated by Michael E. Marmura. Provo: Brigham Young University Press, 2005.

Bacon, Roger. *Fr. Rogeri Bacon Opera hactenus inedita I*. Edited by J.S. Brewer. London: Longman, Green, Longman, and Roberts, 1859.

Basil, *Contra Eunomium*. Patrologia Graeca 29. Turnhout: Brepols, n.d.

———. *De fide*. Patrologia Graeca 31. Turnhout: Brepols, n.d.

Boethius. *De consolatione*. Patrologia Latina 64. Turnhout: Brepols, n.d.

———. *De trinitate*. Patrologia Latina 64. Turnhout: Brepols, n.d.

———. *In Categorias Aristotelis libri quatuor*. Patrologia Latina 64. Turnhout: Brepols, n.d.

———. *In Porphyrium dialogi a Victorino translati*. Patrologia Latina 64. Turnhout: Brepols, n.d.

Bonaventure. *Doctoris Seraphici S. Bonaventurae Opera Omnia.* 10 vols. Quarrachi: Ex Typographia Collegii S. Bonaventurae, 1882–1902.

Denys the Carthusian. *De venustate mundi et pulchritudine dei.* In *Doctoris Ecstatici D. Dionysii Cartusiani Opera Omnia, cura et labore monachorum ordinis
Carthusiensis.* Vol. 34. 223–255. Montreuil-sur-Mer/Tournai/Parkminster, 1907.

Dionysius Areopagita. *Corpus Dionysiacum I: De divinis nominibus.* Edited by
Beate Regina Suchla. Patristische Texte und Studien 33. New York, Berlin:
Walter de Gruyter, 1990.

———. *The Works of Dionysius the Areopagite.* Translated by John D. Parker.
London: James Parker, 1897.

Eriugena, John Scottus. *Periphyseon (De divisione naturae).* Edited by I.P.
Sheldon-Williams and Ludwig Bieler. Dublin: Dublin Institute for Advanced
Studies, 1972.

Gregory Nazianzen. *Orationes.* Edited by Paul Gallay and Justin Mossay. Sources
Chrétiennes 250 and 284. Paris: Les éditions du cerf, 1978 and 1981.

Gregory of Nyssa. *Ad Ablabium.* Patrologia Graeca 45. Turnhout: Brepols, n.d.

———. *Contra Eunomium.* Patrologia Graeca 45. Turnhout: Brepols, n.d.

Hilary of Poitiers. *De trinitate.* Edited by Pieter Frans Smulders. Corpus
Christianorum Series Latina 62–62a. Turnhout: Brepols, 1979.

Hugh of St. Victor. *De sacramentis.* Patrologia Latina 176. Turnhout: Brepols, n.d.

Iamblichus. *De mysteriis.* Translated by Emma C. Clarke, John M. Dillon, and
Jackson P. Hershbell in *Iamblichus: On the Mysteries.* Atlanta: Society of
Biblical Literature, 2003.

Isidore of Seville. *Sentences.* Patrologia Latina 83. Turnhout: Brepols, n.d.

John Damascene. *De fide orthodoxa.* Edited by Bonifatius Kotter, P. Ledrux,
Vassa Kontouma, and Georges-Matthieu Durand. Sources Chrétiennes 540.
Paris: Les éditions du cerf, 2011.

John of La Rochelle. *Quaestiones disputatae de gratia* q. 7. Edited by Ludwig
Hödl in *Die Neuen Quästionen der Gnadentheologie des Johannes von Rupella
OM (†1245) in Cod. lat. Paris 14726.* Munich: Max Hueber Verlag, 1964.

———. *Summa de anima.* Edited by J.-G. Bougerol. Paris: Vrin, 1995.

Julian of Norwich. *A Revelation of Love* in *The Writings of Julian of Norwich.*
Edited by Nicholas Watson and Jacqueline Jenkins. University Park: The
Pennsylvania State University Press, 2016.

Marius Victorinus. *Marii Victorini opera pars I: opera theologica.* Edited by Paul
Henry and Pierre Hadot. *Corpus Scriptorum Ecclesiasticorum Latinorum* 83.1.
Vienna: Hoelder/Pichler/Tempsky, 1971.

Matthew of Aquasparta. *Quaestiones disputatae de gratia.* Edited by Victorin
Doucet. Bibliotheca Franciscana Scholastica Medii Aevi, vol. 11. Ad Claras
Aquas, Florentiae: Ex Typographia Collegii S. Bonaventurae, 1935.

Maximus Confessor. *Ambigua.* Translated and edited by Maximos Constas in
On Difficulties in the Church Fathers: The Ambigua. Dumbarton Oaks
Medieval Library 28–29. Cambridge, MA: Harvard University Press, 2014.

Peter Lombard. *Magistri Petri Lombardi Parisiensis Episcopi Sententiae in IV Libris Distinctae.* Edited by Ignatius Brady. Spicilegium Bonaventurianum 4–5. Grotta-ferrata: Editiones Collegii S. Bonaventurae Ad Claras Aquas, 1971–1981. English translations taken from Guilio Silano's *The Sentences.* Mediaeval Sources in Translation, 42–43, 45, 48. Toronto: Pontifical Institute of Mediaeval Studies, 2007.

Philip the Chancellor. *Quaestio disputata De imagine et similitudine nostra.* Edited by Niklaus Wicki in his *Die Philosophie Philipps des Kanzlers. Ein philosophierender Theologe des frühen 13. Jahrhunderts.* 171–181. Fribourg: Academic Press Fribourg, 2005.

———. *Summa de bono.* 2 vols. Edited by Niklaus Wicki. Corpus Philosophorum medii aevi. Bern: Francke, 1985.

Plato. *Hippias Major.* In *Plato: Cratylus, Parmenides, Greater Hippias, Lesser Hippias.* Translated by Harold North Fowler. Loeb Classical Library 167. Cambridge, MA: Harvard University Press, 1926.

Plotinus. *Enneads.* In *Plotinus: Enneads.* 6 vols. Translated by A. H. Armstrong. Loeb Classical Library 440–468. Cambridge, MA: Harvard University Press, 1969–1988.

Porphyry. *Isagoge.* Greek from *Porphyrii Isagoge et in Aristotelis Categorias Commentarium.* Edited by Adolfus Busse. Berlin: Reimer, 1887. English from *Porphyry: Introduction.* Oxford: Oxford University Press, 2003.

Proclus. *Theology of Plato.* In *Proclus' Theology of Plato.* Volume 3. Translated by Thomas Taylor. London: s.n., 1816.

Richard of St. Victor. *De tribus appropriatis personis in trinitate.* In *Opuscules théologiques: texte critique avec introduction, notes et tables.* Edited by J. Ribaillier. Textes philosophiques du Moyen Age 15. Paris: J. Vrin, 1967.

———. *De trinitate.* Edited by J. Ribaillier. *Textes philosophiques du Moyen Age 6.* Paris: J. Vrin, 1958. English translation by Christopher P. Evans in *Victorine Texts in Translation: Exegesis, Theology and Spirituality from the Abbey of St. Victor: Trinity and Creation.* Edited by Boyd Taylor Coolman and Dale M. Coulter. 195–382. Hyde Park: New City Press, 2011.

Seneca. *Epistle* 58. Translated by Richard M. Gummere in *Seneca the Younger.* Vol 4, *Epistles 1–65.* Loeb Classical Library 75. Cambridge, MA: Harvard University Press, 1917.

Thomas Aquinas. *In librum beati Dionysii De divinis nominibus.* Edited by Ceslai Pera. Turin/Rome: Marietti, 1950.

———. *Quaestiones disputatae de potentia.* In Vol. 2 of *S. Thomae Aquinatis Quaestiones disputatae,* 10th edition. Edited by P.M. Pession, 1–276. Turin: Marietti, 1965.

———. *Quaestiones disputatae de veritate.* Vols. 22.1–3 of *Sancti Thomae Aquinatis opera omnia iussu impensaque Leonis XIII P.M. edita.* Rome: Sancta Sabina, 1972–1975.

———. *Quaestio disputata de spiritualibus creaturis.* In *Sancti Thomae Aquinatis opera omnia iussu impensaque Leonis XIII P.M. edita.* Vol. 24.2. Rome: Commissio Leonina, 2000.

———. *Scriptum super libros sententiarum magistri Petri Lombardi*. Vols. 1–2 edited by R.P. Mandonnet; Vols. 3–4 edited by R.P. Maria Fabianus Moos. Paris: Lethielleux, 1929–1947.

———. *Summa theologiae*. Vols. 4–12 of *Sancti Thomae Aquinatis opera omnia iussu impensaque Leonis XIII P.M. edita*. Rome: Ex Typographia Polyglotta S.C. de Propaganda Fide, 1888–1906.

Ulrich of Strasburg. *De summo bono* II.1–4. *Corpus Philosophorum Teutonicorum Medii Aevi* 1.2. Edited by Alain de Libera. Hamburg: Felix Meiner, 1987.

William of Auxerre. *Summa Aurea*. 5 vols. Spicilegium Bonaventurianum 16–20. Grottaferrata: Editiones Collegii S. Bonaventurae, 1980–86.

2. SECONDARY SOURCES

Acar, Rahim. *Talking about God and Talking about Creation: Avicenna's and Thomas Aquinas's Positions*. Boston/Leiden: Brill Publishers, 2005.

Aertsen, Jan. "Avicenna's Doctrine of the Primary Notions and its Impact on Medieval Philosophy." In *Islamic Thought in the Middle Ages: Studies in Text, Transmission and Translation, in Honor of Hans Daiber*, edited by Anna Akasoy and Wim Raven, 21–42. Boston, Leiden: Brill Publishers, 2008.

———. "Beauty in the Middle Ages: A Forgotten Transcendental?" *Medieval Philosophy and Theology* 1 (1991): 68–97.

———. "The Concept of 'Transcendens' in the Middle Ages: What is Beyond and What Is Common." *Platonic Ideas and Concept Formation in Ancient and Medieval Thought*, edited by G. Van Riel and Caroline Macé, 133–153. Leuven: Leuven University Press, 2004.

———. "Das Schöne." In *Historisches Wörterbuch der Philosophie, Band 8: R–Sc*, edited by Joachim Ritter and Karlfried Gründer, 1351–1358. Basel: Schwabe & Co, 1992.

———. "Die Frage nach der Transzendentalität der Schönheit im Mittelalter." In *Historia Philosophiae Medii Aevi, Festschrift für Kurt Flasch*. Edited by Burkhard Mojsisch and Olaf Pluta. Amsterdam, Philadelphia: B.R. Grüner, 1991: 1–22.

———. *Medieval Philosophy and the Transcendentals: The Case of Thomas Aquinas*. Boston/Leiden: Brill Publishers, 1996.

———. *Medieval Philosophy as Transcendental Thought: From Philip the Chancellor to Francisco Suarez*. Boston/Leiden: Brill Publishers, 2012.

———. "What Is First and Most Fundamental? The Beginnings of Transcendental Philosophy." *Was ist Philosophie im Mittelalter? Que'est-ce que la philosophie au Moyen Âge? What Is Philosophy in the Middle Ages?*, edited by Jan A. Aertsen and Andreas Speer, 177–192. New York, Berlin: Walter de Gruyter, 1998.

———, and Martin Pickavé. *Die Logik des Tranzendentalen: Festschrift für Jan A. Aertsen zu 65. Geburtstag*. New York, Berlin: Walter de Gruyter, 2003.

———. "The Triad True-Good-Beautiful': The Place of Beauty in the Middle Ages." In *Intellect et imagination dans la philosophie médiévale: actes du XIe*

Congrès international de philosophie médiévale de la Société internationale pour l'étude, vol. *1*, edited by Maria Cândida Pachecho and José F. Meirinhos, 415–435. Boston/Leiden: Brill Publishers, 2006.

Anatolios, Khaled. *Retrieving Nicaea: The Development and Meaning of Trinitarian Doctrine*. Grand Rapids: Baker Academic, 2011.

Ashworth, Jennifer. "Philosophy of Language: Words, Concepts, Things, and Non-things." In *Routledge Companion to Sixteenth Century Philosophy*. Edited by Henrik Lagerlund and Benjamin Hill. New York: Routledge, 2017.

Auer, Johann. *Die Entwicklung der Gnadenlehre in der Hochscholastik*. Freiburg im Breisgau: Herder, 1942–1951.

Babcock, William S. "Augustine's Interpretation of Romans (A.D. 394–396)." *Augustinian Studies* 10 (1979): 55–74.

Barnes, Corey L. "Necessary, Fitting, or Possible: The Shape of Scholastic Christology." *Nova et Vetera* 10 (2012): 657–688.

Barth, Karl. *Church Dogmatics* I/1. Translated by Geoffrey William Bromiley. Edinburgh: T&T Clark, 1975.

Bauerschmidt, Frederick Christian. *Thomas Aquinas: Faith, Reason, and Following Christ*. New York: Oxford University Press, 2013.

Bertolacci, Amos. "The Distinction of Essence and Existence in Avicenna's Metaphysics: The Text and Its Context." In *Islamic Philosophy, Science, Culture, and Religion: Essays in Honor of Dimitri Gutas*, edited by Felicitas Opwis and David Reisman. 257–288. Boston, Leiden: Brill Publishers, 2012.

Bieniak, Magdalena. *The Soul-Body Problem at Paris, ca. 1200–1250: Hugh of St-Cher and His Contemporaries*. Leuven: Leuven University Press, 2010.

———. "The Soul-Body Union in the *Summa halensis*." *The Legacy of Early Franciscan Thought*, edited by Lydia Schumacher, 37–49. Berlin, Boston: De Gruyter, 2021.

Blanco, Francisco de Asís Chavero. "La quaestio *De doctrina theologiae* del manuscrito Vat. Lat. 782: introdducción y edición." *Carthaginensia* 15, no. 27 (1999): 31–72.

Blankenhorn, Bernhard. *The Mystery of Union with God: Dionysian Mysticism in Albert the Great and Thomas Aquinas*. Washington, DC: The Catholic University of America Press, 2015.

de Blignieres, Louis-Marie. *Le mystère de l'être: L'approche thomiste de Guérard des Lauriers*. Preface by Serge-Thomas Bonino. Paris: J. Vrin, 2007.

Bogumil, Remec. *De sanctitate et gratia doctrina summae theologicae Alexandri Halensis*. Ljubljana: Domus Societatis Jesu, 1940.

Bourdieu, Pierre. *Pascalian Meditations*. Translated by Richard Nice. Stanford: Stanford University Press, 1997.

Bulgakov, Sergius. *The Comforter*. Translated by Boris Jakim. Grand Rapids: Wm. B. Eerdmans Publishing Co, 2004.

Brady, Ignatius C. "'The 'Summa Theologica' of Alexander of Hales (1924–1948)." *Archivum franciscanum historicum* 70, nos. 3–4 (1977): 437–447.

Brittain, Charles. "No Place for a Platonist Soul in Fifth-Century Gaul? The Case of Mamertus Claudianus." In *Society and Culture in Late Gaul: Revisiting the Sources,* edited by Ralph W. Mathisen and Danuta Shanzer, 239–262. London, New York: Routledge, 2017.

Brown, Stephen F. "Abelard and the Medieval Origins of the Distinction between God's Absolute and Ordained Power. In *Ad litteram: Authoritative Texts and Their Medieval Readers,* edited by Mark D. Jordan and Kent Emery, Jr, 199–215. Notre Dame: University of Notre Dame Press, 1992.

———. "Declarative and Deductive Theology in the Early Fourteenth Century." In *Miscellanea Mediaevalia* 26: *Was ist Philosophie im Mittelalter?,* edited by Jan A. Aertsen and Andreas Speer, 648–655. Edited by Jan A. Aertsen and Andreas Speer. 648–655. New York, Berlin: Walter de Gruyter, 1998.

———. "Medieval Supposition Theory in Its Theological Context." *Medieval Philosophy & Theology* 3 (1993): 121–157.

Brumberg-Chaumont, Julie. "Logico-grammatical Reflections about Individuality in Late Antiquity." In *Individuality in Late Antiquity,* edited by Alexis Torrance and Johannes Zachhuber, 63–91. New York: Routledge, 2016.

De Bruyne, Edgar. *Études d'esthétique médiévale III: Le xiii siècle.* Bruges: De tempel, 1946.

Bychkov, Oleg V. *Aesthetic Revelation: Reading Ancient and Medieval Texts after Hans Urs von Balthasar.* Washington, DC: Catholic University of America, 2010.

———. "The Beautiful after Thomas Aquinas: Questioning Present-Day Concepts." In *Theological Aesthetics after von Balthasar,* edited by Oleg V. Bychkov and James Fodor, 51–57. Burlington: Ashgate, 2008.

———. "Decor ex praesentia mali: Aesthetic Explanation of Evil in Thirteenth-Century Franciscan Thought." *Recherches de théologie et philosophie médiévales* 68, no. 2 (2001): 245–269.

———. "'Metaphysics as Aesthetics': Aquinas' Metaphysics in Present-Day Theological Aesthetics" in *Modern Theology* 31 (2015): 147–178.

———. "The Nature of Theology in Duns Scotus and his Franciscan Predecessors." *Franciscan Studies* 66 (2008): 5–62.

———. "A Propos of Medieval Aesthetics: A Historical Study of Terminology, Sources, and Textual Traditions of Commenting on Beauty in the Thirteenth Century." PhD dissertation, University of Toronto, 1999.

———. "The Reflection of Some Traditional Stoic Ideas in the Thirteenth-Century Scholastic Theories of Beauty." *Vivarium* 34, no. 2 (1996): 141–160.

———. "Russian Religious Aesthetics." In *Encyclopedia of Aesthetics* 4. Edited by M. Kelly, 195–202. 195–202. New York, Oxford: Oxford University Press, 1998.

———. "Suspended Beauty? The Mystery of Aesthetic Experience in the *Summa halensis.*" *The Legacy of Early Franciscan Thought,* edited by Lydia Schumacher, 111–128. Berlin, Boston: De Gruyter, 2021.

———. "What Does Beauty Have to Do with the Trinity? From Augustine to Duns Scotus." *Franciscan Studies* 66 (2008): 197–212.

Cacho, Alejandro Salas. "El Concepto de la Gracia en la Suma Teológica de Alejandro de Hales." Pamplona: Pamplona Universidad Navarra, 1985.

Callus, Daniel A. "The Origins of the Problem of the Unity of Form." *The Thomist* 24 (1961): 257–288.

de Certeau, Michel. "History: Science and Fiction." In *Heterologies: Discourse on the Other*, translated by Brian Massumi, 199–224. Minneapolis: University of Minnesota Press, 2000.

———. *The Writing of History*. Translated by Tom Conley. New York: Columbia University Press, 1988.

Châtillon, Jean. "Unitas, aequalitas, concordia vel connexia. Recherches sur les origines de la théorie thomiste des appropriations." In *Thomas Aquinas 1274–1974. Commemorative Studies*, 337–380. Toronto: Pontifical Institute of Mediaeval Studies, 1974.

Chenu, Marie-Dominique. *Nature, Man, and Society in the Twelfth Century: Essays on New Theological Perspectives in the Latin West*. Edited and translated by Jerome Taylor and Lester K. Little. Toronto: University of Toronto Press, 1997.

Clark, Elizabeth A. *History, Theory, Text: Historians and the Linguistic Turn*. Cambridge, MA: Harvard University Press, 2004.

Clarke, W. Norris. "The Problem of the Reality and Multiplicity of Divine Ideas in Christian Neoplatonism" in *Neoplatonism and Christian Thought*, edited by Dominic J. O'Meara, 109–127. Albany: State University of New York Press, 1982.

Coolman, Boyd Taylor. "The Comprehensive Trinitarianism of the *Summa Halensis*." In *The Summa Halensis: Doctrines and Debates*, edited by Lydia Schumacher, 107–139. Berlin, Boston: Walter de Gruyter, 2020.

———. "'A Cord of Three Strands Is Not Easily Broken'": The Transcendental Brocade of Unity, Truth and Goodness in the Early Franciscan Intellectual Tradition." *Nova et Vetera* 16, no. 2 (2018): 561–586.

———. "Hugh of St. Victor's Influence on the Halensian Definition of Theology." *Franciscan Studies* 70 (2012): 367–384.

———. "Hugh of St. Victor's Influence on the *Summa Halensis*." In *The Summa Halensis: Sources and Context*, edited by Lydia Schumacher, 201–215. Berlin, Boston: Walter de Gruyter, 2020.

———. "'In Whom I Am Well Pleased': Hugh of St. Victor's Trinitarian Aesthetics." *Pro Ecclesia* 23, no. .3 (2014): 331–354.

———. *Knowing God by Experience: The Spiritual Senses in the Theology of William of Auxerre*. Washington, DC: The Catholic University of America Press, 2004

———. *Knowledge, Love, and Ecstasy in the Theology of Thomas Gallus*. Oxford: Oxford University Press, 2017.

———. "On the Subject-Matter of Theology in the *Summa halensis* and St. Thomas Aquinas." *The Thomist* 79, no. 3 (2015): 439–466.

———. "The Pneumatic Finality of Goodness—Metaphysics: Transcendental Pneumatology in the *Summa halensis*." Paper presented at the Works and Worlds of Saint Bonaventure Conference, St. Bonaventure, NY, July 2017.

———. "'The Spirit Comes to Christians through Christ': Capital Grace in the *Summa halensis*." Unpublished paper.

Coyle, Justin Shaun. "Appropriating Apocalypse in Bonaventure's *Breviloquium*." *Franciscan Studies* 76 (2018): 99–135.

———. "Beauty among the Transcendentals in the *Summa halensis*." *Nova et Vetera* 18, no. 3 (2020): 875–907.

Cross, Richard. *Duns Scotus*. Oxford: Oxford University Press, 1999.

———. "Duns Scotus on Disability: Teleology, Divine Willing, and Pure Nature." *Theological Studies* 78, no. 1 (2017): 72–95.

———. *The Metaphysics of the Incarnation: Thomas Aquinas to Duns Scotus*. Oxford: Oxford University Press, 2002.

Cunningham, Francis L.B. *The Indwelling of the Trinity: A Historico-Doctrinal Study of the Theory of St. Thomas Aquinas*. Dubuque: The Priory Press, 1955.

Czapiewski, Winfried. *Das Schöne bei Thomas von Aquin*. Freiburg im Breisgau: Herder, 1964.

Dales, Richard C. *Medieval Discussions of the Eternity of the World*. Boston, Leiden: Brill Publishers, 1989.

———. *The Problem of the Rational Soul in the Thirteenth Century*. Boston, Leiden: Brill Publishers, 1995.

de Libera, Alain. *Albert le Grand et la philosophie. A la recherche de la vérité*. Paris: Vrin, 1990.

———. *Archéologie du sujet*. 2 vols. Paris: J. Vrin, 2007–2008.

———. "When Did the Modern Subject Emerge?" *American Catholic Philosophical Quarterly* 82, no. 2 (2008): 181–220.

Deneffe, August. "Perichoresis, circumincessio, circuminsessio: Eine terminologische Untersuchung." *Zeitschrift für katholische Theologie* 47, no. 4 (1923): 497–532.

Denzinger, Heinrich. *Enchiridion symbolorum definitionum et declarationum de rebus fidei et morum*. 37th ed. Edited by Peter Hünermann. San Francisco: Ignatius Press, 2012.

de Régnon, Theodore. *Études sur la Sainte Trinité*. 4 vols. Paris: Victor Retaux, 1892–1898.

de Villalmonte, Alejandro. "Influjo de los Padres griegos en la doctrina trinitaria de San Buenaventura." In *XIII Semana Española de Teologia, 14–19 Septembre 1953*, 553–557. Madrid: 1954.

Dihle, Albrecht. *The Theory of the Will in Classical Antiquity*. Berkeley: University of California Press, 1982.

Doolan, Gregory T. *Aquinas on the Divine Ideas as Exemplar Causes*. Washington, DC: The Catholic University of America Press, 2008.

Doucet, Victorin. "The History of the Problem of the Authenticity of the *Summa*." *Franciscan Studies* 7 (1947): 26–41, 274–312.

Doyle, Dominic. "Is Charity the Holy Spirit? The Development of Aquinas' Disagreement with Peter Lombard." In *Thomas Aquinas: Questions on Love and Charity*, edited by Robert Miner, 313–335. New Haven, CT: Yale University Press, 2016.

Dumsday, Travis. "Alexander of Hales on Angelic Corporeality." *The Heythrop Journal* 54, no. 3 (2013): 360–370.

Eco, Umberto. *Art and Beauty in the Middle Ages*. New Haven, CT: Yale University Press, 1986.

———. *The Aesthetics of Thomas Aquinas*. Translated by Hugh Bredin. Cambridge, MA: Harvard University Press, 1988.

Emery, Gilles. *The Trinitarian Theology of St. Thomas Aquinas*. Translated by Francesca Aran Murphy. Oxford: Oxford University Press, 2007.

———. *La trinité créatrice. Trinité et création dans les commentaires aux Sentences de Thomas d'Aquin et de ses précurseurs Albert le Grand et Bonaventure*. Paris: J. Vrin, 1995.

———. "Trinité et Unité de Dieu dans la scholastique XIIe–XIVe siècles." In *Le christianisme est-il un monothéisme?*, edited by Pierre Gisel and Gilles Emery, 195–220. Geneva: Labor & Fides, 2001.

———. *Trinity in Aquinas*. Ypsilanti: Sapientia Press, 2003.

Emery, Kent, Jr. "Fondements théoriques de la reception de la beauté dans les écrits de Denys le Chartreux." In *Les Chartreux et l'art: XIVe–XVIIIe siècles: actes du Xe Colloque international d'histoire et de spiritualité cartusiennes*, edited by Daniel Le Blévec and Alain Girard, 307–324. Villeneuve-lès-Avignon: Editions du Cerf, 1989.

———. "The Matter and Order of Philosophy according to Denys the Carthusian." In *Was ist Philosophie im Mittelalter?*, *Qu'est-ce que la philosophie au Moyen Âge?*, *What Is Philosophy in the Middle Ages?*, 674–675. New York, Berlin: Walter de Gruyter, 1998.

Even-Ezra, Ayelet. "The *Summa Halensis*: A Text in Context." In *The Summa Halensis: Sources and Context*, edited by Lydia Schumacher, 219–234. Berlin, Boston: Walter de Gruyter, 2020.

Fokin, Alexey R. "The Doctrine of the 'Intelligible Triad' in Neoplatonism and Patristics," *Studia Patristica* 58 (2013): 45–71.

Fornaro, Italo. *La teologia dell'immagine nella Glossa di Alessandro d'Hales*. Venice: Edizioni L.I.E.F., 1985.

Francis I. *Amoris Laetitia* [Post-Synodal Apostolic Exhortation on Love in the Family], Vatican Website, March 19, 2016, sec. 159, accessed July 20, 2018, https://w2 .vatican.va/content/dam/francesco/pdf/apost_exhortations/documents/papa -francesco_esortazione-ap_20160319_amoris-laetitia_en.pdf.

———. *Laudato Si'* [Encyclical on Care for Our Common Home], Vatican Website, May 24, 2015, sec. 239, accessed July 20, 2018, http://w2.vatican.va

/content/francesco/en/encyclicals/documents/papa-francesco_20150524
_enciclica-laudato-si.html.

Friedman, Russell. "Divergent Traditions in Later-Medieval Trinitarian Theology: Relations, Emanations, and the Use of Philosophical Psychology, 1250–1325." *Studia Theologica* 53 (1999): 13–25.

———. *Intellectual Traditions at the Medieval University: The Use of Philosophical Psychology in Trinitarian Theology among the Franciscans and Dominicans, 1250–1350.* 2 vols. Studien und Texte zur Geistesgeschichte des Mittelalters: Bd. 108. Boston, Leiden: Brill Publishers, 2012.

———. "Medieval Trinitarian Theology from the Late Thirteenth to the Fifteenth Centuries." In *The Oxford Handbook of the Trinity*, edited by Gilles Emery and Matthew Levering, 197–209. New York: Oxford University Press, 2011.

———. *Medieval Trinitarian Thought from Aquinas to Ockham.* Cambridge: Cambridge University Press, 2010.

———. "The Voluntary Emanation of the Holy Spirit: Views of Natural Necessity and Voluntary Freedom at the Turn of the Thirteenth Century." In *Trinitarian Theology in the Medieval West*, e. Edited by Pekka Kärkkäinen, 124–148. Helsinki: Luther-Agricola-Society, 2007.

Fries, Albert. "Zur Problematik der *Summa theologiae* unter dem Namen des Albertus Magnus." *Franziskanische Studien* 70 (1988): 68–91.

Fuchs, Johann. *Die proprietäten des seins bei Alexander von Hales.* Munich: Salensianischen offizin, 1930.

Gadamer, Hans-Georg. "Elements of a Theory of Hermeneutic Experience." In *The Phenomenology Reader*, edited by Dermot Moran and Timothy Mooney, 314–348. New York: Routledge, 2002.

———. *Truth and Method.* London: Bloomsbury Academic, 2013.

Garcia, Jorge J. E. "The Transcendentals in the Middle Ages: An Introduction." *Topoi* 11, no. 2 (1992): 113–120.

Garrigou-Lagrange, Reginald. *Les perfections divins.* Paris: Beauchesne, 1936.

Gies, Aaron. "Alexander of Hales on the Gospel of John: An Epitome of Sacra Doctrina." PhD diss, The Catholic University of America, 2017.

———. "Biblical Exegesis in the *Summa Halensis*" in *The Summa Halensis: Sources and Context*, edited by Lydia Schumacher, 11–31. Berlin, Boston: Walter de Gruyter, 2020.

Gilson, Étienne. *History of Christian Philosophy in the Middle Ages.* New York: Random House, 1955.

Gonzalez, Olegario. *Misterio Trinitario y existencia humana: estudio historico teologico en torno a san Buenaventura.* Madrid: Ediciones Rialp, 1966.

Gorce, Matthieu-Maxime. "Le problème des trois Sommes: Alexandre de Halès, Thomas d'Aquin, Albert le Grand." *Revue Thomiste* 36 (1931): 293–301.

Gössmann, Wilhelm E. "Die Methode der Trinitätslehre in der Summa Halensis." *Münchener Theologische Zeitschrift* 6 (1955): 253–262.

Gössmann, Elisabeth. *Metaphysik und Heilsgeschichte: Eine theologische Untersuchung der Summa Halensis.* Munich: Max Hueber Verlag, 1964.

Griffiths, Paul J. *Intellectual Appetite: A Theological Grammar.* Washington, DC: The Catholic University of America Press, 2009.

———. "Secularity and the *saeculum*." In *Augustine's "City of God": A Critical Guide,* edited by James Wetzel, 33–54. Cambridge: Cambridge University Press, 2012.

Hadot, Pierre. *Porphyre et Victorinus.* Paris: Études augustiniennes, 1968.

Hagendahl, Harald. *Augustine and the Latin Classics.* Stockholm: Almqvist & Wiksell, 1967.

Halcour, Dieter. "Tractatus de transcendentalibus entis conditionibus." *Franziskanische Studien* 41 (1959): 41–106.

Hammond, Jay M. "Appendix: Order in the *Itinerarium mentis in Deum*." In J. A. Wayne Hellmann, *Divine and Created Order in Bonaventure's Theology.* St. Bonaventure: The Franciscan Institute, 2001.

Hankey, Wayne J. "*Ab uno simplici non est nisi unum*: The Place of Natural and Necessary Emanation in Aquinas' Doctrine of Creation." In *Divine Creation in Ancient, Medieval, and Early Modern Thought: Essays Presented to the Rev'd Dr Robert D. Crouse,* edited by Michael Treschow, Willemien Otten, and Walter Hannam, 309–333. Boston, Leiden: Brill Publishers, 2007.

Harkins, Franklin T. "The Embodiment of Angels: A Debate in Mid-Thirteenth-Century Theology." *Recherches de théologie et philosophie médiévales* 78, no. 1 (2011): 25–58.

Harrison, Carol. *Beauty and Revelation in the Thought of Saint Augustine.* Oxford: Clarendon Press, 1992.

Hart, David Bentley. *The Beauty of the Infinite: The Aesthetics of Christian Truth.* Grand Rapids: Wm. B. Eerdmans, 2004.

———. *The Experience of God: Being, Consciousness, Bliss.* New Haven, CT: Yale University Press, 2013.

Hasse, Dag Nikolaus. *Avicenna's De Anima in the Latin West: The Formation of a Peripatetic Philosophy of the Soul 1160–1300.* London: The Warburg Institute, 2000.

Hayes, Zachary. "Bonaventure's Trinitarian Theology in General." In *St. Bonaventure's Disputed Questions on the Mystery of the Trinity.* St. Bonaventure: The Franciscan Institute, 2000.

———. *The General Doctrine of Creation in the Thirteenth Century: With Special Emphasis on Matthew of Aquasparta.* Munich, Vienna: Verlag Ferdinand Schöningh, 1964.

———. "Review of *Metaphysik und Heilsgeschichte: Eine theologische Untersuchung der Summa Halensis* by Elisabeth Gössmann." *Speculum* 41, no. 1 (1966): 134–138.

Hegel, G.W.F. *Lectures on the Philosophy of Religion: One Volume Edition: The Lectures of 1827.* Edited by Peter C. Hodgson. Translated by R. F. Brown,

Peter C. Hodgson, and J. M. Stewart. Berkeley: University of California Press, 1988.

Heim, Karl. *Die Lehre von der* gratia gratis data *nach Alexander Halesius.* Leipzig: M. Heinsius Nachfolger, 1907.

Hellmann, J. A. Wayne. *Divine and Created Order in Bonaventure's Theology.* Translated by Jay Hammond. St. Bonaventure: The Franciscan Institute, 2001.

Hoenen, Maarten. "Being and Thinking in the *'Correctorium Fratris Thomae'* and the *'Correctorium Corruptorii Quare':* Schools of Thought and Philosophical Methodology." In *Nach der Verurleilung von 1277: Philosophie und Theologie an der Universität von Paris im letzten Veirtel des 13. Jahrhunderts. Studien und Texte,* edited by Jan Aertsen, Kent Emery Jr., and Andreas Speer, 417–435. Miscellanea Mediaevalia 28. New York, Berlin: Walter de Gruyter, 2001.

Hunter, Justus. *If Adam Had Not Sinned: The Motive for the Incarnation from Anselm of Canterbury to John Duns Scotus.* Washington, DC: The Catholic University of America Press, 2019.

———. "The Contribution of the *Summa Halensis* to the Reason for the Incarnation" in *The Summa Halensis: Debates and Doctrines,* edited by Lydia Schumacher, 141–152. Berlin, Boston: Walter de Gruyter, 2020.

Imle, Fanny, and Julien Kaup, *Die Theologie des hl. Bonventura. Darstellung seiner dogmatischen Lehren.* Werl: Franziskus-Druckerei, 1931.

Jacobi, Klaus. "*Nomina transcendentia*: Untersuchungen von Logikern des 12. Jahrhunderts über transkategoriale Terme." In *Die Logik des Transzendentalen. Festschrift für Jan A. Aertsen,* edited by Martin Pickavé, 23–36. New York: Miscellanea Mediaevalia 30, 2003.

Jordan, Mark D. "The Evidence of the Transcendentals and the Place of Beauty in Thomas Aquinas." *International Philosophical Quarterly* 29, no. 4 (1989): 393–407.

———. *Ordering Wisdom: The Hierarchy of Philosophical Discourses in Aquinas.* Notre Dame: University of Notre Dame Press, 1986.

———. *Rewritten Theology: Aquinas after His Readers.* Malden, Oxford: Blackwell Publishing, 2006.

———. *Teaching Bodies: Moral Formation in the* Summa *of Thomas Aquinas.* New York: Fordham University Press, 2016.

Jüngel, Eberhard. *God's Being Is in Becoming: The Trinitarian Being of God in the Theology of Karl Barth: A Paraphrase.* Translated by John Webster. Edinburgh: T&T Clark, 2001.

Kasper, Walter. *The Absolute in History: The Philosophy and Theology of History in Schelling's Late Philosophy.* Translated by Sr. Katherine E. Wolff. New York, Mahwah: Paulist Press, 2018.

Keane, Kevin Patrick. "The Logic of Self-Diffusive Goodness in the Trinitarian Theory of the 'Summa fratris Alexandri.'" PhD diss., Fordham University, 1978.

Kierkegaard, Søren. *Either/Or: Part I. Kierkegaard's Writings.* Vol. 3. Translated by Howard V. Hong and Edna H. Hong. Princeton: Princeton University Press, 1987.

Kovach, Francis J. "Divine and Human Beauty in Duns Scotus." In *Deus et Homo ad mentem I. Duns Scoti,* 445–459. Rome: Societas Internationalis Scotistica, 1972.

———. "The Transcendentality of Beauty in Thomas Aquinas." In *Scholastic Challenges to Some Mediaeval and Modern Ideas.* Edited by Francis J. Kovach. Stillwater: Western Publications, 1987.

Kretzmann, Norman. "Trinity and Transcendentals." In *Trinity, Incarnation, and Atonement: Philosophical and Theological Essays,* edited by Ronald Feenstra and Cornelius Plantinga, Jr., 79–109. Notre Dame: University of Notre Dame Press, 1990.

Kobusch, Theo. "'The Summa Halensis': Towards a New Concept of 'Person.'" *The Summa Halensis: Debates and Doctrines,* edited by Lydia Schumacher, 153–170. Berlin, Boston: Walter de Gruyter, 2020.

Ku, John Baptist. *God the Father in the Theology of St. Thomas Aquinas.* New York: Peter Lang, 2013.

Künzle, Pius. *Das Verhältnis der Seele zu ihren Potenzen. Problemgeschichtliche Untersuchungen von Augustin bis und mit Thomas von Aquin.* Freiburg: Universitätsverlag, 1956.

LaNave, Gregory F. "'A Particularly Agitated Topic': Aquinas and the Franciscans on the Subject of Theology in the Mid-Thirteenth Century." *The Thomist* 79, no. 3 (2015): 467–491.

Leo XIII. *Divinum Illud Munus* [Encyclical letter on the Holy Spirit], Vatican Website, May 9, 1897, sec. 6, accessed 20 July 2018. http://w2.vatican.va /content/leo-xiii/en/encyclicals/documents/hf_l-xiii_enc_09051897_divinum -illud-munus.html.

Lottin, Odon. *Psychologie et morale aux XIIe et XIIIe siècles.* Vol. 1. Leuven: Abbaye du Mont César, 1942.

MacDonald, Scott. "The Relation between Being and Goodness." In *Being and Goodness. The Concept of the Good in Metaphysics and Philosophical Theology,* 31–55. Ithaca, NY: Cornell University Press.

Macierowski, Edward M. "Does God Have a Quiddity According to Avicenna?" *The Thomist* 52 (1988): 79–87.

Marc, André. *Dialectique de l'affirmation.* Paris: Desclée de Br., 1952.

Maritain, Jacques. *Art and Scholasticism.* Translated by Joseph Owens. New York: Charles Scribner's Sons, 1962.

Marmura, Michael E. "Avicenna on Primary Concepts in the *Metaphysics* of his *al-Shifa.*" In *Probing Islamic Philosophy: Studies in the Philosophies of Ibn-Sīnā, al-Ghazālī, and Other Major Muslim Thinkers,* 149–168. Binghamton: Global Academic Publishing, 2005.

Marshall, Bruce. *Trinity and Truth.* New York: Cambridge University Press, 2004.

McGinn, Bernard. "Introduction." In *Three Treatises on Man: A Cistercian Anthropology*, 1–100. Kalamazoo: Cistercian Publications, 1977.

McGrath, Alister E. "The Influence of Aristotelian Physics upon St Thomas Aquinas' Discussion of the 'Processus Iustificationis.'" *Recherches de théologie ancienne et médiévale* 51 (1984): 223–229.

———. *Iustitia Dei: A History of the Christian Doctrine of Justification.* 4th ed. New York: Cambridge University Press, 2005.

Metzler, Irina. *Disability in Medieval Europe: Thinking about Physical Impairment during the High Middle Ages, c. 1100–1400.* London: Routledge, 2006.

Mews, Constant. "The World as Text" in *Scripture and Pluralism: Reading the Bible in the Religiously Plural Worlds of the Middle Ages and Renaissance*, edited by Thomas J. Heffernan and Thomas E. Burman, 95–122. Boston, Leiden: Brill Publishers, 2005.

Michael, Emily. "Averroes and the Plurality of Forms." *Franciscan Studies* 52 (1992): 155–182.

Monsour, Daniel. "The Relation Between Uncreated and Created Grace in the Halensian Summa: A Lonergan Reading." PhD diss., University of Toronto, 2000.

Murphy, Francesca Aran. *Christ the Form of Beauty: A Study in Theology and Literature.* London: T&T Clark, 2005.

———. "Hans Urs von Balthasar: Beauty as a Gateway to Love." In *Theological Aesthetics after von Balthasar*, edited by Oleg V. Bychkov and James Fodor, 5–18. Burlington: Ashgate Publishing Company, 2008.

Nichols, Aiden. *Discovering Aquinas: An Introduction to His Life, Work, and Influence.* Grand Rapids, Cambridge: Wm. B. Eerdmans Publishing Co, 2003.

———. *Redeeming Beauty: Soundings in Sacral Aesthetics.* Burlington: Ashgate Publishing, 2007.

Osborne, Kenan B. "Alexander of Hales: Precursor and Promoter of Franciscan Theology." In *The History of Franciscan Theology*, edited by Kenan B. Osborne, 1–38. St. Bonaventure: The Franciscan Institute, 1994.

Ost, David E. "Bonaventure: The Aesthetic Synthesis." *Franciscan Studies* 36 (1976): 233–247.

Paredes, B. G. "Ideas estéticas de Santo Tomás." *La ciencia tomista* 2 (1910–11): 345–357.

Pannenberg, Wolfhart. *Systematic Theology* I. Translated by Geoffrey W. Bromiley. Grand Rapids: Wm. B. Eerdmans Publishing Co, 1991.

Peter, Karl. *Die Lehre der Schönheit nach Bonaventura.* Werl: Dietrich-Coelde-Verlag, 1964.

Philips, Gérard. "La Théologie de la Grâce dans la *Summa Fratris Alexandri*." *Ephemerides Theologicae Lovanienses* 49 (1973): 100–123.

———. *L'union personnelle avec Le Dieu vivant: Essai sur l'origine et le sens la grâce créée*. Leuven: Leuven University Press, 1989.

Pöltner, Gunther. *Schönheit. Eine Untersuchung zum Ursprung des Denkens bei Thomas von Aquin*. Vienna: Herder & Herder, 1978.

Pomplun, Trent. "Notes on Scotist Aesthetics in Light of Gilbert Narcisse's *Les raisons de Dieu*." *Franciscan Studies* 66 (2008): 247–268.

Poirel, Dominique. *Livre de la nature et débate trinitaire au XIIe siècle: Le De tribus diebus de Hughes de Saint-Victor*. Bibliotheca Victorina 14. Turnhout: Brepols, 2002.

———. "Scholastic Reasons, Monastic Mediations, and Victorine Conciliations: The Question of the Unity and Plurality of God in the Twelfth Century." In *The Oxford Handbook of the Trinity*, edited by Gilles Emery and Matthew Levering, 168–181. Oxford: Oxford University Press, 2011.

Pouillon, Henri. "La beauté, propriété transcendentale chez les scolastiques (1220–1270)." In *Archives d'histoire doctrinale et littéraire du Moyen Age*, 263–314. Paris: Librairie Philosophique J. Vrin, 1946.

Primeau, Ernest J. "Doctrina *Summa theologicae* Alexandri Halensis: De Spiritus Sancti apud justos Inhabitatione." Thesis, Seminarium Sanctae Mariae ad Lacum, 1936.

Principe, Walter. *Alexander of Hales' Theology of the Hypostatic Union*. Toronto: Pontifical Institute of Mediaeval Studies, 1967.

———. *Hugh of Saint-Cher's Theology of the Hypostatic Union*. Toronto: Pontifical Institute of Mediaeval Studies, 1970.

———. *Philip the Chancellor's Theology of the Hypostatic Union*. Toronto: Pontifical Institute of Mediaeval Studies, 1975.

———. *William of Auxerre's Theology of the Hypostatic Union*. Toronto: Pontifical Institute of Mediaeval Studies, 1963.

Rahner, Karl. *Foundations of Christian Faith: An Introduction to the Idea of Christianity*. Translated by William V. Dych. New York: The Seabury Press, 1978.

Reynolds, Philip L. "Bonaventure's Theory of Resemblance." *Traditio* 58 (2003): 219–255.

Robinson, Michael A. "The Early 13th-Century Latin-Augustinian Reception of the Peripatetic Agent Intellect and the Historical Constitution of the Self." PhD diss., Boston College, 2012.

Robson, Michael. "Anselm's Influence on the Soteriology of Alexander of Hales: The *Cur deus homo* in the Commentary on the *Sentences*." In *Cur deus homo: Atti del Congresso Anselmiano Internazionale, Roma 21–23 maggio 1998*, edited by Paul Gilbert, Helmut Kohlenberg, and Elmar Salmann, 191–219. Rome: Pontificio Ateno S. Anselmo, 1999.

———. "The Interpretation of Anselm's Teaching on Christ's Satisfaction for Sin in the Franciscan Tradition from Alexander of Hales to Duns Scotus." *Franciscan Studies* 71 (2013): 411–444.

Roest, Bert. *Franciscan Learning, Preaching, and Mission c. 1220–1650.* Boston, Leiden: Brill Publishers, 2015.

Rohmer, Jean. "La théorie de l'abstraction dans l'école franciscaine de Alexandre de Halès à John Peckham." *Archives d'histoire doctrinale et littéraire du moyen-âge* 3 (1928): 105–184.

Romero, Miguel J. "St. Thomas Aquinas and Profound Cognitive Impairment." PhD diss., Duke Divinity School, 2012.

Rosato, Andrew. "Anselm's Influence on the Teaching of the *Summa Halensis* on Redemption." In *The Summa Halensis: Sources and Context,* edited by Lydia Schumacher, 187–200. Berlin, Boston: Walter de Gruyter, 2020.

———. "The Impact of the *Cur deus homo* on the Early Francisan School." In *Anselm: Aosta, Bec, and Canterbury, Papers in Commemoration of the Nine-Hundredth Anniversary of Anselm's Enthronement as Archbishop, 25 September 1093,* edited by D. E. Luscombe and G. R. Evans, 334–347. Sheffield: Sheffield Academic Press, 1996.

Rosemann, Philipp W. "Fraterna dilectio est deus: Peter Lombard's Thesis on Charity as the Holy Spirit." In *Amor amicitiae: On the Love that is Friendship: Essays in Medieval Thought and Beyond in Honor of the Rev. Professor James McEvoy,* edited by Thomas A. F. Kelly and Philipp W. Rosemann, 409–36. Leuven: Peeters, 2004.

———. "*Li* or *Ly,* Marker of Metalanguage in Scholastic Latin." In *Tolle Lege: Essays on Augustine & Medieval Philosophy in Honor of Roland J. Teske, SJ,* edited by Richard C. Taylor, David Twetten, and Michael Wreen, 335–352. Milwaukee: Marquette University Press, 2011.

———. *Understanding Scholastic Thought with Foucault.* New York: St. Martin's Press, 1999.

Rosheger, John P. "Is God a 'What'? Avicenna, William of Auvergne, and Aquinas on the Divine Essence." In *Medieval Philosophy and the Classical Tradition in Islam, Judaism, and Christianity,* edited by John Inglis, 277–296. London, New York: Routledge, 2002.

Rubin, Michael J. "The Meaning of 'Beauty' and Its Transcendental Status in the Metaphysics of Thomas Aquinas." PhD diss., The Catholic University of America, 2016.

Ryan, Denise. "An Examination of a Thirteenth-Century Treatise on the Mind/Body Dichotomy: Jean de La Rochelle on the Soul and its Powers." PhD diss., National University of Ireland Maynooth, 2010.

Rydstrøm-Poulsen, Aage. *The Gracious God: Gratia in Augustine and the Twelfth Century.* Copenhagen: Akademisk Forlag, 2002.

Ryle, Gilbert. "Knowing-How and Knowing-That." *Proceedings of the Aristotelian Society* 46 (1946): 1–16.

Sammon, Brendan. *The God Who Is Beauty: Beauty as a Divine Name in Thomas Aquinas and Dionysius the Areopagite.* Eugene: Pickwick Publications, 2013.

Schindler, D. C. "The Transcendentals." In *Hans Urs von Balthasar and the Dramatic Structure of Truth: A Philosophical Investigation*, 350–421. New York: Fordham University Press, 2004.

Schlenker, Ernst. *Die Lehre von den göttlichen Namen in der Summe Alexanders von Hales*. Freiburg im Breisgau: Herder, 1938.

Schmaus, Michael. *Der Liber Propugnatorius des Thomas Anglicus und die Lehrunterschiede zwischen Thomas von Aquin und Duns Scotus. II Teil, Die Trinitarischen Lehrdifferenzen*. Munster: Aschendorff, 1930.

Schumacher, Lydia. "The *De anima* Tradition in Early Franciscan Thought: A Case Study in Avicenna's Reception." In *The Summa Halensis: Sources and Contexts*, edited by Lydia Schumacher, 155–170. Berlin, Boston: Walter de Gruyter, 2020.

———. *Divine Illumination: The History and Future of Augustine's Theory of Knowledge*. Oxford, Malden: Wiley-Blackwell, 2011.

———. *Early Franciscan Theology: Between Authority and Innovation*. New York: Cambridge University Press, 2019.

———. "Theology as a Science in the *Summa minorum*." *Medioevo Romanzo* (2015): 367–384.

Sesboüé, Bernard. "Appropriations." In *Dictionnaire critique de théologie*, edited by Jean-Yves Lacoste, 83–84. Paris: Presses Universitaires de France, 1998.

Sevier, Christopher Scott. *Aquinas on Beauty*. Lanham: Lexington Books, 2015.

Siemering, Lucia Marie. "Capital Grace of the Word Incarnate according to Saint Thomas Aquinas." *Studia Gilsoniana* 5, no. 2 (2016): 327–343.

Smith, Lesley. "Hugh of St. Cher and Medieval Collaboration." In *Transforming Relations: Essays on Jews and Christians throughout History in Honor of Michael A. Signer*, edited by Franklin T. Harkins, 241–264. Notre Dame: University of Notre Dame Press, 2010.

Sondag, Gérard. "The Conditional Definition of Beauty by Scotus." *Medioevo* 30 (2005): 191–206.

Spargo, Sr. Emma Jane Marie. *The Category of the Aesthetic in the Philosophy of Saint Bonaventure*. St. Bonaventure: The Franciscan Institute, 1953.

Speer, Andreas. "Aesthetics." In *The Oxford Handbook of Medieval Philosophy*, 661–686. New York, Oxford: Oxford University Press, 2012.

Stemmer, Peter. "Perichorese: Zur Geschichte eines Begriffs." In *Archiv für Begriffsgeschichte* 27 (1983): 9–55.

Stohr, Albert. *Die Trinitätslehre des hl. Bonaventura: Eine systematische Darstellung und historische Würdigung. I Teil. Die wissenschaftliche Trinitätslehre*. Munster: Aschendorff-Verlag, 1923.

Strand, Vincent. "The Ontology of Grace in Alexander of Hales and John of La Rochelle." In *The Summa Halensis: Doctrines and Debates*, edited by Lydia Schumacher, 171–192. Berlin, Boston: Walter de Gruyter, 2020.

Swanstrom, Julie. "The Metaphyics of Causation in the Creation Accounts of Avicenna and Aquinas." PhD diss., Purdue University, 2013.

Sylwanowicz, Michael. *Contingent Causality and the Foundation of Duns Scotus' Metaphysics.* Boston, Leiden: Brill Publishers, 1996.

Szabo, Titus. *De ss. trinitate in creaturis refulgente doctrina S. Bonaventura.* Rome: Orbis Catholicus, 1959.

Tallon, Philip. *The Poetics of Evil: Toward an Aesthetic Theodicy.* Oxford: Oxford University Press, 2012.

Tanner, Norman P. *Decrees of the Ecumenical Councils.* Vol. 1. Washington, DC: Georgetown University Press, 1990.

Tatarkiewicz, Władysław. *Medieval Aesthetics.* Vol. 2 of *History of Aesthetics.* Translated by R. M. Montgomery. Edited by C. Barrett. Bristol: Thoemmes Press, 1970.

Van Steenberghen, Fernand. *Thomas Aquinas and Radical Aristotelianism.* Washington, DC: The Catholic University of America Press, 1980.

Venard, Olivier-Thomas. *Thomas D'Aquin, Poète Théologien.* Geneva: Ad Solem, 2002.

Viladesau, Richard. *Theology and the Arts: Encountering God through Music, Art, and Rhetoric.* Mahwah: Paulist Press, 2000.

von Balthasar, Hans Urs. *The Glory of the Lord II: Clerical Styles.* Translated by Andrew Louth, Francis McDonagh, and Brian McNeil. San Francisco: Ignatius Press, 1984.

———. *The Glory of the Lord IV: The Realm of Metaphysics in Antiquity.* Translated by Brian McNeil, Andrew Louth, John Saward, Rowan Williams, and Oliver Davies. Edited by John Riches. San Francisco: Ignatius Press, 1989.

———. *Theo-Logic 3: The Spirit of Truth.* Translated by Graham Harrison. San Francisco: Ignatius Press, 2005.

Waddel, Michael Machias. "Truth Beloved: Thomas Aquinas and the Relational Transcendentals." PhD diss., University of Notre Dame, 2000.

Wass, Meldon Clarence. *The Infinite God and the Summa fratris Alexandri.* Chicago: Franciscan Herald Press, 1964.

Weber, Hubert Philipp. *Sünde und Gnade bei Alexander von Hales: Ein Beitrag zur Entwicklung der theologischen Anthropologie im Mittelalter.* Innsbruck: Tyrolia-Verlag, 2003.

———. "Alexander of Hales's Theology in His Authentic Texts (Commentary on the *Sentences* of Peter Lombard, Various Disputed Questions)." In *The English Province of the Franciscans (1224–c.1350),* edited by Michael J. P. Robson, 273–293. Boston, Leiden: Brill Publishers, 2017.

Wenzel, Paul. *Das wissenschaftliche Anliegen des Güntherianismus. Ein Beitrag zur Theologiegeschichte des 19. Jahrhunderts.* Essen: Ludgerus-Verlag, 1961.

Wicki, Niklaus. *Die Philosophie Philipps des Kanzlers. Ein philosophierender Theologe des frühen 13. Jahrhunderts.* Fribourg: Academic Press Fribourg, 2005.

Wippel, John F. "Norman Kretzmann on Aquinas's Attribution of Will and of Freedom to Create to God." *Religious Studies* 39, vol. 3 (2003): 287–298.

Wisnovksy, Robert. "Final and Efficient Causality in Avicenna's Cosmology and Theology." *Quaestio: The Yearbook of the History of Metaphysics* 2 (2002): 97–123.

Wittgenstein, Ludwig. *Philosophical Investigations.* Translated by G.E.M. Anscombe, P.M.S. Hacker, and Joachim Schulte. 4th ed. Malden, Oxford: Blackwell Publishing, 2009.

———. *Lectures and Conversations on Aesthetics, Psychology, and Religious Belief.* Edited by Cyril Barrett. Berkeley: University of California Press, 1967.

Wolter, Allan B. *The Transcendentals and Their Function in the Metaphysics of Duns Scotus.* Washington, DC: The Catholic University of America Press, 1946.

Woo, Esther. "Theophanic Cosmic Order in Saint Bonaventure." *Franciscan Studies* 32 (1972): 306–330.

Wood, Jacob. "Kataphasis and Apophasis in Thirteenth-Century Theology: The Anthropological Context of the *Triplex Via* in the *Summa fratris Alexandri* and Albert the Great." *The Heythrop Journal* 57, no. 2 (2016): 293–311.

———. "Forging the Analogy of Being: John of La Rochelle's *De divinis nominibus* (Trier, Abtei St. Matthias, 162) and the *Summa Halensis* on Knowing and Naming God." In *The Summa Halensis: Debates and Doctrines,* edited by Lydia Schumacher, 32–57. Berlin, Boston: Walter de Gruyter, 2020.

Wood, Jordan Daniel. "Creation is Incarnation: The Metaphysical Pecularity of the *Logoi* in Maximus Confessor." *Modern Theology* 34, no. 1 (2018): 83–102.

———. "No 'Proto-Father': Negative Causality in Bonaventure's Trinitarian Theology." Paper presented at the Conference on Medieval and Renaissance Studies, Saint Louis, MO, June 2016.

———. "That and How Perichoresis Differs from Participation: The Case of Maximus Confessor." In *Platonism and Christian Thought in Late Antiquity.* Edited by P. G. Pavlos, L. F. Hanby, E. K. Emilsson, and T. T. Tollefsen. London: Routledge, 2019.

Wood, Rega. "Distinct Ideas and Perfect Solicitude: Alexander of Hales, Richard Rufus, and Odo Rigaldus." *Franciscan Studies* 53 (1993): 7–31.

Wrisley Shelby, Katherine. "Part V: On the Grace of the Holy Spirit." In *Bonaventure Revisited: Companion to the* Breviloquium, edited by Dominic Monti and Katherine Wrisley Shelby, 215–244. St. Bonaventure: The Franciscan Institute, 2017.

———. "The *Vir Hierarchicus*: St. Bonaventure's Theology of Grace." PhD diss., Boston College, 2017.

INDEX

Justin Shaun Coyle (PhD, Boston College) is Associate Professor of Theology, Church History, and Philosophy and Associate Academic Dean at Mount Angel Seminary in St. Benedict, Oregon. He is a tonsured reader in the Ukrainian Greek-Catholic Church.

Ronald E. Pepin, *The Vatican Mythographers*

Paul Thom, *The Logic of the Trinity: Augustine to Ockham*

Charles Bolyard and Rondo Keele, eds., *Later Medieval Metaphysics: Ontology, Language, and Logic*

Daniel D. Novotný, *Ens rationis from Suárez to Caramuel: A Study in Scholasticism of the Baroque Era*

John Buridan, *Treatise on Consequences*. Translated by Stephen Read, Introduction by Hubert Hubien

Gyula Klima, ed., *Intentionality, Cognition, and Mental Representation in Medieval Philosophy*

John Duns Scotus, *On Being and Cognition: "Ordinatio" 1.3*. Edited and translated by John van den Bercken

Claude Panaccio, *Mental Language: From Plato to William of Ockham*. Translated by Joshua P. Hochschild and Meredith K. Ziebart

Andrew LaZella, *The Singular Voice of Being: John Duns Scotus and Ultimate Difference*

Lydia Schumacher and Oleg Bychkov, ed. and trans., *A Reader in Early Franciscan Theology: The "Summa Halensis"*

Justin Shaun Coyle, *The Beauty of the Trinity: A Reading of the Summa Halensis*

CPSIA information can be obtained
at www.ICGtesting.com
Printed in the USA
LVHW041924231222
735831LV00013B/180/J